Lecture Notes in Computer Science

Commenced Publication in 1973
Founding and Former Series Editors:
Gerhard Goos, Juris Hartmanis, and Jan van Leeuwen

Christoph Bussler   Malu Castellanos
Umesh Dayal   Sham Navathe (Eds.)

Business Intelligence for the Real-Time Enterprises

First International Workshop, BIRTE 2006
Seoul, Korea, September 11, 2006
Revised Selected Papers

 Springer

Volume Editors

Christoph Bussler
Cisco Systems Inc.
San Jose, CA 95134, USA
E-mail: chbussler@aol.com

Malu Castellanos
Hewlett-Packard
CA 94304, USA
E-mail: malu.castellanos@hp.com

Umesh Dayal
Hewlett-Packard
CA, 94304, USA
E-mail: umeshwar.dayal@hp.com

Sham Navathe
Georgia Institute of Technology
Atlanta, Georgia 30332, USA
E-mail: navathe@yahoo.com

Library of Congress Control Number: 2007931598

CR Subject Classification (1998): H.3.5, H.4.1, H.2.7, H.5.3, K.4.3, K.4.4, K.6, J.1

LNCS Sublibrary: SL 3 – Information Systems and Application, incl. Internet/Web
and HCI

ISSN   0302-9743
ISBN-10   3-540-73949-1 Springer Berlin Heidelberg New York
ISBN-13   978-3-540-73949-4 Springer Berlin Heidelberg New York

Springer is a part of Springer Science+Business Media

springer.com

© Springer-Verlag Berlin Heidelberg 2007
Printed in Germany

Typesetting: Camera-ready by author, data conversion by Scientific Publishing Services, Chennai, India
Printed on acid-free paper   SPIN: 12100705   06/3180   5 4 3 2 1 0

Preface

The 1st Workshop on Business Intelligence for the Real-Time Enterprise (BIRTE 2006) was held on September 11, 2006 in conjunction with the 32nd International Conference on Very Large Data Bases (VLDB 2006) in Seoul, Korea. The co-location with VLDB is very important as the topic of the workshop was centered on different aspects in the lifecycle of business intelligence on very large enterprise-wide operational real-time data sets.

In today's competitive and highly dynamic environment, analyzing data to understand how the business is performing, to predict outcomes and trends, and to improve the effectiveness of business processes underlying business operations has become critical. The traditional approach to reporting is not longer adequate; users now demand easy-to-use intelligent platforms and applications capable of analyzing real-time business data to provide insight and actionable information at the right time. The end goal is to improve the enterprise performance by better and timelier decision making, enabled by the availability of up-to-date, high-quality information.

As a response, the notion of "real-time enterprise" has emerged and is beginning to be recognized in the industry. Gartner defines it as "using up-to-date information, getting rid of delays, and using speed for competitive advantage is what the real-time enterprise is all about... Indeed, the goal of the real-time enterprise is to act on events as they happen."

Although there has been progress in this direction and many companies are introducing products towards making this vision reality, there is still a long way to go. In particular, the whole lifecycle of business intelligence requires new techniques and methodologies capable of dealing with the new requirements imposed by the real-time enterprise. From the capturing of real-time business performance data to the injection of actionable information back into business processes, all the stages of the business intelligence (BI) cycle call for new algorithms and paradigms as the basis of new functionalities including dynamic integration of real-time data feeds from operational sources, evolution of ETL transformations and analytical models, and dynamic generation of adaptive real-time dashboards, just to name a few.

The goal of the BIRTE 2006 workshop was to provide a forum for the discussion of five major aspects of business intelligence for the real-time enterprise: Models and Concepts for Real-Time Enterprise Business Intelligence, Architectures for Real-Time Enterprise Business Intelligence, Uses Cases of Real-Time Enterprise Business Intelligence, Applications of Real-Time Enterprise Business Intelligence and Technologies for the Real-Time Enterprise Business Intelligence.

The workshop started with the keynote "Practical Considerations for Real-Time Business Intelligence" by Donovan Schneider. It continued with several sessions addressing various aspects of real-time data analysis. The first session "Streaming Data" concentrated on data streams as one mechanism for obtaining real-time enterprise data. The second session "Data Loading and Data Warehouse Architectures" addressed data loading and data warehouse architectures that both are a basis for the actual analysis task. The third session "Integration and Data Acquisition" focused on heterogeneous data sources as well as mechanisms for obtaining real-time data. The final session "Business Processes and Contracts" extended the analysis aspect from data to processes. The workshop closed with the interesting panel ""How Real Can Real-Time Business Intelligence Be?" moderated by Malu Castellanos, and Chi-Ming Chen, Mike Franklin, Minos Garofalakis, Wolfgang Lehner, Stuart Madnick and Krithi Ramamrithan as speakers.

The field of business intelligence for the real-time enterprise is fairly new, albeit increasingly important. This first workshop on the topic was meant to be a starting point of a series of several workshops covering various aspects in more detail over time. As academic research and industrial application experience more in-depth insights and use of this technology, an interesting research field opens up as well as an exciting area for practitioners. We encourage researchers and those in industry to continue their exciting work, and we encourage newcomers to enter this challenging and increasingly important field as there is still a lot of exciting work to be done.

We wish to express special thanks to the Program Committee members for providing their technical expertise in reviewing the submitted papers and preparing an interesting program. We are particularly grateful to the keynote speaker, Donovan Schneider, for delighting us with his very interesting keynote. Special recognition goes to the panelists for their enthusiastic participation in presenting their perspectives. To the authors of the accepted papers we express our appreciation for sharing their work and experiences in this workshop. Finally, we would like to extend many thanks to the VLDB 2006 Workshop Co-Chairs, Sang-goo Lee and Ming-Chien Shan, for their support in making this workshop possible.

September 2006

Christoph Bussler
Malu Castellanos
Umesh Dayal
Sham Navathe

Organization

Organizing Committee

General Chair

Umeshwar Dayal, Hewlett-Packard, USA

Program Committee Chairs

Christoph Bussler, Cisco Systems, Inc., USA
Malu Castellanos, Hewlett-Packard, USA
Sham Navathe, Georgia Institute of Technology, USA

Program Committee

Christof Bornhoevd, SAP Labs, USA
Mike Franklin, UC Berkeley, USA
Venkatesh Ganti, Microsoft, USA
Dimitrios Georgakopoulos, Telcordia Technologies, USA
Ramesh Jain, UC Irvine, USA
Meichun Hsu, HP Labs, China
Kamal Karlapalem, IIIT Hyderabad, India
Rajesh Parekh, Yahoo, USA
Torben B. Pedersen, Aalborg University, Denmark
Ee Peng, Nanyang Technological University, Singapore
Krithi Ramamritham, IIT Bombay, India
W.M.P. Van der Alst, Eindhoven University of Technology, The Netherlands
Panos Vassiliadis, University of Ioannina, Greece
Kazi Zaman, Siebel Systems Inc., USA

Publication Chair

Kamalakar Karlapalem, IIIT Hyderabad, India

Reviewers

Bin Zhang

Table of Contents

Practical Considerations for Real-Time Business Intelligence 1
 Donovan A. Schneider

What Can Hierarchies Do for Data Streams? 4
 Xuepeng Yin and Torben Bach Pedersen

Leveraging Distributed Publish/Subscribe Systems for Scalable Stream
Query Processing 20
 Yongluan Zhou, Kian-Lee Tan, and Feng Yu

Transaction Reordering and Grouping for Continuous Data Loading 34
 *Gang Luo, Jeffrey F. Naughton, Curt J. Ellmann, and
 Michael W. Watzke*

A Scalable Heterogeneous Solution for Massive Data Collection and
Database Loading 50
 Uri Shani, Aviad Sela, Alex Akilov, Inna Skarbovski, and David Berk

Two-Phase Data Warehouse Optimized for Data Mining 63
 *Balázs Rácz, Csaba István Sidló, András Lukács, and
 András A. Benczúr*

Document-Centric OLAP in the Schema-Chaos World 77
 Yannis Sismanis, Berthold Reinwald, and Hamid Pirahesh

Callisto: Mergers Without Pain 92
 *Huong Morris, Hui Liao, Sriram Padmanabhan, Sriram Srinivasan,
 Eugene Kawamoto, Phay Lau, Jing Shan, and Ryan Wisnesky*

Real-Time Acquisition of Buyer Behaviour Data – The Smart Shop
Floor Scenario 106
 Bo Yuan, Maria Orlowska, and Shazia Sadiq

Business Process Learning for Real Time Enterprises 118
 Rodion Podorozhny, Anne Ngu, and Dimitrios Georgakopoulos

An Integrated Approach to Process-Driven Business Performance
Monitoring and Analysis for Real-Time Enterprises 133
 *Jonghun Park, Cheolkyu Jee, Kwanho Kim, Seung-Kyun Han,
 Duksoon Im, Wan Lee, and Noyoon Kim*

Quality Contracts for Real-Time Enterprises 143
 Alexandros Labrinidis, Huiming Qu, and Jie Xu

Author Index 157

Practical Considerations for Real-Time Business Intelligence

Donovan A. Schneider

Yahoo! Inc.
701 First Avenue, Sunnyvale, CA 94089
dschneider@yahoo-inc.com

Abstract. The area of real-time business intelligence is ill defined in industry. In this extended abstract we highlight the practical requirements through the use of examples across several domains.

1 Introduction

Real-time Business Intelligence (BI) is an ambiguous area. To be practical in industry, real-time BI must satisfy two requirements:

1. Time is money. It costs money to reduce latency. The decisions to be made on the reduced latency data must justify the investment.
2. Actionable Data. Effective decision making requires rich contextual data.

1.1 Examples

We discuss several examples across different domains to highlight the practical real-time business intelligence requirements. Fraud detection is the canonical example of real-time BI. It involves detecting anomalies, for example, in credit card usage. Detection must be done quickly in order to prevent further fraudulent use. Fraud detection can be thought of as a form of alerting. The time in which to make a decision may be seconds or minutes. However, a surprising amount of context is required to prevent excessive numbers of false positives or false negatives. For example, different alerting applications may require knowledge of days of weeks (e.g., weekday vs. weekend), holidays, geographical location, past behavior and trends, to name a few. Without sufficiently rich context the decision making will be of limited usefulness.

Another illustrative example is real-time marketing. When a customer calls into a call center a decision may be made to pitch a premium service (up-sell) or a related product (cross-sell). The decision of which marketing message to present must be made in seconds (or sub-seconds). Again, in order for the marketing to be effective ample information must be available, including the reason for the current call, previous offers and their acceptance, behavior of similar users, history of the customer, etc. Often this rich contextual data is built offline in the form of models in order to meet the ultra low latency requirements.

C. Bussler et al. (Eds.): BIRTE 2006, LNCS 4365, pp. 1–3, 2007.

Many other forms of traditional business intelligence exist. These require very rich contextual data including role-specific views (e.g., an executive, district manager and a sales representative see different views of the same data) and task specific views (sometimes referred to as guided navigation). Most of these applications do not require decisions to be made in seconds, but rather in minutes. Thus, these types of applications are classified as near real-time, not real-time. When humans are making the decisions a person needs time to analyze the information and make a decision. Even when programs/systems are making the decisions enough data must be available for a useful decision to be made. Examples include incident tracking, inventory management, and sales analytics.

Several interesting examples of BI exist in the domain of web analytics. A common example is a recommendation service where other products (movies, books, etc.) are recommended based on what similar people liked or bought. Behavioral targeting is somewhat similar to this; it involves showing specific advertisements or personalized content to a user based on sophisticated models that may include demographic data (age, gender, income level, etc.), geographic data, and past and present user behavior. The interesting aspect of these examples is that although the decision of the recommendation or advertisement to present must be made in real-time (seconds), the context is often built off-line as part of a sophisticated modeling process. Refinements to the model may be made in real-time.

An interesting marketing area for the web is search engine marketing (SEM). SEM involves bidding on search terms from the search engine vendors (e.g., Yahoo!, Google, and MSN) to lead users to a particular web page, and then analyzing the click-thru and conversion rates of the users. Decisions to buy more or less of a search term must be made quickly. However, latencies of many minutes are common because enough user traffic must be analyzed before an effective decision can be made.

Another category of web analytics is popularity. Although it is possible to update the list of most popular search terms or downloads in real-time, this is often not done because the decisions to be made do not justify the investment and/or because of concerns of abuse (spam, pornography, abuse, etc.).

Experimentation is another common web application. An experiment may involve an A/B test to evaluate whether a new page design is superior. The metrics may involve measuring an increase of time spent on the page, click-thru rate on advertisements, or moving a user to a desired end state such as upgrading to a premium service. In order for an accurate decision to be made, though, enough users must see both versions. Thus, decisions cannot typically be made for at least 15 minutes.

Some common themes can be seen from these examples. First, rich contextual data is needed to make effective decisions. Second, relatively few applications justify true real-time decision making. This is because the cost of providing the data in context does not justify the decision making, or simply because more time is needed to acquire the context to make an informed decision. In many cases, the requirement is for near real-time business intelligence which is measured in minutes, not seconds.

2 Challenges

There are many technical challenges in providing practical real-time or near real-time business intelligence. Because the decisions to be made have been determined to be valuable and must be made with low latency, the underlying systems must be highly available. The rich contextual data often implies a high degree of data integration, access to detailed data, and access to aggregated/trending data. Sophisticated modeling may often be employed in order to classify behavior into similar segments. As the requirements get closer to real-time (seconds), the applications must tolerate some amount of data incompleteness or inaccuracy, as it is often not feasible (financially or technically) to provide 100% of the data within such strict time requirements.

3 Architectures

Several architectures exist for providing business intelligence. The most common solution for real-time business intelligence is to build a custom system. Commercial off the shelf platforms are not typically suited to the ultra low latency access, high availability and integration with detailed and aggregated data.

Commodity solutions for near real-time business intelligence typically involve enterprise data warehouses; these can be virtual or physical. The warehouse environment provides the detailed and aggregated data as well as high availability. The primary challenges are to load the data into the warehouse with low latency and to query it with low latency.

Several startups have emerged to build platforms to support low latency decision making on high volumes of streaming data. The primary challenges are to build a platform that is cost effective for applications that do not require ultra low-latency and to integrate with alternative data sources to provide the rich context necessary for decision making.

4 Summary

Most applications do not require real-time business intelligence which we define as making decisions in seconds or sub-seconds. Rather, given the difficulty and high cost of providing real-time BI, many of these applications can tolerate, or even require, less strict latency requirements.

What Can Hierarchies Do for Data Streams?

Xuepeng Yin and Torben Bach Pedersen

Aalborg University

Abstract. Much effort has been put into building data streams management systems for querying data streams. However, the query languages have mostly been SQL-based and aimed for low-level analysis of base data; therefore, there has been little work on supporting OLAP-like queries that provide real-time multi-dimensional and summarized views of stream data. In this paper, we introduce a multi-dimensional stream query language and its formal semantics. Our approach turns low-level data streams into informative high-level aggregates and enables multi-dimensional and granular OLAP queries against data streams, which supports the requirements of today's real time enterprises much better. A comparison with the STREAM CQL language shows that our approach is more flexible and powerful for high-level OLAP queries, as well as far more compact and concise.

Classification: Real-time OLAP, Streaming data, Real-time decision support.
Submission Category: Regular paper.

1 Introduction

Pervasive Computing is the newest wave within the IT world. Examples are temperature and noise sensors that can measure whether the environment behave as expected, and report irregularities. The data produced by these devices are termed *data streams*. Due to the different characteristics of data streams (e.g., continuous, unbounded, fast, etc.) from those of traditional, static data, it will most often be infeasible to handle the total data stream from a large number of devices using traditional data management technologies, and new techniques must therefore be introduced.

Recent studies have been focusing on building Data Stream Management Systems (DSMS) similar to the traditional DBMS's. However, queries in these systems have to a large extent been based on SQL and targeted for low-level data, and therefore are not suitable in performing OLAP-like operations to provide multi-dimensional and multi-granular summaries of data streams. As the notion of real-time enterprise is more and more recognized in the industry, analyzing data in a timely fashion for effective decision making in today's competitive and highly dynamic environment has become critical. Examples of such technologies are real-time OLAP, real-time Business Activity Monitoring (BAM), and streaming data. The solution presented in this paper is to build a multi-dimensional stream query language with built-in support for hierarchies, enabling the OLAP functionalities such as slice, roll-up and drill-down queries for powerful and timely analysis on data streams, which supports the requirements of today's real time enterprises much better.

Specifically, we present the following novel issues: 1) a new cube algebra that enables multi-dimensional and multi-granular queries against static OLAP cubes. That is,

C. Bussler et al. (Eds.): BIRTE 2006, LNCS 4365, pp. 4–19, 2007.
© Springer-Verlag Berlin Heidelberg 2007

high-level and low-level facts representing summaries and details can be presented together in a query result and different levels of selection criteria can also be applied. 2) conversion operators that transfer a continuous data stream into conventional cubes and also the other way around. 3) stream operators that perform OLAP operations on data streams, e.g., aggregates, roll-ups and drill-downs, with all the powers of the cube operators on static data. 4) comparisons with the Stanford STREAM language for roll-up and drill-down queries. We believe we are the first to present a multi-dimensional stream query language capable of performing typical OLAP operations against data streams, and the concrete query semantics for the above operators. The comparisons with the STREAM CQL query language suggest that our approach is much more compact and concise, and more effective in multi-dimensional and multi-granular analysis.

There has been a substantial amount of work on the general topic of OLAP [1]. Relevant work includes OLAP data modeling and querying [2,3,4,5]. However, all this work builds their solutions for static data, e.g., stored relational data. A more related topic is data integration of OLAP databases with dynamic XML data [6]. However, the system proposed is targeted for B2B business data on the web, which has far smaller data volumes and update frequencies in comparison with data streams. Recent interests in building data stream management system has generated a number of projects, including Aurora [7], Gigascope [8], NiagaraCQ [9], STREAM [10], and TelegraphCQ [11]. The query languages used by these systems generally have SQL-like syntax and the operators are analogous to operators in the relational algebra. Gigascope [12] supports shared fine-granularity aggregation queries to compute multiple coarser aggregation queries with different grouping attributes, which is a maintenance optimization rather than an OLAP extension. Therefore, OLAP-like queries involving hierarchical structures upon the basic stream schema have not yet been supported by current DSMS's.

The following descriptions of our approach is based on a sensor network, where sensor motes are deployed in a building to measure temperature every thirty seconds, producing a data stream with the schema SensorStream(Temperature, Id, Timestamp), capturing the current temperature reading, a unique identifier of the sensor, and the time of measurement. Also, we define the measure Temperature which is characterized by the dimensions Location(All-Floor-Room-Id), and Time(All-Day-Hour-Minute-Second), where the bottom levels are the attributes from the stream schema. A regular OLAP database, SensorCube, contains all the stream data produced on June 15, 2005.

The rest of the paper is organized as follows. Section 2 describes a query algebra and a multi-dimensional query language over a static cube model. Then, Section 3 introduces the stream model and the stream query language. Section 4 compares our language with the STREAM CQL with respect to OLAP-like analysis. Section 5 describes the current implementation. Finally Section 6 concludes the paper.

2   Querying Cubes

This section introduces the terms used in the following descriptions of cube operations. More formal definitions about the data model and the operators can be found in [13].

The Cube Model. A *dimension* D_i has a hierarchy of *levels* $L_{i1}, \ldots, L_{ik_i}$. A level is a set of *dimension values*. There exists a partial order, denoted $\sqsubseteq_i$ such that for two levels in a dimension, L_{il} and L_{ik}, we say $L_{il} \sqsubset_i L_{ik}$ holds if and only if the values of the higher level L_{ik} contain the values of the lower level L_{il}. For example, let D_i be a time dimension, $Day \sqsubset_i Year$ because years contain days. Similarly, a partial order also exists between dimension values. We say that $e_1 \sqsubset_{D_i} e_2$ if e_2 can be said to contain e_1. For example, the year 2004 has the date, Feb. 29th 2004, is denoted 2004-02-29 $\sqsubset_{D_i} 2004$. We also define $\sqsubseteq$ to denote a dimension value contained or equal to another. We use $e_i \in D_i$ to represent an arbitrary value e_i in dimension D_i.

A *measure* M_j is a set of numeric values that are being analyzed, e.g., sales, quantity, etc. A fact contains measure and dimension values, i.e., a tuple with the schema $(M_1, \ldots, M_m, D_1, \ldots, D_n)$ where M_j is a measure and D_i is a dimension. A fact is $r = (v_1, \ldots, v_m, e_1, \ldots, e_n)$, where v_i is a measure value characterized by dimension values $e_1, \ldots, e_n$. Also, a fact can have *any granularity in any dimension*, i.e., $(e_1, \ldots, e_n) \in D_1 \times \ldots \times D_n$. A *fact table* R is a set of facts with the schema $(M_1, \ldots, M_m, D_1, \ldots, D_n)$, such that in each fact, the measure values $v_1, \ldots, v_m$ are characterized by the values from the same set of dimensions $D_1, \ldots, D_n$ at any granular. For example, a fact table could be { (28.0, floor#1, 2005-06-15 08), (29.0, room#11, 2005-06-15 08), (27.0, room#12, 2005-06-15 08)}, where, there exist facts for the hourly temperatures of floors as well as rooms. A *cube* is a three tuple $C = (N, D, R)$ consisting of the name of the cube N, a non-empty set of dimensions $D = \{D_1, \ldots, D_n\}$ and a fact table R.

Querying Cubes. The cube generalized projection operator (Π_{cube}) turns the facts in a cube into higher level facts and aggregates the measures correspondingly. We also allow the result facts to have any granularity in any dimension to enable the roll-up and drill-down effects on certain dimensions in the query results, meaning that there might be multiple combinations of grouping values where the values from the same dimension in different combinations may be from different levels. When compared with the CUBE and ROLLUP operators [3], the cube generalized projection operator is more flexible and powerful in terms of OLAP-like queries. Specifically, the Π_{cube} operator can roll-up the input cube to any combination of levels without having to enumerate a full set of *super-aggregates* (as the CUBE and ROLLUP operators always do) and to specify the subset using conditions on the GROUPING() functions [3]. Moreover, the operator allows roll-up to or drill-down on a specific dimension value to, e.g., monitor anomalies on certain locations, which is not possible for the CUBE and ROLLUP operators. Thus, the cube generalized projection operator serves better for the purpose of our approach.

To ensure correct aggregation and also to be deterministic, we always use the *lowest-level* facts in each group, where in each tuple, every dimension value is from the bottom level. For example, to compute the hourly average temperature of a floor, we use the tuples directly from the sensors with the timestamps at the second level. We say such tuples have the lowest *level-combination* which is (Id, Second). However, sometimes, the tuples with such a level-combination may not be available, e.g., the base tuples are rolled up to higher levels, then the lowest level-combination now contains the lowest available levels in the dimensions of the current tuples. Currently, we assume that there always exists a lowest level-combination (in either sense above) in a group.

Definition 1 (Cube Generalized Projection). *Suppose that $C = (N, D, R)$ is the input cube, the generalized projection operator is defined as:* $\Pi_{cube[\{e_{i_1 1}, \ldots, e_{i_1 n_1}\}, \ldots,}$

$\{e_{i_k1},...,e_{i_kn_k}\}]<f_{j_1}(M_{j_1}),...,f_{j_l}(M_{j_l})>(C) = (N,D,R')$, where N and D are the same as in C, R' is the new fact table, $\{e_{i_h1},...,e_{i_hn_h}\}$ is a set of dimension values from dimension D_{i_h} and $f_{j_1},...,f_{j_l}$ are the given aggregate functions for the specified measures $\{M_{j_1},...,M_{j_l}\}$. Similar to the relational aggregate operator, a combination of the dimension values (i.e. grouping values) from each of the given sets constitutes a group of fact tuples over which the measures are aggregated. A group is denoted as $g_{(e_{i_1j_1},...,e_{i_kj_k})}$ where $(e_{i_1j_1},...,e_{i_kj_k}) \in \{e_{i_11},...,e_{i_1n_1}\} \times ... \times \{e_{i_k1},...,e_{i_kn_k}\}$. A group $g_{(e_{i_1j_1},...,e_{i_kj_k})}$ is the set of tuples such that the values from the dimensions $D_{i_1},...,D_{i_k}$ in the tuple are contained in the values $e_{i_1j_1},...,e_{i_kj_k}$ from the same dimensions, i.e., $g_{(e_{i_1j_1},...,e_{i_kj_k})} = \{(v_1,...,v_m,e_1,...,e_n) \in F | \exists e_{i_1},...,e_{i_k} \in \{e_1,...,e_n\}(e_{i_1} \sqsubseteq_{D_{i_1}} e_{i_1j_1} \wedge ... \wedge e_{i_k} \sqsubseteq_{D_{i_k}} e_{i_kj_k})\}$.

Each group produces one fact tuple consisting of the measures calculated over the tuples in the group. A fact is a lowest-level fact, if for any dimension value e_{i_h} in such a tuple, no descendants of e_{i_h} exists in any other fact of the group, and the group of such tuples is g_{lowest}, i.e., for a group $g_{(e_{i_1j_1},...,e_{i_kj_k})}$, $g_{lowest} = \{(v_1,...,v_m,e_1,...,e_n) \in g_{(e_{i_1j_1},...,e_{i_kj_k})} | \nexists(v'_1,...,v'_m,e'_1,...,e'_n) \in g_{(e_{i_1j_1},...,e_{i_kj_k})}, e'_{i_h} \in \{e'_1,...,e'_n\}, e_{i_h} \in \{e_1,...,e_n\}(e'_{i_h} \sqsubset e_{i_h})\}$. The fact tuple produced over the group is $r = (v'_{j_1},...,v'_{j_l}, e_{i_1j_1},...,e_{i_kj_k})$, where $v'_{j_q} = f_{M_{j_q}}(\{v_{j_q} | (v_1,...,v_{j_q},...,v_m,e_1,...,e_n) \in g_{lowest}\})$ and the input to the aggregate function is a multiset. We use $g_{(e_{i_1j_1},...,e_{i_kj_k})} \mapsto r$ to denote the relation between the group and the result tuple. The result fact table is $R' = \{r | g \in G \wedge g \mapsto r\}$, where G is the set of all the non-empty groups, i.e., $G = \{g_{(e_{i_1j_1},...,e_{i_kj_k})} | (e_{i_1j_1},...,e_{i_kj_k}) \in \{e_{i_11},...,e_{i_1n_1}\} \times ... \times \{e_{i_k1},...,e_{i_kn_k}\} \wedge g_{(e_{i_1j_1},...,e_{i_kj_k})} \neq \emptyset\}$.

Temperature	Location	Time
28.0	s#1	2005-06-15 08:00:00
28.0	s#2	2005-06-15 08:00:00
27.0	s#3	2005-06-15 08:00:00
27.0	s#4	2005-06-15 08:00:00
28.2	s#1	2005-06-15 08:00:30
28.2	s#2	2005-06-15 08:00:30
27.2	s#3	2005-06-15 08:00:30
27.2	s#4	2005-06-15 08:00:30

(a) The fact table before selection

Temperature	Location	Time
27.6	floor#1	2005-06-15 08:00
28.1	room#11	2005-06-15 08:00
27.1	room#12	2005-06-15 08:00

(b) The fact table after the operation

Fig. 1. The fact tables before and after the cube generalized projection

Example 1. Let the table in Figure 1(a) be the current fact table of SensorCube. The cube generalized projection $\Pi_{cube[\{floor\#1, room\#11, room\#12\}, \{2005\text{-}06\text{-}15\ 08:00\}]}(SensorCube)$ computes the average temperature per minute for floor#1, room#11, and room#12. The fact table after the operation is shown in Figure 1(b). The average floor temperature is computed over all the tuples in Figure 1(a), which are directly from the sensors and all at the lowest-level. Similarly, the average temperature of room#11 is computed over all the tuples sent by sensors s#1 and s#2 (the sensors in room#11), whereas the temperature of room#12 is computed over the tuples sent by s#3 and s#4 (the sensors in room#12).

Similarly to the relational selection operator σ, the *cube selection* operator σ_{cube} is used to process the facts, where measure values of a fact as well as the dimension values characterizing the measures must satisfy certain criteria to be selected into the result. Specially, levels of any granularity from any dimensions can be involved in the predicates; thus, a cube selection is capable of selecting multi-granular facts. That is, the predicate is true if the fact contains the value that satisfies the condition (e.g., room#11 in the above predicate) or descendants of the satisfying value (e.g., s#1 or s#2). In this way, we can easily specify the scopes of the interesting tuples to be analyzed without enumerating a long list of low-level details.

Definition 2 (Cube Selection). *Suppose the input cube is $C = (N, D, R)$, the selection operator is: $\sigma_{cube[\theta]}(C) = (N, D, R')$, where the cube name N and the dimensions D are not changed, and the output fact table is $R' = \{r | r \in R \wedge \theta(r) = true\}$.*

The Multi-dimensional SQL Language: SQL$_M$ The query below,

SELECT	AVG(Temperature), Room, Minute
FROM	SensorCube
WHERE	Time.Hour BETWEEN 8 AND 9
	AND Room in ('room#11', 'room#12')
DRILLDOWN DESCENDANTS('room#11', Location.Id)	

calculates the average temperature per minute for not only room#11 and room#12 but also the sensors in room#11 between 08:00:00 and 09:00:00. The DESCENDANTS function in the DRILLDOWN clause drills down to the Id level of the Location dimension for room#11, whose corresponding descendants are the sensors, s#1 and s#2. The optional DRILLDOWN clause is used to enable data analysis at a finer level for some specific dimension values, which are at the level given in the SELECT clause. Note that the first argument of DESCENDANTS can be a level, meaning drill-downs to the second argument level for all the values on the first level. The algebra expression for the above query is: $\Pi_{cube[\{room\#11,\,room\#12,\,s\#1,\,s\#2\},\{08:00,...,08:59\}]<AVG(Temperature)>}(\sigma_{cube[}$ $_{Time.Hour\ BETWEEN\ 8\ AND\ 9\ \wedge\ Room\ IN\ ('room\#11',\ 'room\#12']}((SensorCube))$. The operator σ_{cube} filters the cube and only passes on the sensor data emitted in room#11 and room#12 between 08:00:00 and 09:00:00. The parameters of the operator Π_{cube} contain the set of values at different levels from the Location dimension and the set of timestamps at the Minute level in the specified range. The filtered tuples are grouped according to the combinations of the values from the two sets. The cube generalized projection operator then computes the aggregated result tuple for each group.

The SELECT, WHERE, and FROM clauses are similar to the respective clauses in SQL, except that users do not need to specify join predicates in the WHERE or FROM clauses if column names in the SELECT clause are from different tables. The DRILL-DOWN clause allows drilldown to lower levels of the same dimensions, to which the levels given in the SELECT clause also belong. A drilldown operation is specified by the DESCENDANTS function, which is similar to the DESCENDANTS function in MS MDX[14]. The general form of a SQL$_M$ query can be stated as follows:

SELECT $\quad L_{i_1r_1},\ldots,L_{i_kr_k},f_{j_1}(M_{j_1}),\ldots,f_{j_l}(M_{j_l})$
FROM $\quad\quad C$
[WHERE $\quad\theta_1$]
[DRILLDOWN DESCENDANTS($e_{i_1r_1s_1},L_{i_1p_1}$),..., DESCENDANTS($e_{i_1r_1t_1},L_{i_1q_1}$),

$$\cdots$$

DESCENDANTS($e_{i_kr_ks_k},L_{i_kp_k}$),..., DESCENDANTS($e_{i_kr_kt_k},L_{i_kq_k}$)]

where, $L_{i_1r_1},\ldots,L_{i_kr_k}$ are dimension levels from dimensions $D_{i_1},\ldots,D_{i_k}$, $f_{j_1},\ldots,$ f_{j_l} are aggregate functions on measures $M_{j_1},\ldots,M_{j_l}$, and C is the input cube. θ_1 is the select predicate on dimensions and base measures. Note that the WHERE clause is optional. $e_{i_hr_hs_h},\ldots,e_{i_hr_ht_h}$ are some dimension values from the level $L_{i_hr_h}$ in the SELECT clause. $L_{i_hp_h}$ in DESCENDANTS($e_{i_hr_hs_h},L_{i_hp_h}$) is another level lower than $L_{i_hr_h}$ in the same dimension D_{i_h}. Note that the DRILLDOWN clause is also optional.

For each query on this form, we define the query semantics to be $\Pi_{cube[\{e_{i_11},\ldots,e_{i_1n_1}\}}$ $_{,\ldots,\{e_{i_k1},\ldots,e_{i_kn_k}\}]<f_{j_1}(M_{j_1}),\ldots,f_{j_l}(M_{j_l})>}(\sigma_{cube[\theta_1]}(C))$, where $\sigma_{cube[\theta_1]}$ is optional, and $\{e_{i_h1},\ldots,e_{i_hn_h}\}$ is a set of dimension values from the dimension D_{i_h}, which consists of all the dimension values from the level $L_{i_hr_h}$ as specified in the SELECT clause if the DRILLDOWN clause is not present, otherwise it also contains the descendant dimension values for $e_{i_hr_hs_h},\ldots,e_{i_hr_ht_h}$ from the levels $L_{i_hp_h},\ldots,L_{i_hq_h}$, respectively, as specified in the DRILLDOWN clause.

3　Querying Data Streams

The Streams Data Model. A *stream fact* is a timestamped regular fact where the timestamps are from the dimension of *application time*, which is assigned by the data sources. For example, sensor readings include the timestamps denoting the time at which a reading was taken, e.g., 2005-06-15 07:01:00,000 in the pattern of yyyy-mm-dd hh:mm:ss.xxx. Like a regular fact, a stream fact can have any granularity in any dimension. Therefore, a timestamp may refer to a time value coarser than the basic timestamps. That is, a time period associated with aggregated measure values. For example, 2005-06-15 07 represents the duration of an hour from 7:00AM, which includes 60 minutes directly as child values. 2005-06-15 07:01 represents the duration of a minute from 7:01AM, which includes 60 seconds as child values.

A *punctuation* is a special stream fact, which denotes the end of a subset of stream facts. Same as in [15], a fact r is said to *match* a punctuation p when the function: $match(r,p)$ returns ture. A punctuation is represented as a series of patterns over data items in the stream facts. The defined patterns are as following: 1) $*$ for the wildcard matching any value, 2) c for a constant that matches only c, and 3) e_i for any dimension value v with a partial order relationship to e_i, i.e., $v\sqsubseteq_{D_i}e_i$ along dimension D_i. Here, we assume that the stream sources, such as sensors, are smart enough to embed punctuations into the stream data when emissions of special subsets of stream tuples are finished. An example punctuation is in the form $p=(*,\ldots,*,t_p)$ and no stream facts with timestamps $t\sqsubseteq_T t_p$ will come after p and all the facts that come later all have timestamps $t>t_p$. Here, t might be a descendant of a larger value on the same level as t_p or the large value itself. For example, 2005-06-15 09:01 > 2005-06-15 08 because 2005-06-15 09 > 2005-06-15 08 and 2005-06-15 09:01 $\sqsubseteq_T$ 2005-06-15 09.

A *fact stream* S is an ordered multiset of stream facts $\{r_1, \ldots, r_k\}$ where facts are aligned from left to right in the sequence of their arrivals in the stream. Moreover, facts in the stream have the schema $(M_1, \ldots, M_m, D_1, \ldots, D_n)$, where measures in each stream fact are characterized by the same set of dimensions.

Conversion Operators. The multi-dimensional SQL queries and the cube operators above are *one-time* operations, i.e., they consume input and produce output only once in their lifetime. Based on these notions, we view the execution of stream queries as continuously consecutive runs of one-time queries on a data stream; therefore, streams are first converted to cubes then processed by the cube operators, which, when looked as one process, can be triggered by time-based or tuple-based events. Next, we introduce the conversion operators (i.e., stream-to-cube and cube-to-stream operators).

The stream-to-cube operator, when executed, produces a cube using the data from the input stream. Intuitively, the cube is a multi-dimensional snapshot of the input stream, i.e., columns of the stream tuples are divided into measures and dimensions and hierarchical data including the dimension values in the stream tuples are used to characterize the measure values. In some sense, the snapshots constructed by the stream-to-cube operator are time-based windows when the execution frequency of the cube operators is triggered by time, or tuple-based windows when the executions are triggered by a certain number of tuples. The snapshot contains either all the stream tuples in the current stream which are then processed to reveal the latest status or some tuples that satisfy certain conditions (e.g., punctuations marking the end of a set of tuples have arrived). We say that the stream-to-cube operators converting the entire input stream are in CONTINUOUS mode and non-blocking, and those with constraints on input facts in PERIODIC mode and blocking.

Definition 3 (Stream-to-Cube). *The stream-to-cube operator takes a fact stream S with the schema $(M_1, \ldots, M_m, D_1, \ldots, D_n)$ as input and generates a cube. Formally, a stream-to-cube operator is defined as: $SC_{[\{t_1,\ldots,t_k\}, MODE]}(S) = C$, where $\{t_1, \ldots, t_k\}$ are the timestamps representing the time periods to divide the input stream facts into subsets. The timestamps are inherited from the cube operators for which the input stream is converted. Moreover, $C = (N, D, R)$ is the new cube, where N is the new cube name, $D = \{D_1, \ldots, D_n\}$ are the dimensions characterizing the measures of the stream facts, and R is the fact table which contains the facts that are selected from the input stream according to the parameter MODE. In the following, suppose $r = (v_1, \ldots, v_m, e_1, \ldots, e_{n-1}, t_r)$ is a stream fact and t_r is the timestamp, P is the set of punctuations in S, $p \in P$ is a punctuation, and t_p is the timestamp of p marking the end of a subset of stream facts.*

When MODE=PERIODIC, the operator is blocking for the facts emitted in a given time period until their punctuations are received. In other words, for each execution, if all the stream facts having the timestamps within the specified periods of time are received, i.e., the subsets for the parameters are complete, they are converted into cube facts, and those without matching punctuations will be left in the input stream until, at a later execution, the operator finds that the subset they belong to is complete. Formally, suppose $S_{t_1}, \ldots, S_{t_k}$ are the subsets for the time parameters $t_1, \ldots, t_k$, respectively. i.e., $S_{t_1} = \{r | r \in S \wedge t_r \sqsubseteq_T t_1\}, \ldots, S_{t_k} = \{r | r \in S \wedge t_r \sqsubseteq_T t_k\}$. Among them, the complete sets are $S_{t_j}, \ldots, S_{t_l}$ ($1 \leq j \leq l \leq k$) where $\forall r \in S_{t_i} \exists p \in S(match(r, p) \wedge$

$t_p \geq t_i$) when $t_i \in \{t_j, \ldots, t_l\}$, whereas the incomplete sets are $S_{t_m}, \ldots, S_{t_n}$ ($1 \leq m \leq n \leq k$) where $\forall r \in S_{t_i} \not\exists p \in S(match(r,p) \wedge t_p \geq t_i)$ when $t_i \in \{t_m, \ldots, t_n\}$. Then, the fact table of the result cube is $R = S_{t_j} \cup \ldots \cup S_{t_l}$. The input stream after the operation is $S' = S_{t_m} \cup \ldots \cup S_{t_n}$.

When MODE=CONTINUOUS, the operator is non-blocking. That is to say, whenever the operator is invoked, all the facts except the punctuations in the input stream will be output to the result cube, which is defined as $R = S \backslash P$. When the set of the timestamps is empty, i.e., the operator is $SC_{[\{\}, CONTINUOUS]}$, then the input stream after the operation is $S' = \emptyset$, i.e., everything is moved to the result cube. Otherwise, the input stream is the same as in PERIODIC mode.

Example 2. This example shows how a stream is converted into cubes containing the facts produced from 2005-06-15 08:00:00 to 2005-06-15 08:02:00. Figure 2 shows the input and the output facts for just two working sensors, where facts in the top blocks are from the input stream and those at the bottom are the facts in the result cubes (the same alignment also appears in Figure 3.) Note that in the following examples the Year-Month-Day part of the timestamps is omitted to save space. For each execution, the selected facts on the left are the results of the PERIODIC mode and those on the right are results of the CONTINUOUS mode. The stream-to-cube operators producing the cubes to be aggregated upon behave as follows, respectively:

When $SC_{[\{2005-6-15\ 08:00,\ 2005-6-15\ 08:01\}, PERIODIC]}(S)$ is invoked, it outputs a cube containing the stream facts from the complete subsets for the past minutes. Suppose the operator is invoked at 08:01:20, the stream facts $r1$, $r2$, $r3$, and $r4$ with timestamps included in the minute 08:00 (i.e., 08:00:00-08:00:59), and $r5$ and $r6$ with timestamps included in 08:01 (i.e., 08:01:00-08:01:59) have been received; thus, the facts in the input stream are divided into $S_{08:00} = \{r1, r2, r3, r4\}$, and $S_{08:01} = \{r5, r6\}$. Because $p1$ and $p2$ mark the set $S_{08:00}$ complete and the punctuations for the facts in $S_{08:01}$ have not been received, the facts in the result cube are $\{r1, r2, r3, r4\}$. $r5$ and $r6$ are left in the input stream. At 08:02:32, the complete set is $S_{08:01} = \{r5, r6, r7, r8\}$. The punctuations $p3$ and $p4$ mark the end of the facts emitted before 08:02:00. Therefore, the result cube of the second execution contains the facts $\{r5, r6, r7, r8\}$. At this point, no more timestamps are left in the parameters and the operation is done.

When the CONTINUOUS output mode is applied, the operator $SC_{[\{2005-6-15\ 08:00, 2005-6-15\ 08:01\}, CONTINUOUS]}(S)$ outputs a cube containing all the facts in the current input stream every time the operator is invoked. Like the PERIODIC execution, facts from the incomplete subsets are remained in the input; thus, $r5$ and $r6$ are kept in the input stream for the next execution. At 08:02:32, all facts are copied to the result cube and there is no more incomplete sets according to the parameters. The operation is done.

The stream-to-cube operator does the conversion the other way around, which enables the aggregated/selected cubes to be presented in a streamed fashion; thus, historical data can participate in a stream query together with fresh data, thereby providing more powerful analysis on data streams. The two conversion operators are symmetric, which means one operator produces the data that can be accepted by the other. Because a cube does not contain punctuations, a cube-to-stream operator explicitly generates punctuation tuples for the output stream.

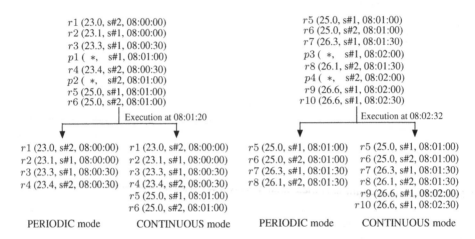

Fig. 2. Stream-to-cube operator at 08:01:20/08:02:32

Definition 4 (Cube-to-Stream). *A cube-to-stream operator takes a cube as a parameter and appends the fact tuples into a fact stream. Moreover, for each fact in the cube, a matching punctuation is also appended to the output cube. Suppose $C = (N, D, R)$ is the input cube, O is the output stream, a cube-to-stream operator is defined as: $CS(C) = O'$, where O' is the output stream with the new facts. Formally, $O' = append(O, sort(R \cup R_p))$, where R_p is the set of punctuations for the facts in R, i.e., $R_p = \{(*_1, \ldots, *_m, e_1, \ldots, e_n) | (v_1, \ldots, v_m, e_1, \ldots, e_n) \in R\}$. The function, sort, is used to transform a regular set of facts into an ordered multiset. Here, the result multiset just has the sequence as they appear in R on the physical storage and each punctuation fact is placed after the fact with the same dimension values (see below). The function specification could be application dependent, which means the tuples in the result can also be sorted by attribute(s) in the tuples, e.g., timestamp. The function, append, appends each fact in the sorted multiset to the end of O.*

Punctuations duplicate the facts except for the measure values, because we might not have pre-knowledge about the cube data. For example, the cube facts may have been aggregated, divided into subsets or selected by some criteria; thus there are no general patterns that can summarize the facts. Also, a punctuation defined as above identifies a unique fact, which also holds when streams are merged.

Stream Operators. The operators for stream queries are *stream-to-stream* (*stream* in short) operators whose inputs and outputs are streams. Unlike the STREAM project, we explicitly introduce stream-to-stream operators so that the data-flows in a query plan of such operators are always streams. With the inter-operator data flows, it is possible to physically distribute and execute the operators of a query plan on different computing devices; thus, instead of sharing the limited resources on one location, stream query execution can take the advantage of multiple processing and memory units. Also, the streaming input and output allow Gigascope's [12] two-layer architecture for query processing to be applied, i.e., a stream query (in our case, an operator as well) can be split into two parts communicating with streams: 1) simple low-level queries/operators to reduce data volumes, and 2) (potentially complex) high-level queries/operators over the results from the first part. Specifically, intermediate outputs of the stream operators of some queries can be redirected to other operators, thereby also giving the potentials for multiple-query optimization. Therefore, for a plan of stream operators, query evaluation is more flexible than for a plan with a stream-to-cube operator at the bottom, a cube-to-stream operator at the top, and cube operators in between. All in all, stream operators make a plan much easier to construct and understand, and also give a potential for more effective intermediate data sharing and query optimization. Note that in the following we define the semantics of stream operators using the conversion and cube operators to get well defined correspondence.

Definition 5 (Stream Selection). *The stream selection operator takes a stream I as input and outputs the result in a stream O. The formal definition is: $\sigma_{stream[\theta]}(I) = O$, where O is the output stream with the selected stream facts. The stream selection operator can be interpreted as a composition of a bottom stream-to-cube operator transferring subsets of stream facts from the input stream into a cube, a cube selection operator in the middle filtering the cube, and a top cube-to-stream operator converting the filtered cube into the output stream. Formally, $O = CS(\sigma_{cube[\theta]}(SC_{[\{\,\},CONTINUOUS]}(I)))$.*

Definition 6 (Stream Generalized Projection (SGP)). *Suppose the input and output streams of the SGP operators are I and O respectively. The operator is defined as: $\Pi_{stream[(\{e_{i_1 1},...,e_{i_1 n_1}\},...,\{e_{i_k 1},...,e_{i_k n_k}\},\{t_p,...,t_q\}),MODE]<f_{j_1}(M_{j_1}),...,f_{j_l}(M_{j_l})>}(I) = O$, where $t_p,\ldots,t_q$ are the timestamps from the time dimension, i.e., time periods to divide the stream facts into subsets, O is the output stream with the aggregated facts, and MODE is PERIODIC or CONTINUOUS. Similar to the stream selection operator, the SGP operator is also interpreted as a stream-to-cube operator at the bottom, a cube generalized projection operator in the middle, and a top cube-to-stream operator The output is $O = CS(\Pi_{cube[\{e_{i_1 1},...,e_{i_1 n_1}\},...,\{e_{i_k 1},...,e_{i_k n_k}\},\{t_p,...,t_q\}]<f_{j_1}(M_{j_1}),...,f_{j_l}(M_{j_l})>}(SC_{[\{t_p,...,t_q\}, MODE]}(I)))$.*

Example 3. Figure 3 shows the two executions of the SGP operator in different modes. The SGP operator in PERIODIC mode, $\Pi_{stream[(\{room\#11\},\{2005\text{-}6\text{-}15\,08,\,2005\text{-}6\text{-}15\,09\}),}$ PERIODIC]<AVG(temperature)>(SensorStream), produces the streamed output as $CS(\Pi_{cube[\{}$ room#11}, {2005-6-15 08, 2005-6-15 09}] <AVG(temperature) > $(SC_{[\{2005\text{-}6\text{-}15\,08,\,2005\text{-}6\text{-}15\,09\},PERIODIC]}($ SensorStream))). Each execution in PERIODIC mode only outputs one fact, which contains the average temperature value aggregated over the entire subset of the stream facts emitted in 08:00:00-08:59:59 or 09:00:00-09:59:59.

The SGP operator in CONTINUOUS mode, $\Pi_{stream[(\{room\#11\},\{2005\text{-}6\text{-}15\,08,\,2005\text{-}6\text{-}15}}$ 09})),CONTINUOUS]<AVG(temperature)>(SensorStream), produces the streamed output as $CS(\Pi_{cube[\{room\#11\},\{2005\text{-}6\text{-}15\,08,\,2005\text{-}6\text{-}15\,09\}]<AVG(temperature)>}(SC_{[\{2005\text{-}6\text{-}15\,08,\,2005\text{-}6\text{-}15\,09\},}$ CONTINUOUS]$(SensorStream)))$. In Figure 3, the execution in CONTINUOUS mode at 09:25:00 produces two facts, where $r1'$ is the same as the $r1'$ in PERIODIC mode since $p1$ and $p2$ for both sensors in room#11 have arrived. However, $r2'$ is produced using the received stream facts in 09:00:00-09:25:00 and contains the temperature value showing the latest status. After the punctuations for $r5$, $r6$, $r7$ and $r8$ have arrived, the second execution updates $r2'$, which reflects the exact average temperature for the hour.

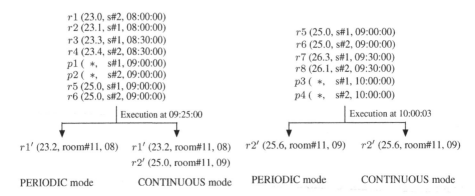

Fig. 3. The SGP operator at 09:25:00/10:00:03

The Multi-dimensional Stream Query Language[1]: SQL$_{MS}$ Section 2 shows the SQL$_M$ query on stored sensor data, whereas a similar SQL$_{MS}$ query can be issued on the continuous stream emitted by the same sensors. The query (below) calculates the average temperature per minute for each room between 8 AM and 9 AM. The algebra

```
SELECT       PERIODIC AVG(Temperature), Room, Minute
FROM         SensorStream
WHERE        Time.Hour BETWEEN 8 AND 9
             AND Room in ('room#11', 'room#12')
DRILLDOWN DESCENDANTS('room#11', Location.Id)
```

expression is: $\Pi_{stream[(\{room\#11, room\#12, s\#1, s\#2\}, \{08:00,...,08:59\}), PERIODIC]<AVG(Temperature)>}$ $(\sigma_{stream[Time.Hour\ BETWEEN\ 8\ AND\ 9 \wedge\ Room\ IN('room\#11',\ 'room\#12')]}(SensorStream))$. The parameters of the stream operators are constructed in the same way as for the cube operators, given the query and the dimensions. The selection operator σ_{stream} filters the received stream facts in a non-blocking manner and appends all the satisfying facts to the output stream, which is the input stream of the SGP operator. The PERIODIC SGP operator divides the complete subsets into groups according to the four location values and computes the result fact over each group, and then waits for the next execution.

Given the input stream I, the general form of a SQL$_{MS}$ query is:

```
SELECT       {PERIODIC|CONTINUOUS} L_{i_1 r_1},..., L_{i_k r_k}, f_{j_1}(M_{j_1}),..., f_{j_l}(M_{j_l})
FROM         I
[WHERE       θ_1 ]
[DRILLDOWN DESCENDANTS(e_{i_1 r_1 s_1}, L_{i_1 p_1}),..., DESCENDANTS(e_{i_1 r_1 t_1}, L_{i_1 q_1}),
                    ...
             DESCENDANTS(e_{i_k r_k s_k}, L_{i_k p_k}),..., DESCENDANTS(e_{i_k r_k t_k}, L_{i_k q_k}) ]
```

where, PERIODIC and CONTINUOUS are the new keywords that control the behaviors of the generalized projection operator. The parameters are the same as in the general

---

[1] Due the space limit, we omit the WITH clause and the SQL style HAVING clause of the original SQL$_{MS}$ in the full paper [13], where the WITH clause adds new dimensions to the stream cube based on external data, e.g., XML, to enable analysis of the facts in different scales and perspectives.

form of SQL_M (see [13] for more details about formal semantics). For each SQL_{MS} query on this form, we define the query semantics to be: $\Pi_{stream[(\{e_{i_1 1},...,e_{i_1 n_1}\},...,\{e_{i_k 1}, ...,e_{i_k n_k}\}),\text{OUTPUT\_MODE}]<f_{j_1}(M_{j_1}),...,f_{j_l}(M_{j_l})>}(\sigma_{stream[\theta_1]}(I))$, which is similar to that of SQL_M queries except that the operators are stream operators, and OUTPUT_MODE represents PERIODIC or CONTINUOUS.

4   Comparison with STREAM CQL

A SQL_{MS} query uses dimension levels in its clauses and predicates, whereas the Continuous Query Language (CQL) from the STREAM project uses only the columns defined in the stream schema (*basic columns* in short). When performing analysis requiring multiple views and different levels of details on stream data, the multi-dimensional and multi-granular characteristics of SQL_{MS} are considerably more powerful. In comparison, CQL, whose semantics to a large extent is based on SQL, does not fit the requirements of complex analysis over data stream very well.

SELECT	Rstream(AVG(Temperature) AS temp, NULL AS room, NULL AS floor, 'Overall' AS building)
FROM	SensorStream[Range 1 H, Slide 1 H]
	UNION
SELECT	Rstream(AVG(Temperature) AS temp, NULL AS room, floor AS floor, NULL AS building)
FROM	SensorStream[Range 1 H, Slide 1 H] SensorLocation
WHERE	SensorStream.location=SensorLocation.location
GROUP BY floor	
	UNION
SELECT	Rstream(AVG(Temperature) AS temp, room AS room, NULL AS floor, NULL AS building)
FROM	SensorStream[Range 1 H, Slide 1 H] , SensorLocation
WHERE	SensorStream.location=SensorLocation.location AND SensorLocation.floor='floor#2'
GROUP BY room	
	UNION
	(The union of the same three queries as above but using the sliding window of 1 minute)

Fig. 4. The CQL query

An example is shown to compare the two languages in the wireless sensor networks application (see [13] for more comparisons). The task, "show the average temperatures per hour and minute for the entire building, all the floors and the rooms on floor two", can be performed in both languages but with different complexity. The CQL query in Figure 4 unions six tables for the combinations of two time units and three levels of sensor locations. The predicate for selecting the sensor readings from floor two appears in two sub-queries whenever the temperature values are aggregated for the rooms. In comparison, the SQL_{MS} query in Figure 5 is considerably more compact and concise for the drill-down operations. The arguments in the SELECT clause indicate the coarsest granularity of the output along each dimension. In addition, through the DESCENDANTS functions, the DRILLDOWN clause specifies other lower levels that will be used to group the input stream facts. Therefore, aggregates can be performed on the groups formed by the combinations of Hour or Minute in the time dimension and the top level (the whole building), Floor or Room in the location dimension. Specially, to restrict the temperatures of the rooms not on floor#2 from being computed, the SQL_{MS} query specifies the drill-down operation on floor#2 explicitly using the DESCENDANTS function, which is much more concise than the predicates used in the sub-queries of the CQL query. The schema of the CQL result set is (temp, room, floor, building, timestamp) where two of the three columns representing different levels of locations are always NULL. The schema of the SQL_{MS} is (Temperature, Location, Time), where Location is a dimension and locations of any granularity are allowed to be present in this column, thereby leaving no NULL values in the output. The two queries return the same number of tuples (see [13]); thus, the SQL_{MS} output is much more dense than the CQL's.

SELECT PERIODIC   AVG(Temperature), Location.All, Time.Hour
FROM   SensorStream
DRILLDOWN DESCENDANTS(Location.All, Location.Floor),
               DESCENDANTS(Location.'floor#2', Location.Room),
               DESCENDANTS(Time.Hour, Time.Minute)

Fig. 5. The SQL_{MS} query

We discuss two more examples in the following to compare the languages: task 2) "show the average temperature per hour per floor" and task 3) "if the average temperature of the whole building exceeds 30°C, then show the floors with average temperatures higher than 32°C, and also the temperatures of each room on these floors." Table 1 shows the complexities of the six queries, where "# of lines" is the number of lines of each query, "# of unions" is the number of sub–queries unioned together, "# of characters" is the number of characters in each query, and "# of cells" is the number of the cells in the output (lines×columns). In summary, we can see that the multi-dimensional and multi-granular features of SQL_{MS} queries are more intuitive and make the OLAP-like queries more compact and considerably easier to construct, e.g., the SQL_{MS} query

Table 1. Complexity comparisons

		# of lines	# of unions	# of characters	# of cells
Task 1	CQL	31	6	990	6125
	SQL_{MS}	5	0	199	3675
Task 2	CQL	4	0	142	12
	SQL_{MS}	2	0	77	12
Task 3	CQL	27	3	834	40
	SQL_{MS}	6	0	255	24

for task 1 is 5-6 times less complicated than the CQL query for the same task. This also gives a potential for more efficient query evaluation.

5 Implementation

We implemented a prototypical stream query engine in C# with Microsoft Visual Studio .NET 2003 on Microsoft Windows XP Pro. SP2, which supports all the queries given in this paper. Specifically, the roll-up and drill-down operations are essentially look-ups in hashtables, which are the dimensions loaded into the main memory during starting-up. A dimension value and a level constitute a key in the hashtables and the corresponding bucket stores the ancestor of the dimension value in the given level. A selection operator is first positioned upon the input stream if the WHERE clause is present. Roll-up's are involved when the select predicates reference non-bottom levels. Ancestor values in the referenced levels must be found for each input fact to evaluate the predicates. To aggregate over the desired levels (i.e., levels referenced by the SELECT clause and the second argument(s) of the DESENDANTS functions), ancestor values in these levels are also needed for each input fact. Measures are then aggregated for each combination of the ancestor values from different dimensions. A new entry is added in the hashtable for aggregation if it does not already exist. Also, the query engine supports measure dimensions, meaning that the values of a measure can be divided into ranges and used as a regular dimension to characterize other measures.

SELECT CONTINUOUS AVG(Humidity), Room, Minute   FROM SensorStream
SELECT CONTINUOUS AVG(Humidity), Section, Minute   FROM SensorStream
SELECT CONTINUOUS AVG(Humidity), Area, Minute   FROM SensorStream
SELECT CONTINUOUS AVG(Humidity), Room, Minute   FROM SensorStream WHERE Area='outer' AND Temprange='cold'
SELECT CONTINUOUS AVG(Humidity), Section, Minute   FROM SensorStream WHERE Area='outer' AND Temprange='cold'
SELECT CONTINUOUS AVG(Humidity), Area, Minute   FROM SensorStream WHERE Area='outer' AND Temprange='cold'
SELECT   CONTINUOUS AVG(Humidity), Area, Minute   FROM SensorStream WHERE   Area='outer' AND Temprange='cold' DRILLDOWN DESCENDANTS('outer',Moteid)
SELECT   CONTINUOUS AVG(Humidity), Area, Minute   FROM SensorStream WHERE   Area='outer' AND Temprange='cold' DRILLDOWN DESCENDANTS('outer',Room)
SELECT   CONTINUOUS AVG(Humidity), Area, Minute   FROM SensorStream WHERE   Area='outer' AND Temprange='cold' DRILLDOWN DESCENDANTS('outer',Section)

Preliminary experiments have shown that the performance is promising. The table below shows nine example queries. Their execution times are around 1.5 seconds (on an Intel Pentium 1.86GHz laptop with 1.5GB of RAM) for 50,000 tuples of Intel Lab Data [16]. Here, the hierarchy of the dimension Location is (ALL-Area-Section-Room-Moteid) and Temperature(ALL-Temprange-Temperature) is a measure dimension.

Temprange contains the values: freezing, cold, warm, and hot. The input facts are filtered on the fly, where the predicate "Area='outer'" selects the sections adjacent to the wall, but the aggregation is only performed when no more data can be received. The experiments are preliminary at this point, but it shows that the algorithms can handle at least 30,000 facts/second.

6   Conclusion

Stream data gives more interesting and valuable information when analyzed at appropriate levels of abstraction. Due to its distinct characteristics (e.g., continuous, unbounded, fast, etc.), traditional data analysis systems are not suitable. Recent DSMS's are to a large extent SQL-based and do not support OLAP-like stream analysis.

In this paper, we have introduced an approach to perform real-time OLAP-like analysis on data streams. Specifically, we presented the new cube operators that support multi-granular analysis on persistent data and then using the new conversion operators, we defined the new stream operators that view the input stream as cubes and support OLAP-like real-time multi-dimensional and granular stream queries.

We believe we are the first to present a multi-dimensional stream query language and the concrete semantics of the stream operators. Our next step is to study the performance of the prototype and exploit optimization techniques (e.g., data-reduction by multi-level aggregations, reuse of finer-granular pre-aggregations, approximations, etc.) to maximize the stream query engine's throughput and minimize resource consumption. Details about experiments and implementation of the operators will be documented.

Acknowledgements

This work was supported by the Danish Research Council for Technology and Production Sciences under grant no. 26-02-0277.

References

1. Codd, E.F., Codd, S.B., Salley, C.T.: Providing OLAP (Online Analytical Processing) to User-Analysts: An IT Mandate (2005) (Current as of May 8, 2006)
   `www.essbase.com/ resource_library/white_papers/providing_olap_touser_analysts_0.cfm`
2. Chatziantoniou, D., Ross, K.A.: Querying Multiple Features of Groups in Relational Databases. In: Proc. of VLDB, pp. 295–306 (1996)
3. Gray J., et al.: Data Cube: A Relational Aggregation Operator Generalizing Group-By, Cross-Tab, and Sub-Total. In: Proc. of ICDE, pp. 152–159 (1996)
4. Jagadish, H.V., Lakshmanan, L.V.S., Srivastava, D.: What can Hierarchies do for Data Warehouses? In: Proc. of VLDB, pp. 530–541 (1999)
5. Pedersen, D., Riis, K., Pedersen, T.B.: XML-Extended OLAP querying. In: Proc. of SSDBM, pp. 195–206 (2002)
6. Yin, X., Pedersen, T.B.: Evaluating XML-Extended OLAP Queries Based on a Physical Algebra. In: Proc. of DOLAP, pp. 73–82 (2004)

7. Carney D., et al.: Monitoring Streams - A New Class of Data Management Applications. In: Proc. of VLDB, 215–226 (2002)
8. Cranor, C.D., et al.: Gigascope: High Performance Network Monitoring with an SQL Interface. In: Proc. of SIGMOD, p. 623 (2002)
9. Chen, J., et al.: NiagaraCQ: A Scalable Continuous Query System for Internet Databases. In: Proc. of SIGMOD, pp. 379–390 (2000)
10. The STREAM group: STREAM: The Stanford Stream Data Manager. IEEE Data Engineering Bulletin, vol. 26(1), pp. 19–26 (2003)
11. Chandrasekaran, S., et al.: TelegraphCQ: Continuous Dataflow Processing for an Uncertain World. In: Proc. of CIDR, pp. 269–280 (2003)
12. Zhang, R., et al.: Multiple Aggregations Over Data Streams. In: Proc. of SIGMOD, pp. 299–310 (2005)
13. Yin, X., Pedersen, T.B.: What can Hierarchies do for Data Streams. Technical Report TR-12 (2005) (Current as of May 8, 2006) http://www.cs.auc.dk/DBTR
14. Spofford, G.: MDX Solutions. Wiley, New York (2001)
15. Tucker, P.A., Maier, D., Sheard, T.: Applying Punctuation Schemes to Queries Over Continuous Data Streams. IEEE Data. Engineering Bulletin 26(1), 33–40 (2003)
16. Intel Berkeley Research lab: Intel lab data (2004) berkeley.intel-research.net/labdata

Leveraging Distributed Publish/Subscribe Systems for Scalable Stream Query Processing

Yongluan Zhou, Kian-Lee Tan, and Feng Yu

National University of Singapore

Abstract. Existing distributed publish/subscribe systems (DPSS) offer loosely coupled and easy to deploy content-based stream delivery services to a large number of users. However, the lack of query expressiveness limits their application scope. On the other hand, distributed stream processing engines (DSPE) provide efficient processing services for complex stream queries. Nevertheless, these systems are typically tightly coupled, platform dependent, difficult to deploy and maintain, and less scalable to the number of users. In this paper, we propose a new architectural design for a scalable distributed stream processing system, which provides services to evaluate continuous queries for a large number of clients. It is built by placing a query layer on top of a DPSS architecture. In particular, we focus on solving the query distribution problem in the query layer.

1 Introduction

Emerging monitoring applications, such as financial monitoring, sensor network monitoring, network management etc., have fueled much research interest in designing distributed publish/subscribe systems (DPSS) [1,5,10] and distributed stream processing engines (DSPE) [2,7,11,13,17]. DPSS, which is mostly developed by the networking community, aims at providing scalable content-based stream delivery service to a large number of users. It can be applied in applications such as stock/sports tickers, news feed etc. Such systems adopt a loosely coupled architecture and hence are easy to deploy. In such an architecture, data sources continuously publish data to the network without specifying the destinations. Hence the destinations are independent of the data sources. Instead, the distributed brokers will cooperatively route the data to the interested users based on the data content. In summary, DPSSs are efficient in content-based data delivery to a vast number of users.

On the other hand, existing DSPEs, which are mainly built by the data management community, are targeted at supporting complex continuous queries over data streams. Example applications include network management, sensor network monitoring etc. In these applications, the number of users is relatively smaller and the queries are much more complex than those of the DPSS applications (e.g., user queries are specified in SQL-like statements). Moreover, in DSPEs, the processors are coupled more tightly to enhance the processing efficiency. Query operators are allocated to the distributed processors to optimize

C. Bussler et al. (Eds.): BIRTE 2006, LNCS 4365, pp. 20–33, 2007.

the system performance. Each processor evaluates the local operators and forward the results to the downstream processors or the end users. In short, DSPEs are efficient in complex stream query evaluations.

The above two types of systems target different application scenarios and hence adopt different architectures. However, there are emerging applications (e.g., finanacial market monitoring) that require the strengths of both systems. http://www.traderbot.com illustrates an example of such applications. It provides continuous query processing services over real time data such as stock trades, financial news etc. This kind of service has a potentially large number of users and hence the DPSS architecture is desirable to scale up the data delivery service. However, the user queries require a query interface with much more features than that can be provided by a DPSS. On the other hand, existing DSPEs are not scalable to the large user number of these applications.

In this paper, we propose a new architectural design to bridge the gap between these two types of systems and to leverage their strengths. To handle both the streaming data and streaming queries, the system adopts a two-layered architecture. The data layer resembles the DPSS architecture and is responsible for disseminating source data streams among the processors as well as the result streams to the users. The query layer distributes the streaming queries to a number of distributed nodes for processing. The goal of query distribution is to achieve load balance and minimum communication cost. We model the problem as a graph partitioning problem and develop an efficient query distribution algorithm. Our performance study shows the efficiency of our techniques.

The rest of the paper is organized as follows. Section 2 presents the model and the challenges of the system. Sections 3 and 4 present the query distribution techniques. Representative experimental results are also presented in Section 4. Section 5 concludes the paper.

2   System Model and Challenges

Figure 1 shows the overview of our scalable distributed stream processing system, COSMOS (COoperative and Self-tuning Management Of Streaming data). The service is backed by a number of distributed processors interconnected with a widely distributed overlay network. These processors may be under independent administrations and may join or leave the system anytime. A number of data sources continuously publish their data to the network through the processors. User queries submitted to the system are specified in high level SQL-like language statements. For simplicity, we only consider continuous queries and assume they do not involve stored tables.

There are two major challenges in the system: data stream delivery and query processing. Two layers of services, the data layer and query layer, are provided to address these two problems respectively. Figure 2 shows the architecture of a processor in the system. The delivery of both the raw streams and the result streams, is handled by the data layer module. The raw streams received by the data layer module will be transformed and cleaned by the data cleaner and then

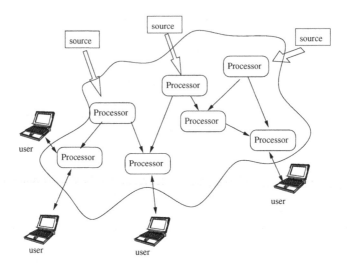

Fig. 1. Overview of COSMOS

pushed to the stream processing engine (SPE) for processing. Existing single site SPE such as TelegraphCQ [6], STREAM [15] and Aurora [4], can be adopted in our system. The following subsections present more details and identify the challenges in both layers.

2.1 Data Layer

Given the user queries, the system should route the source data streams to the processors to feed the queries and deliver the result streams to the users. Existing DPSS architecture is employed to support this service. DPSS provides a scalable content-based stream delivery service. The service is backed by a number of brokers, which are organized into multiple dissemination trees. Data sources can just push their data into the network through their root brokers without the need to specify the destinations. Data destinations are identified by their data interest, which is specified by their profiles. A profile typically contains a set of predicates over the attributes of the data. Upon receiving a data item, a broker checks if its neighboring brokers or its local users are interested in the data item and only forwards it to those interested parties.

The data layer module of a processor in COSMOS plays the role of the brokers in the DPSS architecture. The data interest profiles used by this module is extracted from the local user queries by the query management module. More specifically, the selection predicates of each query are extracted and used to compose the profile. :w

As for the data delivery scheme, we adopt a similar scheme as SemCast [10]. In this scheme, the data space is partitioned into multiple subspaces by dividing each stream into multiple substreams. We denote the total set of substreams in the system as $SS = \{ss_1, ss_2, \ldots, ss_{|SS|}\}$. Logically, the data interest of a node

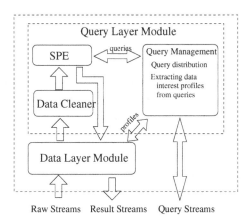

Fig. 2. Architecture of a processor

can be represented as a bit vector $q \in \{0, 1\}^{|SS|}$, where $|SS|$ is the total number of substreams.

$$q[i] = \begin{cases} 1 & \text{if substream } ss_i \text{ overlaps with the data interest of } q, \\ 0 & \text{otherwise.} \end{cases}$$

When a tuple arrives, it is matched to a substream and then sent to those destinations that are interested in the substream. Matching a tuple to a substream is actually searching the subspace (the substream) that covers a specific point (the tuple) in the data space. This can be solved by using existing techniques, such as R*-tree [3].

To maximize the filtering efficiency, the data space partitioning strategy is critical. In SemCast [10], the authors proposed a semantic approach to partition the stream spaces based on the user profiles. As a first cut, we simply adopt this approach. As the focus of this paper is on the design of the query layer, we shall not discuss the data layer any further.

2.2   Query Layer

COSMOS is designed to support a large number of clients. Therefore, we have to distribute a large number of queries to the processors for processing. To enhance the processing efficiency, two objectives have to be considered. (1) To achieve maximum system utilization and minimum processing latencies, load balancing among the processors is desirable. (2) Due to the large volumes and continuity of streaming data, minimizing the communication cost in the system is also very important.

Unfortunately, typical DPSS does not consider load balancing and simply allocate user queries to the closest brokers. The DSPEs proposed in [13,17] employed load balancing techniques for a cluster of locally distributed processors, but they did not consider the communication cost. Thus, they are not suitable for a widely distributed network. On the other hand, in [2,11], optimization algorithms were proposed to distribute the query operators across a set of widely distributed processors to minimize the communication cost. The processors are assumed to employ the same processing model and data model. However, these techniques failed to address the load balancing problem. Hence, they are suited for applications where the system is under a central administration and there are only a relatively smaller number of complex queries to process. [14] studied the static operator placement problem in a hierarchical stream acquisition architecture, which cannot be applied in our architecture. Load balancing is also ignored in this piece of work.

In this paper, we opt to distribute queries to processors instead of operators. In other words, we adopt a query level load distribution scheme (instead of an operator level scheme). Several reasons prompted this design decision. First, it is simpler (than an operator-based scheme) and practical. As nodes in a DPSS architecture may be under independent administrations, they may install different stream processing engines or different versions of the same engine. Hence distributing query load at the operator level may be infeasible. For instance, moving a window join operator from the STREAM system to a TelegrahCQ system is hard to implement, because it relies on a special data structure "synopsis" implemented in STREAM which is not only manipulated by the join operator itself but also other operators before or after the join operator. Furthermore, even if the processors use the same engine, one may upgrade its engine without informing the others. This might also give rise to problems unless forward and backward compatibility is implemented. Second, operator level load distribution may tighten the coupling of the processors. Besides adopting the same processing model and data model, the processors may also have to synchronize with each other during the processing of a query. Third, distributing at the operator level would be too complex to be scalable to a large number of query streams.

In addition, our query-level distribution scheme is essentially non-intrusive - existing single site processing engines can fit into our system without much extra software (re)development.

There are two problems to be addressed: (1) How to scale up the query distribution algorithm to a large number of user queries. (2) How to distribute queries to achieve the objectives mentioned above. These two problems are addressed in the following sections respectively.

3   Coordinator Network Construction

To enhance the scalability of the query distribution algorithm, we deploy a number of coordinators to perform this task. Among the processors in our system, we select a few of them as coordinators. Each such processor performs two separate logical roles: the stream processor and the coordinator, while others perform only the stream processor role. We assume that separate resources of these processors are reserved for these two roles. Hereafter, the words "processor" and "coordinator" refer to the logical roles.

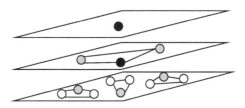

Fig. 3. Hierarchical Coordinator Structure

To scale to fast streaming rate of queries, we organize the coordinators into a hierarchical structure. An example of this structure is illustrated in Figure 3. All the processors are clustered into multiple close-by (in terms of communication latency) clusters. Within each cluster, a processor, say x, is elected as the parent of the cluster, which is responsible for distributing queries to processors within this cluster. In this way, x only has to maintain the information of the processors in its cluster (e.g., statistics of the queries running in the processors etc.). For example, in the bottom plane of Figure 3, the processors are organized into three clusters, and one coordinator (drawn in gray) is selected within each cluster. The coordinators are also clustered level by level in a similar way. An interior coordinator manages a set of close-by coordinators (its children) and is responsible for distributing the queries to them for further distribution. It has to maintain a larger scope of information which is the total scope of its children. To enhance the scalability, the information in the parent is much coarser than those in the children (Section 4). Queries are first submitted to the root coordinator and then are distributed down one level at a time until a processor is reached.

4   Query Distribution

In this section, we present how queries are distributed to the processors. We try to achieve two goals:

- Balance the load among the processors. In this paper, we only focus on the CPU load. We assume the relative computational capability (the CPU speed) of each processor is known. For example, we can set the capability of one processor as the basic capability and associate it with a value 1. If a processor is l times more powerful than this basic processor, its capability is valued as l. Furthermore, the load of a query is estimated as the CPU time that the query will consume per unit time in the basic processor. Hence if the total query load is L and the total capability of the processors is C, the desirable load that should be allocated to a processor with capability value l is $l \cdot \frac{L}{C}$.
- Minimize the total communication cost. The communication cost can be divided into two parts: (1) transferring source streams from the sources to the processors; (2) transferring query results from the processors to the users. Following existing work [2,11], we use the weighted unit-time communication

cost, i.e. the per unit time message transfer rate of each link times the transfer latency of the link, to measure the communication effciency. Here, we use the transfer latency to estimate the distance between two processors.

To minimize this cost, there are two issues to be addressed. First, the total message rate in the system should be minimized. Hence, for each tuple that has to be disseminated, it is desirable to disseminate it to as few processors as possible. That means we should minimize the overlap of the data interest of the processors. Second, we should avoid transferring data through links with long distances as far as possible. This suggests we should maintain data flow locality. For example, if a few queries have very large overlap in their data interest, distributing them to a few nearby processors can achieve better data flow locality than distributing them to a few faraway nodes as the nearby processors can cooperatively disseminate the data that are of interests to them.

To achieve the above two goals, we dynamically partition the queries into N partitions, where N is the total number of processors, and allocate them to the processors. The scheme balances the load among the processors while minimizes the overlap of the data interest between the partitions and maintains the data flow locality.

4.1   Problem Modeling

4.1.1   Simple Approach

To solve the problem, we model it as a graph partitioning problem. More specifically, we construct a *query graph* as follows. Each vertex in the graph represents a query and there is one edge between every two vertices that have overlap in their data interest. Each edge is weighted with the estimated arrival rate (bytes/second) of the data of interest to both end vertices (queries). The weight of a vertex is equal to the estimated load that would be incurred by the query at the processor with the basic capacity. These weights can be estimated based on previously collected statistics and may be re-estimated at runtime based on the new statistics. By doing so, we can model the query distribution problem as a graph partitioning problem:

Given a graph $G = (V, E)$ and the weights on the vertices and edges, partition V into N disjoint partitions such that each partition has a specified amount of vertex weights and the weighted edge cut, i.e. the total weight of the edges connecting vertices in different partitions, is minimized.

Figure 4.1 illustrates an example query graph that comprises 5 queries. The weights of the vertices and edges are drawn around them. If, for example, we have to allocate the queries to two processors, we can consider two plans: (a) allocate Q_3 and Q_4 to one processor and the rest to another; (b) allocate Q_3 and Q_5 to one processor and the others to another. Both the two plans can achieve load balance. However, plan (b) has a better communication efficiency, where only 3 (bytes/second) of data are transferred twice, while in plan (a) 8 (bytes/second) of duplicate data are transferred. Note that only considering allocating similar queries together may not result in good performance. As can be seen from this

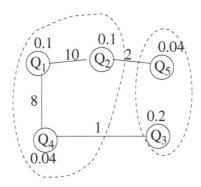

Fig. 4. A simple query graph model

example, Q_3 and Q_5 are not similar in their data interest but allocating them together results in a better scheme.

4.1.2 Extended Approach

The above simple model, unfortunately, does not capture the cost of transmitting the result streams to the users. To solve this problem, we extend the above model as follows.

First, we adopt the same assumption as a DPSS that a user is allocated to his closest processor when he joins the system in the first place. The user and the processor are said to be local to each other. Since the result stream of a query is routed to the user by the DPSS architecture of the data layer, it will be first routed to the user's local processors and then to the user. Therefore, the cost of transferring the query result from the processor to its local users are unavoidable.

Second, for each processor, we add one additional vertex into the query graph. We refer to such additional vertices as processor vertices. The weights of these vertices are set to zero. One edge is also added between each processor and each of its local queries (i.e., queries initiated from the processor). Each such edge is weighted by the estimated result stream rate (bytes/second) of the corresponding query.

Third, the graph partitioning problem statement is revised as follows: *Given a graph $G = (V, E)$ and the weights on the vertices and edges, partition V into N disjoint partitions such that each partition has exactly one processor vertex and a specified amount of vertex weights and the weighted edge cut is minimized.* All queries within a partition are allocated to the processor in that partition.

Figure 4.1 illustrates an extended query graph. In comparison to Figure 4.1, there are two additional processor vertices, which are drawn in rectangles, and five additional edges between them and their local queries. Here, contrary to the prior conclusion, allocating Q_3 and Q_4 to P_1 and the rest to P_2 is a better plan.

4.1.3 Challenges

The graph partitioning problem is an NP-hard problem but has been extensively studied in a lot of application areas, such as parallel scientific computing, VLSI design etc. [12] provides a survey of the graph partitioning algorithms in the application of scientific computing. To enhance the scalability, parallel

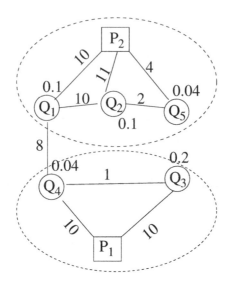

Fig. 5. An extended query graph model

algorithms have also been proposed [8,16]. Unfortunately, the problem in our context bears a few important differences from these previous studies:

(a) The semantics of the graph is different. In our problem, the edges between the query vertices represent the overlap relationship of the data interest among different queries, while, in prior work, they model the amount of communication between the vertices. Furthermore, there is no notion of processor vertices in prior work.

(b) Traditional graph partitioning algorithms do not consider how to assign the resulting partitions to the processors. That is because processors are all connected by fast local network and identical in terms of network locations. However, in a widely distributed network, maintaining data flow locality is critical to minimizing communication cost.

(c) To enhance the scalability of the partitioning algorithm, a distributed or parallel algorithm is needed. In prior work, processors are assumed to be connected by a fast local network [12]. Hence they employ parallel algorithms that require frequent communication between the processors. However, our system is a widely distributed large scale system and the communication cost among even the coordinators could be very high. Hence the existing parallel algorithm is unsuitable for our problem.

The above differences render the existing solutions inadequate for our problem.

4.2   Proposed Approach

In this section, we present the proposed solution. Unlike the previously proposed parallel algorithms, which allow frequent communication between any pair of

---

Algorithm 1. Graph Coarsening

```
1  while |V| > v_max do
2  |   Set all the vertices as unmatched;
3  |   while ∃ unmatched vertices & |V| > v_max do
4  |   |   Randomly select an unmatched vertex u;
5  |   |   A ← adj(u) − mat(adj(u)) ;
6  |   |   if pro(u) then A ← A − {v|v ∈ adj(u) & pro(v) & v.tag! = u.tag};
7  |   |   Select a vertex v from A such that the edge e(u, v) is of the maximum
   |   |   weight;
8  |   |   Collapse u and v into a new vertex w;
9  |   |   Set w as matched;
10 |   |   w.weight ← u.weight + v.weight;
11 |   |   Re-estimate the weights of the edges connected to w;
12 |   |   if pro(u) OR pro(v) then
13 |   |   |   pro(w) ← true;
14 |   |   |   w.tag = pro(u)?u.tag : v.tag;
```

---

coordinators, we employ a *hierarchical graph partitioning* algorithm that is run on our hierarchical coordinator tree. Each leaf coordinator first collects the query specifications from its child processors. These queries are tagged with their original locations. A query graph is then generated over the queries in each leaf coordinator. The edge weight between a pair of vertices can be efficiently estimated by summing up the rates of the substreams of interest to both end vertices. The common interest of two queries can be determined easily based on their data interest vectors (Section 2.1).

Each coordinator (except the root) will perform Algorithm 1 to coarsen its local query graph before submitting to the parent. This algorithm repeatedly collapses two selected vertices until the number of vertices are smaller than or equal to v_{max}. The weights of the corresponding edges and the merged vertex are adjusted accordingly. We set v_{max} as $|V|/f$, where $|V|$ is the total number of vertices and f is the fanout of the parent coordinator. For ease of presentation, we define the following functions:

(1) $adj(u)$ returns the set of adjacent nodes of u;
(2) $pro(u)$ returns true if u is a processor vertex;
(3) $matched(A)$ returns all the matched vertices from a set of vertices A.

In the algorithm, a vertex u tends to collapse with a neighbor v which has an edge $e(u, v)$ with a larger weight. Two processor vertices with different tags will not be merged together. That is because they belong to different child clusters and hence they should be put into different partitions and allocated to different clusters of processors.

The vertices in the coarsened graph are tagged with the current coordinator's name and then the graph is submitted to the parent, who will perform the same procedure after receiving all the coarsened graphs from its children. Note that the procedure can run in parallel in different subtrees, which can accelerate the whole procedure.

Finally, when the root coordinator receives all the graphs from its children, it will generate a global query graph and then partition it into f partitions, one for each of its children. The partitioning is done based on the total computational capabilities of the processors within the scope of each child. Here we can apply any of the traditional graph partitioning algorithms [12] while ensuring the constraint that two processor vertices with different tags cannot be put into the same partition. In our experiments, we use the algorithm in [9]. Each child coordinator will then uncoarsen the subgraph assigned to it one level back. Based on the tags of the vertices, the information of the finer-grained vertices can be retrieved from the corresponding coordinator. Finally, the uncoarsened graph is partitioned as in the root coordinator. This procedure repeats at each level until all the queries are assigned to the processors.

We can see that, at each level of the above procedure, the queries are distributed to minimize the overlap of data interest between different regions of the network. Furthermore, the higher the result stream rate of a query, the more likely that the query is put close to its local processor. These help maintain data flow locality.

4.3 Experiments

In this section, we present a performance study of the proposed techniques. A network topology with 4096 nodes is generated using the GT-ITM topology generator. The Transit-Stub model, which resembles the internet structure, is used. Among these nodes, 100 nodes are chosen as the data stream sources, and 256 nodes are selected as the stream processors, and the remaining nodes act as the routers. Our algorithms are implemented in C and the communication between the processors is simulated. The experiments are run on a Linux Server with an Intel 2.8GHz CPU.

The default cluster size parameter k used in the coordinator tree construction is set to 4. All the streams are partitioned into $20,000$ substreams and they are randomly distributed to the sources. The arrival rate of each substream is randomly chosen from 1 to 10 (bytes/seconds). As it is hard to collect large number of real query workload, we use synthetic query workload in our experiments. To simulate clustering effect of user behaviors, $g = 20$ groups of user queries are generated and each group has different data hot spots. For the queries within every group, the probability that a substream is selected conforms to a zipfian distribution with $\theta = 0.8$. To model different groups having different hot spots, we generate g number of random permutations of the substreams.

We compare our approach with three other approaches: (a) Naive: allocate the queries to the processors to balance the load without considering their data interest. (b) Greedy: an expected load limit is computed for each processor. If the capability value of a processor is l, then the expected load limit to it is $(1+a) \cdot l \cdot \frac{L}{C}$ (Recall Section 4), where a is a tunable parameter to ensure all the queries can be accommodated. Then queries are distributed one by one to the

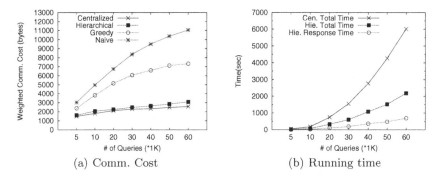

(a) Comm. Cost   (b) Running time

Fig. 6. Initial Distribution

processors. Each query is distributed such that the current communication cost is minimized and the load limit of each processor is not violated. (c) Centralized: all queries are collected to a centralized node and distributed using a centralized graph partitioning algorithm. We use unit-time communication cost - the per unit time message transfer rate of each link times the transfer latency of this link, as the metric to evaluate the query distribution schemes. Figure 6(a) presents the unit-time communication cost of all the four approaches. It can be seen that Naive performs the worst because it cannot identify the data interest of the queries and optimize their locations. Greedy works a lot better by taking the data interest of queries into account. The two graph partitioning algorithms perform the best and their performances are similar. This also verifies that the graph coarsening procedure in our hierarchical partitioning algorithm does not incur much errors. We also report the response time and total time of the centralized and hierarchical graph partitioning algorithms in Figure 6(b). It is shown that both the response time and total time of the hierarchical approach are much less than the centralized one. The hierarchical approach has shorter response time because the coordinators in different branches can work in parallel. To understand why the hierarchical approach also performs better in total time, let us look at an example query graph with n nodes. The complexity of graph partitioning is $k \cdot n^2$, where k is a constant. Hence if, for example, we partition the graph into 2 sub-graphs with sizes of n_1 and n_2 and process them separately, then the complexity is $k \cdot (n_1^2 + n_2^2) < k \cdot n^2$. Since in the hierarchical algorithm, an interior coordinator partitions the query graph into subgraphs and passes them to the child nodes for further partitioning, the total time is also reduced in comparison to the centralized approach.

5   Conclusion and Future Work

In this paper, we propose a new architectural design to leverage the strength of distributed publish/subscribe systems to support scalable continuous query processing over data streams. This architecture retains the loose coupling and easy to deploy merits of a DPSS, while obtaining the processing capabilities of a DSPE. To handle both the query stream and data stream, two layers of services, query layer and data layer, are provided, respectively, by two functional modules. Solutions are proposed to solve the load distribution in the new architecture and performance study are performed to shows their effectiveness. Based on the current results, there are a few directions that we will explore.

Adaptive Query Distribution

The proposed approach in this paper only considers static query distribution. However, in a continuous query context, the system parameters such as data rates, communication bandwidth, workload of the processors, the running user queries etc., are subject to changes in the midst of the query execution. Hence the initial distribution of queries may become suboptimal and an re-optimization is required. The simplest way to perform re-optimization is to re-run our query distribution algorithm from scratch. However, this may incur large overheads in both running the optimization algorithm and migrating the states of the queries. An adaptive algorithm that can minimize the number of query migration as well as optimizing the query distribution quality.

Heterogeneity of Query Engines

Since COSMOS allows different processors employ different query engines, it is possible that a processor can only process certain types of queries and different processors may have different query interfaces and different query semantics. Hence a query wrapper is required to be plugged into each processor to translate the query between the universal query language and the local query language. Furthermore, a user query may not be able to be executed at any processor. Therefore, query distribution algorithm that is aware of this kind of constraints is required.

Computation Sharing

By adopting the DPSS architecture and optimizing the query distribution, COS-MOS minimizes the communication cost by exploiting the sharing of the communication among different queries. We can achieve better system performance by exploiting the opportunities to share the computations among the queries. A processor can publish the intermediate result streams to the system and other processors can subscribe to it if their running queries have similar operations.

Fault Tolerance

Fault tolerance is an important feature for such a service oriented system. It should be supported by both layers in the system with a different target. The fault tolerance module at the data layer is targeted at providing highly available data delivery service while the one at the query layer is aimed to provide highly available query processing service. Different techniques should be developed for these two layers respectively.

To date, we have implemented the proposed algorithms in this paper. We are now trying to incorporate various stream processing engines and then plan to deploy it onto real network environment.

References

1. Aguilera, M.K., Strom, R.E., Sturman, D.C., Astley, M., Chandra, T.D.: Matching events in a content-based subscription system. In: PODC (1999)
2. Ahmad, Y., Çetintemel, U.: Networked query processing for distributed stream-based applications. In: VLDB, pp. 456–467 (2004)
3. Beckmann, N., Kriegel, H.-P., Schneider, R., Seeger, B.: The R*-tree: An efficient and robust access method for points and rectangles. In: SIGMOD Conference (1990)
4. Carney, D., et al.: Monitoring streams: A new class of data management applications. In: VLDB (2002)
5. Carzaniga, A., Rosenblum, D.S., Wolf, A.L.: Design and evaluation of a wide-area event notification service. ACM Transactions on Computer Systems 19(3), 332–383 (2001)
6. Chandrasekaran, S., et al.: TelegraphCQ: Continuous dataflow processing for an uncertain world. In: CIDR (2003)
7. Cherniack, M., et al.: Scalable distributed stream processing. In: CIDR (2003)
8. Karypis, G., Kumar, V.: A coarse-grain parallel formulation of multilevel k-way graph partitioning algorithm. In: PPSC (1997)
9. Karypis, G., Kumar, V.: Multilevel k-way partitioning scheme for irregular graphs. Journal of Parallel and Distributed Computing 48(1), 96–129 (1998)
10. Papaemmanouil, O., Çetintemel, U.: Semcast: Semantic multicast for content-based data dissemination. In: ICDE (2005)
11. Pietzuch, P., et al.: Network-aware operator placement for stream-processing systems. In: ICDE (2006)
12. Schloegel, K., Karypis, G., Kumar, V.: Graph partitioning for high-performance scientific simulations, pp. 491–541 (2003)
13. Shah, M.A., Hellerstein, J.M., Chandrasekaran, S., Franklin, M.J.: Flux: An adaptive partitioning operator for continuous query systems. In: ICDE (2003)
14. Srivastava, U., et al.: Operator Placement for In-Network Stream Query Processin. In: PODS (2005)
15. The STREAM Group. STREAM: The stanford stream data manager. IEEE Data Engineering Bulletin (2003)
16. Walshaw, C., Cross, M., Everett, M.G.: Parallel dynamic graph partitioning for adaptive unstructured meshes. J. Parallel Distrib. Comput. 47(2), 102–108 (1997)
17. Xing, Y., Zdonik, S.B., Hwang, J.-H.: Dynamic load distribution in the borealis stream processor. In: ICDE, pp. 791–802 (2005)

Transaction Reordering and Grouping for Continuous Data Loading

Gang Luo[1], Jeffrey F. Naughton[2], Curt J. Ellmann[2], and Michael W. Watzke[3]

[1] IBM T.J. Watson Research Center
[2] University of Wisconsin-Madison
[3] NCR
luog@us.ibm.com, naughton@cs.wisc.edu,
ellmann@wisc.edu, michael.watzke@ncr.com

Abstract. With the increasing popularity of operational data warehousing, the ability to load data quickly and continuously into an RDBMS is becoming more and more important. However, in the presence of materialized join views, loading data concurrently into multiple base relations of the same materialized join view can cause a severe deadlock problem. To solve this problem, we propose reordering the data to be loaded so that at any time, for any materialized join view, data is only loaded into one of its base relations. Also, for load transactions on the relations that contain "aggregate" attributes, we propose using pre-aggregation to reduce the number of SQL statements in the load transactions. The advantages of our methods are demonstrated through experiments with a commercial parallel RDBMS.

1 Introduction

Today's business market is becoming more and more versatile and competitive. To become and remain successful, an enterprise has to make real-time decisions about its day-to-day operations in response to the fast changes happening all the time in the world [6]. As a result, enterprises are starting to use operational data warehouses to provide fresher data and faster queries [4]. In an operational data warehouse, the stored information is updated in real time or close to it. Also, materialized views are used to speed query processing. This poses some technical challenges. In this paper, we consider a challenge that arises in the context of continuous data loading in the presence of materialized views.

Fig. 1. Operational data warehouse architecture

C. Bussler et al. (Eds.): BIRTE 2006, LNCS 4365, pp. 34–49, 2007.

Figure 1 shows the architecture of a typical operational data warehouse [4] (Wal-Mart's data warehouse uses this architecture [22]). Clients store new data into operational data stores in real time, where an operational data store is an OLTP database, a message queue [3], or anything else that is suitable for an OLTP workload. The purpose of these operational data stores is to acknowledge the clients' input immediately while ensuring the durability of this data. As quickly as feasible, this new data is transferred by continuous load utilities from operational data stores into a centralized operational data warehouse, where it is typically managed by an RDBMS. Then clients can query this operational data warehouse, which is the only place that global information is available.

Note: The continuous load utilities are not used for arbitrary applications. Rather, they are used to synchronize the centralized operational data warehouse with the operational data stores. As a result, the state-of-the-art commercial continuous load utilities (e.g., Oracle [16], Teradata [20]) have certain characteristics that are not valid in some applications. We will describe these characteristics in Section 2.1 below.

For performance reasons, existing continuous load utilities often load data into the RDBMS through multiple concurrent sessions. In the presence of materialized join views, a deadlock problem can occur during immediate materialized join view maintenance. This is because a materialized join view JV links together multiple base relations. When a base relation used in the definition of JV is updated, in order to maintain JV, all other base relations in its definition must be read. Hence, transactions updating different base relations in the definition of JV can deadlock due to their lock requests on these base relations.

A simple solution to the above deadlock problem is to do materialized join view maintenance in a deferred manner rather than immediately. That is, an update is inserted into the base relation as soon as possible; but the materialized join views that refer to that base relation only see the update at some later time, when the materialized join views are updated in a batch operation. Unfortunately, this makes the materialized join views at least temporarily inconsistent with the base relations. The resulting semantic uncertainty may not be acceptable to all applications. This observation has been made elsewhere. For example, [11] emphasizes that consistency is important for materialized views that are used to make real-time decisions. As another example, in the TPC-R benchmark, maintaining materialized views immediately with transactional consistency is a mandatory requirement [18], presumably as a reflection of some real world application demands. As a third example, as argued in [11], materialized views are like indexes. Since indexes are always maintained immediately, immediate materialized view maintenance should also be desirable in many cases.

The reader might wonder whether using a multi-version concurrency control method can solve the above deadlock problem. In general, a multi-version concurrency control method can avoid conflicts between a pure read transaction and a write transaction (or a transaction that does both reads and writes) [2, 11]. However, in our case, the immediate materialized join view maintenance transactions do both reads and writes. As a result, a multi-version concurrency control method cannot avoid the conflicts between these transactions [2, 11]. In fact, [11] proposed a multi-version concurrency control method to avoid conflicts between pure read transactions on materialized join views and immediate materialized join view maintenance transactions. For this reason, in this paper, we do not discuss pure read transactions on materialized join views.

To solve the deadlock problem without sacrificing consistency between the materialized join views and the base relations, we propose reordering the data to be loaded so that at any time, for any materialized join view *JV*, data is only loaded into one of its base relations. (As we describe in Section 2.3, in the context of continuous load operations, standard partitioning techniques can be used to guarantee that there are no deadlocks among transactions updating the same base relation. Also, as we describe in Sections 2.1 and 2.3, reordering is allowed in the state-of-the-art continuous load utilities.)

Reordering transactions may cause slight delays in the processing of load transactions that have been moved later in the load schedule. On balance, these delays will be offset by the corresponding transactions that were moved earlier in the schedule to take the place of these delayed transactions. For some applications, this reordering is preferable to the inconsistencies that result from deferred materialized view maintenance. These are the target applications for our reordering technique.

Reordering transactions is not a new idea. For example, [15] proposed reordering queries to improve the buffer pool hit ratio. Also, in practice, some data warehouse users reorder transactions themselves in their applications to avoid contention among the transactions [5]. However, to our knowledge the published literature has not considered an automatic, general purpose transaction reordering method that attempts to reduce deadlocks in continuous data loading applications.

In addition to reordering transactions, we propose a second method to improve the efficiency of continuous data loading. For relations with attributes representing aggregate information (e.g., quantity, amount), we use pre-aggregation to reduce the number of SQL statements in the load transactions. In our experiments, we observed that pre-aggregation can greatly increase the continuous data loading speed.

Of course, the techniques proposed in this paper do not solve all the problems encountered in continuous data loading in the presence of materialized views. Other problems exist, e.g., concurrency control conflicts on materialized views [11, 12], excessive resource usage during materialized view maintenance [13]. However, we believe our techniques form one part of the solution that is required for continuous data loading in the presence of materialized views.

The rest of this paper is organized as follows. In Section 2, we provide some background for continuous data loading. In Section 3, we explore the deadlock problem with existing continuous load utilities in the presence of materialized join views, and show how this problem can be avoided using the reordering method. In Section 4, we explore the use of pre-aggregation to reduce the number of SQL statements in the load transactions. Section 5 investigates the performance of our method through an evaluation in a commercial parallel RDBMS. We conclude in Section 6.

2 Continuous Data Loading

Since loading data into a database is a general requirement of database applications, most commercial RDBMS vendors provide load utilities, each of which have (somewhat) different functionality. Some are continuous load utilities, while others only support batch bulk load. The functionality of certain load utilities can be implemented by applications. However, since a large number of applications need such functionality, RDBMS vendors typically provide this functionality as a package for application developers to use directly. In the rest of this paper, we do not differentiate between the load utilities provided by the RDBMS vendors and the applications written by the application developers that provide data loading functionality. We refer to both of them as load utilities, and our discussion holds for both.

In this section, we describe how existing continuous load utilities typically work (minor differences in implementation details will not influence our general discussion).

2.1 Workload Specification

Figure 2 shows a typical architecture for loading data continuously into an RDBMS [19, 20]. Data comes from multiple data sources (files, OLTP databases, message queues, pipes, etc.) in the form of modification operations (insert, delete, or update). Then a continuous load utility loads the data into the RDBMS using update transactions. Each update transaction contains one or more modification operations.

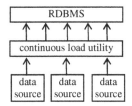

Fig. 2. Continuous data loading architecture

As is the case in data stream applications, the system has no control over the order in which modification operations arrive [1]. To decide which transformations are valid on the stream of load transactions, we discuss the semantics of continuous data loading. The state-of-the-art two popular commercial continuous load utilities (Oracle [16], Teradata [20]) make the following assumptions for continuous data loading:

(a) The RDBMS is running with standard ACID properties for transactions. The continuous load utility looks to the RDBMS like a series of transactions, each containing a single modification operation (insert, delete, or update) on a single relation. Hence, load transactions submitted by continuous load utilities will not cause inconsistency for transactions submitted by other applications.

(b) The RDBMS neither imposes nor assumes any particular order for these load transactions – indeed, their order is determined by the (potentially multiple) external systems "feeding" the load process. Hence, the load process is free to arbitrarily reorder these transactions.

(c) The RDBMS has no requirement on whether multiple modification operations can or cannot commit/abort together. Hence, for efficiency purposes, the load process is free to arbitrarily group these single-modification-operation transactions.

In this paper, we make the same assumptions. Hence, in our techniques, we can do reordering and grouping arbitrarily.

The alert reader may notice that arbitrary reordering can cause certain anomalies. For example, such an anomaly arises if the deletion of a tuple t is moved before the updating of tuple t. In practice, some applications tolerate such anomalies [5]. In other cases, the application ensures that the order in which modification operations arrive at the continuous load utility will not allow such anomalies [5]. For example, before the continuous load utility acknowledges the completion of updating tuple t, the operation of deleting tuple t is not submitted to the continuous load utility. In either case, the continuous load utility does not need to worry about these anomalies.

In this paper, we make the further assumption that some locking mechanism is used to provide concurrency control. More specifically, we assume that:

(a) The system uses strict two-phase locking.
(b) The system uses tuple-level locks. The extension to multiple-granularity locking [9] is straightforward.

To increase concurrency, a continuous load utility typically opens multiple sessions to the RDBMS (at any time, each session can have at most one running transaction [10, page 320]). These sessions are usually maintained for a long time so that they do not need to be re-established for each use. For efficiency, within a transaction, all the SQL statements corresponding to modification operations are usually pre-compiled into a stored procedure whose execution plan is stored in the RDBMS. This not only reduces the network overhead (transmitting a stored procedure requires a much smaller message than transmitting multiple SQL statements) but also eliminates the overhead of repeatedly parsing and optimizing SQL statements.

2.2 Grouping Modification Operations

Continuous load utilities usually combine multiple modification operations into a single transaction rather than applying each modification operation in a separate transaction [19, 20]. This is because of the per transaction overhead. Using a large transaction can amortize this overhead over multiple modification operations. In the rest of this paper, we refer to the number of modification operations that are combined into a single transaction as the *grouping factor*.

2.3 The Partitioning Method

As mentioned in Section 2.1, to increase concurrency, a continuous load utility typically opens multiple sessions to the RDBMS. In this section, we review the standard approach used to avoid deadlock in continuous load operations in the absence of materialized views.

Suppose the continuous load utility opens $k \geq 2$ sessions S_i ($1 \leq i \leq k$) to the RDBMS. If we randomly distribute the modification operations among the k sessions, transactions from different sessions can easily deadlock on X lock requests on the base relations. This is because these transactions may modify the same tuples concurrently [20]. A simple solution to this deadlock problem is to partition (e.g., hash on some attribute) the tuples among different sessions so that modification operations on the same tuple are always sent through the same session [20]. In this way, the deadlock condition (transactions from different sessions modify the same tuple) no longer exists and deadlocks will not occur. (Note: the partitioning method may change the order that the tuples arrive at the RDBMS. However, as mentioned in Section 2.1, such reordering is allowed in existing continuous load utilities.)

3 The Reordering Method

In this section, we consider the general case in which materialized views are maintained in the RDBMS, and show that in this case the partitioning method of Section 2.3 is not sufficient to avoid deadlocks. We focus on an important class of materialized views called *join views*. In an extended relational algebra, by a join view

JV, we mean either an ordinary join view $\pi(\sigma(R_1 \bowtie R_2 \bowtie \ldots \bowtie R_h))$ or an aggregate join

view $\gamma(\pi(\sigma(R_1 \bowtie R_2 \bowtie \ldots \bowtie R_h)))$, where γ is an aggregate operator. SQL allows the aggregate operators *COUNT*, *SUM*, *AVG*, *MIN*, and *MAX*. However, because *MIN* and *MAX* cannot be maintained incrementally (the problem is deletes [8]), we restrict our attention to the three aggregate operators that make the most sense for materialized aggregates: *COUNT*, *SUM*, and *AVG*.

3.1 Impact of Immediate Materialized View Maintenance

In continuous data loading, we allow data to be loaded into multiple base relations concurrently. This is necessary if we want to keep the data in the RDBMS as up-to-date as possible. However, if a join view is defined on multiple base relations, deadlocks are likely to occur. This is because a join view JV links different base relations. When a base relation of JV is updated, to maintain JV, all the other base relations in the definition of JV are read. That is, the introduction of the join view changes the update transactions into update-read transactions. These reads can conflict with concurrent writes to the other base relations of JV. For example, consider the following two base relations: $A(a, c)$ and $B(d, e)$. Suppose a join view

$JV=A \bowtie B$ is defined on A and B, where the join condition is $A.c=B.d$. Consider the following two modification operations:

(1) O_1: Modify a tuple t_1 in base relation A whose $c=v$.
(2) O_2: Modify a tuple t_2 in base relation B whose $d=v$.

These modification operations require the following tuple-level locks on base relations A and B:

O_1:   (L_{11}) A tuple-level X lock on A for tuple t_1.
      (L_{12}) Several tuple-level S locks on B for all the tuples in B whose $d=v$ (for join view maintenance purpose).
O_2:   (L_{21}) A tuple-level X lock on B for tuple t_2.
      (L_{22}) Several tuple-level S locks on A for all the tuples in A whose $c=v$.

Suppose operation O_1 is executed by transaction T_1 through session S_1, while operation O_2 is executed by transaction T_2 through session S_2. If transactions T_1 and T_2 request the locks in the order

Step 1: T_1 requests L_{11}.   **Step 2:** T_2 requests L_{21}.
Step 3: T_1 requests L_{12}.   **Step 4:** T_2 requests L_{22}.

a deadlock occurs. This is because L_{11} (L_{22}) contains a tuple-level X (S) lock on A for tuple t_1. Also, L_{21} (L_{12}) contains a tuple-level X (S) lock on B for tuple t_2.

Allowing dirty reads is a standard technique to improve the concurrency of read-only queries. Since materialized join view maintenance has at its heart a join query, it is natural to wonder if dirty reads can be used here. Unfortunately, in the context of materialized view maintenance, allowing dirty reads is problematic. This is because using dirty reads to maintain join views makes the results of these dirty reads permanent in the join views [21]. Thus, although dirty reads would avoid the deadlock problem, they cannot be used.

It is also natural to question whether some extension of the partitioning method described in Section 2.3 can be used to avoid deadlocks in the presence of materialized join views. In certain cases, the answer is yes. For example, suppose we use the same partitioning function to partition the tuples of A and B among different sessions according to the join attributes $A.c$ and $B.d$, respectively. Then for immediate materialized view maintenance, the deadlock problem will not occur. This is because in this case, "conflicting" transactions are always submitted through the same session. Also, at any time, one session can have at most one running transaction [10, page 320]. Unfortunately, in practice, such an appropriate partitioning method is not always possible:

(1) In continuous data loading, modification operations on a base relation R usually specify some (e.g., the primary key) but not all attribute values of R [20]. We can only partition the tuples of base relation R among different sessions according to (some of) those attributes whose values are specified by the modification operations on R. This is because we use the same attributes to partition the modification operations on base relation R among different sessions. Suppose that base relation R is a base relation of a join view. Also, suppose the join attribute of R is not one of those attributes whose values are specified by the modification operations on R. Then we cannot partition the tuples of base relation R among different sessions according to the join attribute of R.

(2) If multiple join views with different join attributes are defined on the same base relation R, then it is impossible to partition the tuples of base relation R among different sessions according to these join attributes simultaneously.

(3) If within the same join view (e.g., $JV = A \bowtie R \bowtie B$), a base relation R is joined with multiple other base relations (e.g., A and B) on different join attributes, then it is impossible to partition the tuples of base relation R among different sessions according to these join attributes simultaneously.

3.2 Solution with Reordering

The deadlock problem occurs because we allow data to be concurrently loaded into multiple base relations of the same join view. Hence, a natural question is if this were not allowed, would the deadlock problem still occur? Luckily, the answer is "no" if we set the following rules:

(1) **Rule 1:** At any time, for any join view JV, data can only be loaded into one base relation of JV.
(2) **Rule 2:** Modification operations (insert, delete, update) on the same base relation use the partitioning method discussed in Section 2.3.
(3) **Rule 3:** The system uses a high concurrency locking protocol (e.g., the V locking protocol [12], or the locking protocol in [11]) on join views so that lock conflicts on the join views can be avoided.

The reason is as follows.

(1) Using rules 1 and 2, all deadlocks resulting from lock conflicts on the base relations are avoided.
(2) Using rule 3, all deadlocks resulting from lock conflicts on the join views can be avoided (e.g., in the V locking protocol [12], V locks are compatible with themselves; in the locking protocol in [11], E locks are compatible with themselves).

Since all possible deadlock conditions are eliminated, deadlocks no longer occur.

We now consider how to implement rules 1-3. It is easy to enforce rules 2 and 3. To enforce rule 1, we can use the following reordering method to reorder the modification operations. Recall in Section 2.1, the semantics of the workload allows us to reorder modification operations arbitrarily. Consider a database with d base relations R_1, R_2, ..., and R_d and e join views JV_1, JV_2, ..., and JV_e. We keep an array J that contains d elements J_i ($1 \leq i \leq d$). For each i ($1 \leq i \leq d$), J_i records the number of transactions that modify base relation R_i and are currently being executed. Each J_i ($1 \leq i \leq d$) is initialized to zero. For each m ($1 \leq m \leq k$), we maintain a queue Q_m recording transactions waiting to be run through session S_m. Each Q_m ($1 \leq m \leq k$) is initialized to empty. During grouping (see Section 2.2), we only combine modification operations on the same base relation into a single transaction.

If base relations R_i and R_j ($1 \leq i, j \leq d$, $i \neq j$) are base relations of the same join view, we say that R_i and R_j conflict with each other. Two transactions modifying conflicting base relations are said to conflict with each other. We call transaction T a "desirable transaction" if it does not conflict with any currently running transaction. Consider a particular base relation R_i ($1 \leq i \leq d$). Suppose R_{s_1}, R_{s_2}, ..., and R_{s_w} ($w \geq 0$) are all the other base relations that conflict with base relation R_i. At any time, if either $w=0$ or all the $J_{s_u} = 0$ ($1 \leq u \leq w$), then a transaction T modifying base relation R_i ($1 \leq i \leq d$) is a desirable transaction.

We schedule transactions as follows:

(1) **Action 1:** For each session S_m ($1 \leq m \leq k$), as discussed in Section 2.2, whenever the continuous load utility has collected n modification operations on a base relation R_i ($1 \leq i \leq d$), we combine these operations into a single transaction T and insert transaction T to the end of Q_m. Here, n is the pre-defined grouping factor that is specified by the user who sets up the continuous load utility. If session S_m

is free, we try to schedule a transaction to the RDBMS for execution through session S_m.

(2) **Action 2:** When some transaction T modifying base relation R_i ($1 \leq i \leq d$) finishes execution and frees session S_m ($1 \leq m \leq k$), we do the following:
  (a) We decrement J_i by one.
  (b) If Q_m is not empty, we schedule a transaction to the RDBMS for execution through session S_m.
  (c) Suppose J_i is decremented to zero (so that some waiting transaction possibly becomes desirable). For each g ($1 \leq g \leq k$, $g \neq m$), if session S_g is free and Q_g is not empty, we try to schedule a transaction to the RDBMS for execution through session S_g.

(3) **Action 3:** Whenever we try to schedule a transaction to the RDBMS for execution through session S_m ($1 \leq m \leq k$), we do the following:
  (a) We search Q_m sequentially until either a desirable transaction T is found or all the transactions in Q_m have been scanned, whichever comes first.
  (b) In the case that a desirable transaction T modifying base relation R_i ($1 \leq i \leq d$) is found, we increment J_i by one and send transaction T to the RDBMS for execution.

The above discussion does not address starvation. There are several starvation prevention techniques that can be integrated into the transaction reordering method. We list one of them as follows. The idea is to use a special header transaction to prevent the first transaction in any Q_g from starvation ($1 \leq g \leq k$). We keep a pointer r whose value is always between 0 and k. r is initialized to 0. If every Q_m ($1 \leq m \leq k$) is empty, $r=0$. At any time, if $r=0$ and a transaction is inserted into some Q_m ($1 \leq m \leq k$), we set $r=m$. If $r=m$ ($1 \leq m \leq k$) and the first transaction of Q_m leaves Q_m for execution, r is incremented by one (if $m=k$, we set $r=1$). If Q_r is empty, we keep incrementing r until either Q_r is not empty or we discover that every Q_m ($1 \leq m \leq k$) is empty. In the later case, we set $r=0$. We make use of a pre-defined timestamp TS determined by application requirements. If pointer r has stayed at some v ($1 \leq v \leq k$) longer than TS, the first transaction of Q_v becomes the header transaction. Whenever we are searching for a desirable transaction in some Q_m ($1 \leq m \leq k$) and we find transaction T, if the header transaction exists, we ensure that either T is the header transaction or T does not conflict with the header transaction. Otherwise transaction T is still not desirable and we continue the search.

4 The Pre-aggregation Method

A large number of data warehouses have relations with certain attributes representing aggregate information (e.g., *quantity* or *amount*). In many cases, updates to these relations increment or decrement the aggregate attribute values [7]. As discussed in Section 2.2, when we load data continuously into these relations, we combine multiple modification operations into a single load transaction. This creates an opportunity for optimization: by pre-aggregation, we can reduce the number of SQL statements in the load transactions on these relations.

For example, consider a relation R in the database whose $R.b$ attribute represents aggregate information. Suppose the following two modification operations O_1 and O_2 are combined into a single load transaction T:

(1) O_1: update R set R.b=R.b+b_1 where R.a=v;
(2) O_2: update R set R.b=R.b+b_2 where R.a=v;

If we let $b_3=b_1+b_2$, then transaction T can be transformed into an equivalent transaction T' that contains only a single SQL statement:

> update R set R.b=R.b+b_3 where R.a=v;

Compared to transaction T, transaction T' saves one SQL statement. Hence, transaction T' is more efficient. The reason is that executing a SQL statement is much more expensive than aggregating the two values b_1 and b_2 into a single value b_3.

4.1 Algorithm Description

We call the above method the pre-aggregation method. The general pre-aggregation method works in the following way. Consider a base relation R with one or multiple "aggregate" attributes. Assume that in the grouping method discussed in Section 2.2, all modification operations combined in a single transaction are on the same base relation. For each load transaction on relation R, we do the following operations:

(1) Find all the modification operations that increment/decrement the "aggregate" attribute values. Move these modification operations to the beginning of the transaction (i.e., ahead of all the other modification operations). Suppose each such modification operation can be represented as a pair $<a, b>$, where a denotes the tuple (set of tuples) to be modified, and b denotes the amount that will be added to (or subtracted from) the "aggregate" attribute value(s) of the tuple(s).
(2) Sort these modification operations so that modification operations on the same tuple (set of tuples) are adjacent to each other.
(3) Among these modification operations, combine multiple adjacent modification operations $<a, b_1>$, $<a, b_2>$, ..., and $<a, b_m>$ on the same tuple (set of tuples) into a single modification operation $<a, c>$, where $c=b_1+b_2+...+b_m$. In the extreme case that $c=0$, the single modification operation $<a, c>$ can be omitted.

The above procedure can be easily extended to handle the UPSERT/MERGE SQL statement [17].

The pre-aggregation method has the following advantages:

(1) The processing load of the database engine is reduced.
(2) The transaction execution/response time is reduced. This may further improve database concurrency, as the period that transactions hold locks is reduced.

These advantages come from the fact that pre-aggregation outside of the database engine followed by executing fewer SQL statements inside the database engine is more efficient than executing all the SQL statements inside the database engine.

5 Performance Evaluation

In this section, we describe experiments that were performed on the commercial IBM DB2 parallel RDBMS. Our measurements were performed with the database client application and server running on an Intel x86 Family 6 Model 5 Stepping 3 workstation with four 400MHz processors, 1GB main memory, six 8GB disks, and running the Microsoft Windows 2000 operating system. We allocated a processor and a disk for each data server, so there were at most four data servers on each workstation.

5.1 Experiment Description

The relations used for the tests model a real world scenario. Customers interact with a retailer via phone/web to make a purchase. The purchase involves browsing available merchandise items and possibly selecting an item to purchase. The following events occur:

(1) Customer indicates desire for a specific item and event is recorded in the *demand* relation.
(2) The *inventory* relation is checked for item availability.
(3) If the desired item is on hand, a customer order is placed and the *inventory* relation is updated; otherwise a vendor order is placed.

The schemas of the *demand* and *inventory* relations are listed as follows:

demand (partkey, date, quantity, <u>custkey</u>, comment),
inventory (<u>partkey</u>, <u>date</u>, quantity, extended_cost, extended_price).

The underscore indicates the partitioning attributes. For each relation, we built an index on the partitioning attribute(s). In our tests, each *inventory* tuple matches 4 *demand* tuples on the attributes *partkey* and *date*. Also, different *demand* tuples have different *custkey* values. In practice, there can be a large number of different parts. However, for any given day, most transactions only focus on a small portion of them (the "active" parts). In our testing, we assume that s parts are active today. We only consider today's transactions that are related to these active parts. We believe that our conclusion would remain much the same if all transactions related to both active and inactive parts were considered. This is because in this case, the number of deadlocks caused by the transactions that are related to the active parts would remain much the same.

Table 1. Test data set

	number of tuples	total size
demand	8M	910MB
inventory	2M	77MB

Suppose that the *demand* and *inventory* relations are frequently queried for sales forecasting, lost sales analysis, and assortment planning applications, so a join view *onhand_demand* is built as the join result of *demand* and *inventory* on the join attributes *partkey* and *date*:

create join view onhand_demand as select d.partkey, d.date, d.quantity, d.custkey, i.quantity

from demand d, inventory i where d.partkey=i.partkey and d.date=i.date partitioned on d.custkey;

There are two kinds of modification operations that we used for testing, both of which are related to today's activities:

(1) O_1: Insert one tuple (with today's *date*) into the *demand* relation. This new tuple matches 1 *inventory* tuple on the attributes *partkey* and *date*.
(2) O_2: Update one tuple in the *inventory* relation with a specific *partkey* value and today's *date*.

We created an auxiliary relation for the *demand* relation that is partitioned on the (*partkey*, *date*) attributes to change expensive all-node join operations for join view maintenance to cheap single-node join operations [13].

We evaluated the performance of the reordering method and the naive method in the following way:

(1) We tested the largest available hardware configuration with four data server nodes.
(2) We executed a stream of modification operations. A fraction p of these modification operations are O_1. The other $1-p$ of the modification operations are O_2. Each O_1 inserts a tuple into the *demand* relation with a random *partkey* value. Each O_2 updates a tuple in the *inventory* relation with a random *partkey* value.
(3) In both the reordering method and the naive method, we only combine modification operations on the same base relation into a single transaction. Each transaction has the same grouping factor n.
(4) In the naive method, if a transaction deadlocked and aborted, we automatically re-executed it until it committed.
(5) We performed a concurrency test. We fixed $p=50\%$ and the number of active parts $s=10,000$. In both the reordering method and the naive method, we tested four cases: $k=2$, $k=4$, $k=8$, and $k=16$, where k is the number of sessions. In each case, we let the grouping factor n vary from 1 to 128.

5.2 Concurrency Test Results

The throughput (number of modification operations per second) is an important performance metric of the continuous load utility. For the naive method, to see how deadlocks influence its performance, we investigated the relationship between the throughput and the deadlock probability.

By definition, when the deadlock probability becomes close to 1, almost every transaction will deadlock. Deadlock has the following negative influences on throughout:

(1) Deadlock detection/resolution is a time-consuming process. During this period, the deadlocked transactions cannot make any progress.
(2) The deadlocked transactions will be aborted and re-executed. During re-execution, these transactions may deadlock again. This wastes system resources.

Hence, once the system starts to deadlock, the deadlock problem tends to become worse and worse. Eventually, the throughput of the naive method deteriorates significantly.

We show the throughput of the naive method in Figure 3. For a given number of sessions k, when the grouping factor n is small, the throughput of the naive method keeps increasing with n. This is because executing a large transaction is more efficient than executing a large number of small transactions, as discussed in Section 2.2. (In our testing, the performance advantages of having a large grouping factor n are not very large. This is mainly due to the fact that due to software restrictions, we could only run the database client application and server on the same computer. In this case, the overhead per transaction is fairly low. Amortizing such a small overhead with a large n cannot bring much benefit.) When n becomes large enough, if the naive method does not run into the deadlock problem, the throughput of the naive method approaches a constant, where the system resources become fully utilized. The larger k:

(1) the higher concurrency in the RDBMS and the larger the constant.
(2) the easier it becomes to achieve full utilization of system resources and the smaller n is needed for the throughput to achieve that constant.

When n becomes too large, the naive method runs into the deadlock problem. The larger k, the smaller n is needed for the naive method to run into the deadlock problem. Once the deadlock problem occurs, the throughput of the naive method deteriorates significantly. Actually, it decreases as n increases. This is because the larger n, the more transactions are aborted and re-executed due to deadlock.

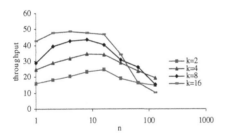 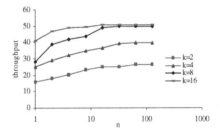

Fig. 3. Throughput of the naive method (concurrency test)   **Fig. 4.** Throughput of the reordering method (concurrency test)

For a given n, before the deadlock problem occurs, the throughput of the naive method increases with k. This is because the larger k, the higher concurrency in the RDBMS. However, when n is large enough (e.g., $n=128$) and the naive method runs into the deadlock problem, due to the extreme overhead of repeated transaction abortion and re-execution, the throughput of the naive method may decrease as k increases.

We show the throughput of the reordering method in Figure 4. The general trend of the throughput of the reordering method is similar to that of the naive method (before the deadlock problem occurs). That is, the throughput of the reordering method increases with both n and k. For a given k, as n becomes large, the throughput of the reordering method approaches a constant. However, the reordering method never deadlocks. For a given k, the throughput of the reordering method keeps approaching that constant no matter how large n is. Once the naive method runs into the deadlock problem, the reordering method exhibits great performance advantages over the naive method, as the throughput of the naive method in this case deteriorates significantly.

In both the $k=8$ case and the $k=16$ case, when n becomes large enough, the throughput of the reordering method approaches (almost) the same constant. This is because in these two cases, all data server nodes (e.g., disk I/Os) become fully utilized. In our testing, if we had a larger hardware configuration with more data server nodes, the constant for the $k=16$ case would be larger than that for the $k=8$ case.

We show the ratio of the throughput of the reordering method to that of the naive method in Figure 5. Before the naive method runs into the deadlock problem, the throughput of the reordering method is smaller than that of the naive method. This is because the reordering method has some overhead in performing reordering and synchronization (i.e., switching from executing one type of transactions (say, transactions updating the *inventory* relation) to executing another type of transactions (say, transactions updating the *demand* relation)). However, such overhead is not significant. In our tests, the throughput of the reordering method is never lower than 96% of that of the naive method.

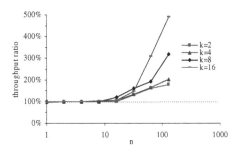

Fig. 5. Throughput improvement gained by the reordering method (concurrency test)

When the naive method runs into the deadlock problem, the throughput of the reordering method does not drop while the throughput of the naive method is significantly worse. In this case, the ratio of the throughput of the reordering method to that of the naive method is greater than 1. For example, when $n=32$, for any k, this ratio is at least 1.3. When $n=64$, for any k, this ratio is at least 1.6. In the extreme case when $k=16$ and $n=128$, this ratio is 4.9. In general, when the naive method runs into the deadlock problem, this ratio increases with both k and n. This is because the larger k or n, the easier the transactions deadlock in the naive method. The extreme overhead of repeated transaction abortion and re-execution exceeds the benefit of the higher concurrency (efficiency) brought by a larger k (n). However, there are two exceptions. When $n=16$ or $n=32$, the ratio curve for $k=16$ is below the ratio curve for $k=8$. This is because in these two cases, for the reordering method, all data server nodes (e.g., disk I/Os) become fully utilized and the throughput is almost independent of both k and n. By comparison, in the naive method, as there are not enough transaction aborts, the throughput for the $k=16$ case is higher than that for the $k=8$ case.

Due to space constraints, we put the performance study of the pre-aggregation method into the full version of this paper [14].

6 Conclusion

This paper proposes two techniques to improve the efficiency of existing continuous load utilities:

(1) In the presence of join views in an RDBMS, we reorder the data load operations to avoid deadlocks.

(2) We use pre-aggregation to reduce the number of SQL statements in the load transactions.

Our experiments with a commercial system are promising, showing that these two techniques can significantly improve throughput for certain workloads.

Acknowledgements

We would like to thank Henry F. Korth for helpful discussions.

References

[1] Babcock, B., Babu, S., Datar, M., et al.: Models and Issues in Data Stream Systems. PODS 2002, pp. 1–16 (2002)

[2] Bernstein, P.A., Hadzilacos, V., Goodman, N.: Concurrency Control and Recovery in Database Systems. Addison-Wesley, Reading (1987)

[3] Bernstein, P.A., Hsu, M., Mann, B.: Implementing Recoverable Requests Using Queues. SIGMOD Conf. 1990, pp. 112–122 (1990)

[4] Brobst, S., Rarey, J.: The Five Stages of an Active Data Warehouse Evolution (2001) http://www.ncr.com/online_periodicals/brobst.pdf

[5] Brobst, S.: Personal communication (2003)

[6] Dver, A.: Real-time Enterprise. Business week December 2, 2002 issue (2002)

[7] Gawlick, D.: Processing "Hot Spots" in High Performance Systems. In: Proc. IEEE Compcon Spring '85 (1985)

[8] J. Gehrke, F. Korn, and D. Srivastava. On Computing Correlated Aggregates over Continual Data Streams. SIGMOD Conf. 2001, pp. 13–24 (2001)

[9] Gray, J., Lorie, R.A., Putzolu, G.R., et al.: Granularity of Locks and Degrees of Consistency in a Shared Data Base. IFIP Working Conference on Modeling in Data Base Management Systems 1976, pp. 365–394 (1976)

[10] Gray, J., Reuter, A.: Transaction Processing: Concepts and Techniques. Morgan Kaufmann Publishers, San Francisco (1993)

[11] Graefe, G., Zwilling, M.J.: Transaction Support for Indexed Views. SIGMOD Conf.2004 (2004)

[12] Luo, G., Naughton, J.F., Ellmann, C.J., et al.: Locking Protocols for Materialized Aggregate Join Views. VLDB 2003, pp. 596–607 (2003)

[13] Luo, G., Naughton, J.F., Ellmann, C.J., et al.: A Comparison of Three Methods for Join View Maintenance in Parallel RDBMS. ICDE 2003, pp. 177–188 (2003)

[14] Luo, G., Naughton, J.F., Ellmann, C.J., et al.: Transaction Reordering and Grouping for Continuous Data Loading. Full version (2006) available at http://www.cs.wisc.edu/~gangluo/tpump_full.pdf

[15] O'Gorman, K., Abbadi, A.E., Agrawal, D.: Multiple Query Optimization by Cache-Aware Middleware using Query Teamwork. ICDE 2002, p. 274 (2002)

[16] Oracle Streams (2002) http://otn.oracle.com/products/dataint/htdocs/streams_fo.html

[17] Oracle9i Database Daily Feature - MERGE Statement (2002) http://technet.oracle.com/products/oracle9i/daily/Aug24.html

[18] Poess, M., Floyd, C.: New TPC Benchmarks for Decision Support and Web Commerce. SIGMOD Record 29(4), 64–71 (2000)

[19] Pooloth, K.: High Performance Inserts on DB2 UDB EEE using Java (2002) http:// www7b.boulder.ibm.com/dmdd/library/techarticle/0204pooloth/0204pooloth.html#overview

[20] Teradata Parallel Data Pump Reference (2002) http://www.info.ncr.com/ eDownload.cfm?itemid=023390001

[21] Zhuge, Y., Garcia-Molina, H., Wiener, J.L.: The Strobe Algorithms for Multi-Source Warehouse Consistency. PDIS 1996, pp. 146–157 (1996)

[22] Zimmerman, E. Nelson. In Hour of Peril, Americans Moved to Stock up on Guns and TV Sets. Wall Street Journal Newsletter (September 18, 2001) http://www.swcollege.com/ econ/ street/html/sept01/sept18_2001.html

A Scalable Heterogeneous Solution for Massive Data Collection and Database Loading

Uri Shani[1], Aviad Sela[1], Alex Akilov[1], Inna Skarbovski[1], and David Berk[2]

[1] IBM Haifa Research Lab
[2] IBM Israel BCS
Haifa University Campus, Carmel Mountain, Haifa, 31905 Israel
shani@il.ibm.com

Abstract. Massive collection of data at high rates is critical for many industries. Typically, a massive stream of records is gathered from the business information network at a very high rate. Because of the complexity of the collection process, the classical database solution falls short. The high volume and rate of records involved requires a heterogeneous pipeline comprised of two major parts: a system that carries out massive collection and then uploads the information to a database, and a subsequent data analysis and management system consisting of an Extract Transform and Load component. We developed a massive collection and loading system, based on a highly scalable heterogeneous architecture solution. The solution has been applied successfully for Telco revenue assurance, and can be applied to other industrial areas. The solution was successful in scaling up a Telco client system to handle streams of records ten times larger than was previously possible.

1 Introduction

For many of today's industries, massive collection of data at high rates is critical. The Telco industry is one such example, where the rate of network activity records may generate up to a billion Call Detail Records (CDRs) per day. Systems that handle this data must include mediation and billing system. However, enterprise data warehouses, fraud control, business intelligence and revenue assurance systems are commonly needed for a healthy business management. Typically, a massive stream of records, which we term in general Event Detail Records (EDRs), is gathered from the business information network at a very high rate. The records are collected, undergoing validation, cleansing, normalization and other similar transformations, based on business rules. The records are then uploaded to a database for further processing. While this sounds like a common Extract Transform and Load (ETL) activity, the classical database solution falls short. The high volume and rate of records involved requires a heterogeneous pipeline comprised of two major parts: a system that carries out massive collection and then uploads the information to a database, and a subsequent data analysis and management system consisting of an ETL component. We developed a massive collection and loading system, based on a highly scalable heterogeneous architecture solution. The solution consists of a WebSphere Application Server cluster (WAS 6[1], which is IBM's J2EE[5] enterprise middleware), and a highly parallel and

C. Bussler et al. (Eds.): BIRTE 2006, LNCS 4365, pp. 50–62, 2007.
© Springer-Verlag Berlin Heidelberg 2007

scalable database using IBM's DB2[6] partitioned DBMS. The solution has been applied successfully for Telco revenue assurance where events are CDRs. The solution can be applied to other Telco problem areas, as well as control and assurance for business information systems. The solution was applied at a client site where it was successful in scaling up the system to handle streams of records ten times larger than was previously possible without the collection system.

Call Detail Records (CDRs) in Telco are the events from which billing can be done and revenues for the service provider can be generated. The switches which generates these records are not standard and different vendors may use different formats and packing for the data fields. Nevertheless, all switches share the same terminology and their CDR fields share common semantics. For instance, A-number and B-number are the caller and called phone numbers respectively, each switch has an ID that is unique over the network, all CDRs operate within a single phone numbering system measure time in the same way, and so forth.

Usually, a mediation system processes the CDRs as part of the billing process. Revenue assurance systems parallel the mediation system and provide comparable results by which further analysis will identify mismatches that are indicative of errors causing revenue leakages. In the Telco industry, these revenue leakages have been estimated as high as 6%.

1.1   The Massive Collection System (MCS)

We characterize massive collection systems by the amount and size of data they need to process. The IBM Massive Collection System (MCS) was developed as part of a multi-tier architecture, as illustrated in **Fig 1**.

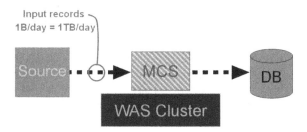

Fig. 1. MCS multi-tier architecture

The MCS middle tier solves a very important problem by enabling the system to scale in places where it previously inhibited the loading of data onto the database – plainly due to the shear size and the pre-processing.

The heterogeneous solution depicted above relies on the ability of the WebSphere Application Server (WAS) middleware – IBM's J2EE implementation – to support a very high level of scalability while providing high availability, recoverability and full transaction support. When working on a cluster spread over several hardware platforms (machines), the system also provides failover support to recover from crashes of single machines.

The IBM MCS system is a J2EE application written in Java. The entire system was developed using IBM Rational Software Architect, which is an IBM Integrated Development Environment for WAS applications in Java, based on the Eclipse platform. The Eclipse Modeling Framework (EMF) was used to model a specific domain language, which we discuss only briefly.

In this paper, we provide a short description of the technological tools that make up our system, including the J2EE and RDBMS platforms. We continue with a description of the MCS solution and its deployment on these platforms. We conclude with some results obtained in a limited early deployment.

2   Technology Background

2.1   WebSphere Application Server Cluster Middleware

MCS uses the WebSphere 6.0 Workload Management (WLM) feature to improve the application's performance, scalability, and reliability. It accomplishes this by providing failover when servers are not available.

Messaging: WAS includes a messaging integration bus (SIB) implementing the standard Java Messaging Services (JMS). SIB is an integral part of WLM allowing it to distribute messages in a balanced policy among all participating servers, where messages are triggers which initiate resource-eager data processing threads.

Scalability: WLM improves scalability by using a cluster configuration that allows the overall system to service a higher data load than that provided by the simple one server configuration. To a certain practical limit it is possible to service any given load by simply adding the appropriate number of application servers to act as cluster members.

Load-balancing: WLM ensures that each machine or server in the cluster processes a fair share of the overall data load being processed by the system. In other words, it prevents a situation where one machine is overloaded while another machine remains mostly idle. It doesn't matter whether all machines are used at 50% of their capacity or 100% of their capacity, the long-term relative wait of data processing on each machine will be the same.

Failover: Using multiple servers in a cluster, and perhaps on multiple independent machines, leads naturally to the potential for the system failover. If any one machine or server in the system were to fail for any reason, the system should be able to continue operating with the remaining servers. The load-balancing property should ensure that the processing load gets redistributed to the remaining N-1 servers, each of which will henceforth process a proportionately higher percentage of the total load.

Workload management is most effective when the deployment topology is comprised of application servers on multiple machines, since such a topology provides both failover and improved scalability. It can also be used to improve scalability in topologies where a system is comprised of multiple servers on a single, high-capacity machine. In either case, it enables the system to make the most effective use of the available computing resources.

2.2 Database

The physical design relies heavily on the technology and functionality of the IBM DB2 UDB product, including its Data Partitioning Facility (DPF). DPF offers a near linear scalability of large database applications by enabling a large number of DB2 database engines to operate in parallel on several UNIX operating systems, while providing a single logical view of the data for application and user access. With DPF, one or more database engines are started in each participating operating system.

Each database engine manages its own resources such as database control files, log files and table-spaces (raw disks or UNIX file system containers) in which table data is stored. When defining tables, the database administrator specifies a partitioning key, which is a set of table columns. Whenever a row is added to a table, the partitioning key columns are mapped by a hashing algorithm to one of the database engines called DB partitions, which stores the row in table-space container owned by the respective partition. The quality of the IBM supplied hashing algorithm ensures that very high cardinality partitioning keys supply an almost uniform distribution of large table rows between the database partitions.

The applications involved can subsequently connect to any DB partition and issue DML statements to query/update the database. The partition handling the connection ships access requests to all partitions that participate in storing data for the requested tables. It then coordinates the processing across the partitions. For example, if a DML statement requires the scanning and/or updating of 1,000,000 rows distributed (by DB2's hashing algorithm) almost uniformly among 20 database partitions , the database will automatically initiate 20 tasks (one on each of the 20 partitions) that will concurrently completes the necessary database processing in 5% of the time required by a single database engine. Section 4.3 provides more detailed examples of the leveraging of DPF's parallel processing in the MCS application.

The DPF functions utilized are: Fast Load, Parallel processing of collocated DML, and Multi Dimensional Clustering (MDC), which provides a physical separation of records with common values in the leading dimensions is another DB2 performance improvement technology levered in the MCS implementation. When defining a table, the DBA has the option of specifying a list of low cardinality "dimension columns" which are commonly used to filter rows in SQL queries. The rows of the database table will be physically separated into groups (called Cells) defined by the permutations of values of these columns. In the case of DPF, the physical grouping will exist in every database partition. For example, assume that MDC is defined on the "transaction_date" column. If a table stores 100,000 transactions per day for 90 days, a table-space scan limited by an SQL predicate to a single day will need to physically scan only 100,000 records instead of 9 million records. The above DPF deployment (20 partitions) will perform 20 concurrent scans of only 5000 records each, in each partition.

Thus by leveraging MDC and DPF we are able to deploy a data base design that reduces table-space scanning by a factor of $1/(MDC\_CARDINALITY * N\_partitions)$ where MDC_cardinality is the expected permutations of values in commonly used predicates and N_partitions is the number of DB2 database partitions deployed in the DB2 database instance.

3 MCS Description

3.1 MCS Execution Model

The MCS execution model was designed to efficiently utilize the scalability, load balancing and failover capabilities of the WebSphere Application Server. To this end, MCS supports breaking down an end to end global process (logical) into several sub-processes (concrete) while maintaining the context of the global process. Each sub-process is triggered by a message, and all those active at a given moment execute in parallel on as many threads as configured on each of the different cluster server member assigned by the Work load Management (WLM) facility.

The MCS execution model assigns to each concrete process a corresponding persistent Data Object (DO) element which represents its state. This design allows each concrete process to execute in several consecutive steps, each of which may run on a different thread. The interactions among the different concrete sub-processes needed to carry out the end to end global logical process is managed by the MCS Business Process Flow & Control Engine (BPFC) described later in this paper.

Presently, the MCS logical process consists of the following concrete processes:

- Massive pre-processing of CDRs according to specific business rules. This is achieved by a set of transformations applied to each CDR, resulting in validated, enriched and normalized output. The set of transformation is composed into a Processing Plan – see section 4.2 below.
- Massive uploading of the processed data to the database.
- Massive broadcasting of the uploaded data to subsequent dependent business components.
- Recovery and exception handling.

MCS BPFC engine is designed to be easily modified to support new business process requirements. This enables the MCS execution model to be applied to other business domains aside from its current subject domain.

3.2 Sources, Target Destinations, and MCS Entities

The MCS data model was designed to support maximum flexibility of input data and their corresponding target output destinations. The massive input stream of record is apportioned into manageable quantities in the following sense. MCS applies transactional data integrity on the partitioned data borders. Currently, each portion is provided as a single file.

When there are logical reasons to associate records across files, MCS defines an Envelope entity, which represents one or more file sharing the same transactional integrity. The single file is processed in a restartable MCS Task entity. This means that in case of failures the file can be reprocessed or disposed as erroneous.

Each input file is associated with a certain processing plan (see below) according to its type. As a result, one or more collection of output records are generated and associated with certain destination. MCS Destination is a logical entity which is associated with a real-world resource, which in general will be a database table. MCS Destinations may also be files, while in general MCS uses files as an intermediate storage for its massive database uploading mechanism.

The MCS massive uploading is carried out in a concrete sub process called a Package. A MCS manages one or more package entities each of which is responsible for uploading into a specific MCS target table destination. The package may upload data produced by one or more envelopes sharing the same MCS destination.

To summarize this section, MCS manages concrete processes of four types: A Poller (described in the sequel), Envelopes, Tasks and Packages.

3.3 Domain Specification Language and Base Operations

To perform pre-processing of CDRs, MCS applies a domain language processor specifically developed for the application. The language uses terminology that is easy to understand in the limited context of preparing CDRs for the subject domain. Without going into too much details, suffice is to say that the language defines the structure of input and output records, types of fields, means for temporary storage, mechanisms for efficient data base table lookups, and sequences of extendable transformations from input fields to output fields. MCS language made it possible for a domain expert to write a Processing Plan according to a required set of business rules. The processing plan is written during an offline Authoring phase. In fact, experts in the CDR pre-processing, familiar with the domain were able to easily write processing plans for several different kinds of records, coming from different sources. No programming skills are required of plans authors.

Fig. 2. MCS IDE screen shots

All input records are pre-mediated to convert the distinct record coding and packaging of the different vendors to unified ASCII format files. Each file consists of a collection of records, where each record occupies a fixed length in bytes.

We developed the language processor using the Eclipse Modeling Framework (EMF)[7] and wrote plans on the Eclipse platform[8] via an MCS plug-in; this provided a GUI editor for writing and testing the plans. EMF was also used to model the language and to generate all the Java classes.

3.4 Operational Data Object (DO) Elements

The integrity of the global process and its concrete processes is maintained by persistent Data Object (DO) elements. The DO persistency is kept in specific MCS database tables. The MCS BPFC manages the concrete process execution and transactions via the WebSphere Application Server transaction support.

MCS currently defines five basic DOs, four of which are used to maintain state of MCS concrete process entities: Poller, Envelope, Task, and Package, and another to maintain state of the MCS destinations. Since for all practical reasons each destination is associated with file storage, the MCS term for destinations is OutputFile.

The Poller DO is a singleton across the entire cluster and is responsible for monitoring the incoming input CDR data, issuing new job requests for the Envelope, and monitoring the health of the MCS runtime environment. The Envelope represents in MCS the end to end global process. This starts from the point where the Poller identifies an input, to the point where all output records resulting from processing this input, are safely stored in their destinations.

The Task DO maintains the state of the Task entity responsible for pre-processing a concrete input CDR file. This consists of invoking the specific domain language processor, communicating with the associated Envelope entity, and the generation of the appropriate OutputFile destinations. MCS maintains a repository of compiled plans, which are fully re-entrant and thread-safe for massive concurrent invocation. Each plan is compiled on its first encounter; MCS plans perform rapid and massive table lookups. For that purpose, MCS maintains an efficient and optimal cache of these tables from the database, which can serve shared access by a highly concurrent plans execution.

There are several Package DOs, each representing a cluster-wide singleton responsible for uploading processed data into a specific database table destination, and which may originate from several Envelopes sharing the same destination.

The OutputFile DO maintains the state of concrete destination instances (i.e., files), throughout their lifecycle from generation to completion of database uploading. This DO is used by the relevant Envelope and Package entities to synchronize their activity. If a destination is not associated with a database table, it reaches its final state as soon as it is successfully generated.

The following diagram represents the flow of incoming CDR data through the MCS entities.

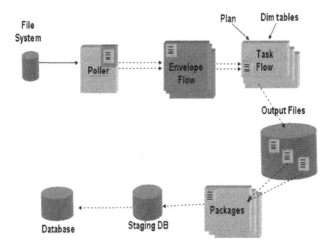

Fig. 3. MCS dataflow

3.5 Business Process Flow Control (BPFC)

The MCS BPFC Engine is written using J2EE building blocks, such as stateless session beans (EJBs), message driven beans (MDBs) and many other resources supported by the WebSphere Application Server.

The MCS BPFC Engine foundation consists of the following concepts:

- A general-purpose State Machine Engine, flexible and versatile for representing composite state hierarchy and corresponding set of transitions between states to form a State Machine Diagram. This diagram also declares the set of domain specific actions taken either during a transition or within the state scope.
- A State Machine Arbiter controls any number of different state machine diagrams allowing interaction across different diagrams. Basically, each state machine diagram is a server-wide singleton referred to as a State Machine Object. The arbiter deciphers incoming Trigger messages uploads the corresponding DO, which represents a concrete MCS entity of a certain type, represented by the respective State Machine Diagram. The Arbiter than dispatches the trigger and the DO to the target State Machine Object. The Arbiter wraps this process within a transaction control over the transition and the state actions, thus maintaining DO persistency and integrity.
- A Trigger Facility generates triggers which can carry any type of message payload to any target State Machine Object, for any of its concrete entity instances, on any of the servers and machines within the MCS WAS cluster.
- A general purpose Dispatcher responsible for sending Triggers carrying message to a target State Machine Object. The Dispatcher utilizes WAS load balance management (WLM).
- WebSphere Application Server Messaging Layer declaring multiple Queues for holding dispatched trigger messages. Together with message driven beans

entry points the MCS architecture allows fine tuning of the flow and its resource allocation addressing the business model massive requirements.

The BPFC execution model differentiates between two types of actions: State Flow Process Action and Transition Action. The transition action is designed to be 'short' (e.g. in the order of few milliseconds). On the other hand, the state actions may be 'long term' (e.g., in the order of minutes). It is the responsibility of the action writer to adhere to these design guide-lines.

3.6 Scalability, Parallelism, Persistency, and More

The MCS architecture of associating database persistent DOs with the BPFC engine makes it highly scalable, to the WAS cluster limits. In fact, as many Envelop and Task concrete entity instances can operate in parallel, as much as the WAS-controlled resources permit on the specific platform configuration on which MCS works.

MCS supports three levels of recovery. The first level is implemented programmatically in the state-machine diagrams. For instance, a failure is detected as a transient, identified as a "soft" failure and is retried. Repeated soft failure is designated by the state-machine as a "hard" failure if it occurs more than a preset threshold. Failures not identified as "soft" are automatically categorized as "hard". Hard failures will mean that the specific concrete entity will be disposed as erroneous. This may mean a specific Task (i.e., an input file), or an entire Envelope.

The second recovery level is applied at the state-machine arbiter mechanism which is integrated with the WAS transaction management. Failures that cannot be handled by the WAS transaction management are propagated to an exception-handling mechanism. As a result, corresponding concrete entities are triggered to handle severe failures – which in general are programmatically handled as "hard" failures.

The third recovery level handles hard platform crashes. This is provided by the WAS recovery and failover facility which ensures continuity of service in face of partial hardware/platform faults.

4 Deployment on the Platforms

4.1 MCS on the WAS Cluster

The MCS execution model is supported by two logical components: MCS Poller and MCS Worker. The MCS Poller holds the Poller singleton DO and assumes its responsibilities. The MCS Worker executes the Business Process Flow & Control components responsible for the Envelope, Task, and Package DOs. Both these components are capable of running in a clustered environment or single server environment.

The MCS Workload Management (WLM) capabilities are achieved with a cluster configuration that consists of two distinct clusters. The first cluster is the MCS Poller cluster, where the MCS Poller execution model is deployed on one or more servers to provide failover capabilities. The second cluster is the MCS Worker cluster, where the MCS Worker execution model is deployed on one or more servers to provide scalability and load balancing. The exact number of servers in each cluster and the resource allocation depends on the physical machine capabilities and even more strongly on the analysis of the Telco revenue assurance business model requirements.

The system configuration is scalable and users can increase the processing capabilities of MCS by using additional physical machines; these machines can be used to install additional Worker application servers that are joined to the MCS Worker cluster, thus providing more processing units for the data.

The configuration in Figure 5-1 demonstrates the interaction between MCS Poller and MCS Worker clusters. MCS Poller cluster contains a number of application servers. Only one of these servers will be active at any point in time; this is ensured programmatically by the MCS Poller implementation. The other servers are used for failover, if needed. The Poller application servers each have a messaging engine, which is part of the MCS SIB bus. When the MCS Poller application identifies a new unit of work, it sends a message to the appropriate queue on this bus. The message is received by one of the Worker application servers and the processing begins. These Worker application servers also have messaging engines and are bus members on MCS SIB bus; these are declared listeners on MCS queues. The load-balancing is therefore achieved by using the JMS WLM mechanism, since the load of messages arriving at a queue is distributed evenly among all the listeners on this queue. Scalability is achieved by adding Worker application servers to the Worker clusters, wherever needed and physically possible. Fault-tolerance is achieved inherently, since even if one Worker server fails, the others continue to process the load.

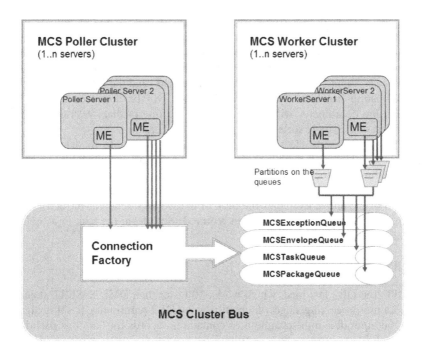

Fig. 4. MCS Poller and Worker clusters

4.2 Database Design

The design of the RDBMS population component allows the MCS to provide an optimal, highly scalable solution for collection systems with the following RDBMS processing requirements:

- Collection of massive amounts of detail records to be stored for a defined retention period before archival and deletion, without update in the RDBMS.
- Filtering of duplicate records that can arrive due to defects in either the digital event collection components or IS operations.

Staging of summary information derived from the arriving detail data that is incorporated into a heavily accessed, query oriented database. The database is designed to enable users to focus on a subset of detailed records by providing values to a small set of leading dimension columns which must include a time dimension column. In the initial Telco application the leading dimension columns are the ID of the digital component generating a CDR and the ID of a 15 minute time interval when the CDR was produced.

4.3 Parallel Processing of Collocated DML

Parallel processing of DML (SELECT, INSERT, UPDATE and DELETE Statements) is enabled by the DB2 optimizer whenever possible and there is no need for developers' coding non standard SQL. Database designers and administrators, on the other hand, must design for parallelism by collocating tables that participate in multi table DML statements in order to achieve the throughput of required by MCS.

For example, a query producing a sorted row result set of 500 rows requiring the scanning of one million rows will be sent to 20 partitions where each partition will scan and filter about 50 thousand rows in parallel and send the intermediary results to the coordinating partition. The bulk of the work will be done concurrently on 20 nodes and the coordinator will merge and sort the intermediary results totaling 500 rows and present a single sorted result set to the application.

Similarly, an Insert-Select statement from a staging table to detail transaction tables that are collocated (having the same partitioning key columns) will be executed in parallel thus the processing of a one million row staging table will automatically be divided among 20 data base engines which will select and insert 50,000 rows each.

In both of the above examples the bulk of the work is done concurrently in 5% of the elapsed time that would have been required to perform the task in a traditional, single database engine environment.

4.4 DB2Fast Load

With DPF, the DB2 fast load, which works 10 faster than DML INSERT statements, executes a pre-processing stage which utilizes the DB2 partitioning hashing algorithm to split the input data into separate files containing records for only one partition and "ships" each file to its respective partition.

The MCS DB load component uses the DB2 fast load to the formatted output data file into a staging table which is collocated with the target detail table. A series of collocated Insert-Select containing Left Outer Joins is used to filter duplicates, Insert Duplicates into an error table and Insert the non duplicate records into the detail table.

Aggregate records of the non duplicate data in the staging table are computed and inserted into a staging table of summary data which will be used to update the query database at end of day processing.

4.5 Multi Dimensional Clustering (MDC)

Multi Dimensional Clustering (MDC) provides physical separation of records with common values in the leading dimensions. In our Telco application, all detail records generated by the same digital component in the same 15 minute interval were stored in a single physical container. This alignment of logical and physical structure enables fast loading, fast retrieval and fast maintenance (when deleting/archiving at end of retention period).

5 Summary

This paper describes a heterogeneous highly scalable collection system in which a massive flow of event detailed records are collected and pre-processed using a special domain-specific language. The data is then uploaded to a highly partitioned database where subsequent post processing is performed.

The target performance for the system using a cluster of machines is in the order of one billion records a day, which translates to a TB a day. Current tests demonstrated a performance reaching 100 million records a day. These deployment tests use a smaller configuration consisting of only three machines: one for MCS and two for DB2. The target and test machines are IBM RISC System 6000 platforms (IBM System p5 ™) having eight CPUs and 32 GB of RAM, running the AIX operating system. It is assumed that the addition of further machines will enable the system to process the target volume.

Acknowledgements

Thanks to Dagan Gilat, Pnina Vortman, and Yoel Arditi for their visionary drive in this project. To Yaakov Dolgov who contributed to the implementation and design of the solution, and to Chani Sacharen and Hanan Singer for editing/formating the manuscript.

References

1. WebSphere Application Server V6 Scalability and Performance Handbook, IBM Redbook, SG24-6392-00, ISBN: 0738490601
2. WebSphere Application Server V6 Technical Overview, by Carla Sadtler, IBM Redbook, REDP-3918-00
3. WebSphere Application Server V6 Planning and Design WebSphere Handbook Series, IBM Redbook, SG24-6446-00, ISBN: 0738492183

4. Java™ Message Service Specification Version 1.1, Sun Microsystems® (April 2002) http://java.sun.com/products/jms/docs.html
5. Java™ 2 Platform Enterprise Edition Specification, v1.4, Sun Microsystems® (November 2003) http://java.sun.com./j2ee/j2ee-1_4fr-spev.pdf
6. IBM DB2 Information Management (Accessed January 29, 2007) http://www.redbooks.ibm.com/portals/Data
7. The Eclipse Modeling Framework (Accessed Janurary 29, 2007) http://www.eclipse.org/modeling/emf/?project=emf
8. The Eclipse project organization (Accessed January 29, 2007) http://www.eclipse.org

Two-Phase Data Warehouse Optimized for Data Mining*

Balázs Rácz, Csaba István Sidló, András Lukács, and András A. Benczúr

Data Mining and Web Search Research Group, Informatics Laboratory
Computer and Automation Research Institute of the Hungarian Academy of Sciences
Kende u. 13-17., 1111 Budapest, Hungary
bracz+v6@math.bme.hu, scs@elte.hu, alukacs@sztaki.hu,
benczur@ilab.sztaki.hu

Abstract. We propose a new, heterogeneous data warehouse architecture where a first phase traditional relational OLAP warehouse coexist with a second phase data in compressed form optimized for data mining. Aggregations and metadata for the entire time frame are stored in the first phase relational database. The main advantage of the second phase is its reduced I/O requirement that enables very high throughput processing by sequential read-only data stream algorithms. It becomes feasible to run speed optimized queries and data mining operations on the entire time frame of most granular data. The second phase also enables long term data storage and analysis using a very efficient compressed format at low storage costs even for historical data. The proposed architecture fits existing data warehouse solutions. We show the effectiveness of the two-phase data warehouse through a case study of a large web portal.

1 Introduction

In this paper we address the efficiency of telecommunication log data warehouses with vital data mining functionalities such as recommender systems [6], web site usage patterns [20] or user community analysis [9]. We observe rapid expansion in the amount of data; several millions of new records per day that reach tens of gigabytes in its raw form are quite common. It is increasingly hard to keep long-term analytical aggregates and data mining models real time without ever increasing the computing and storage capacities.

We propose a *two-phase data warehouse* solution for improved data availability in mining algorithms. While it is widely accepted that database management systems are the appropriate source for data mining [15, p. 172], we put the coupling [25] between the database management system (DBMS) and the mining algorithm into a new view by introducing another *second phase* source of data

---

* The research was partially supported by the Inter-University Center for Telecommunications and Informatics (ETIK), by the National Office for Research and Technology under the grants GVOP-3.1.1.-2004-05-0054/3.0 and NKFP2-00004/2005 and by the Hungarian Scientific Research Fund (OTKA) grant no. T042706.

C. Bussler et al. (Eds.): BIRTE 2006, LNCS 4365, pp. 63–76, 2007.

in addition to the (first phase) DBMS that operates similar to a nearline solution [18]. We achieve loose coupling with the DBMS but tight coupling with
the compressed second phase storage. This provides optimized access to archive
data as in a nearline solution, and also optimized data access for data mining.
We hence combine the advantages of existing loosely coupled data mining and
external nearline solutions.

The motivation of introducing a second phase is based on the observation
that storing large amount of long-term data for on-line analysis requires huge
efforts in a data warehouse environment. Scalability of the standard data warehouse techniques makes the all-time expansions of the system more and more
costly, while the functionality provided by the warehouse remains partly idle.
In addition, data mining algorithms perform poorly in standard data warehouse
environments. We conclude that the special needs of long-term, on-line, data
mining enabled data storage is a supplementary data source in a large scale
integration with the existing data warehouse.

Our model for the knowledge discovery process uses a query language that
describe the execution plan of the knowledge discovery process by giving the
interconnection of the data manipulating and modeling algorithms via a standard
interface. Comparing this approach to the mainstream concept of DMQL has
some similarity to comparing the programming language C to other high level
languages. The data mining pipeline offers a low-level control, allowing a very
effective planning and management of resources utilized.

We demonstrate the applicability of our architecture for the case of Web server
log analysis, an active area of research surveyed by [27]. The log files are typically
very sparse datasets that cover only extremely small part of their state space with
attribute values following very skewed distributions [12,5]. Particular advantage
of our solution lies in our compression method [24]; compression techniques in
commercial database engines often perform poorly for sparse data cubes and
result in large amounts of inefficiently utilized storage. While Web usage analysis
using relational OLAP methods is worked out in detail [29], commercial web
usage mining tools typically do not utilize the data warehouse.

The paper is organized in the following way. After describing related architectures next, in Section 2 the outline of the proposed architecture is presented.
Section 3 provides the case study of the leading Hungarian Web portal. In Section 4 we discuss the detailed functionality and applicability of our second phase
implementation including long-term storage, data mining support and other advanced features. Performance measurement results are displayed in Section 5.

1.1 Related Results and Architectures

Efficiency of traditional OLAP and data warehouse techniques [11,32] is considered by several authors [16] who invest huge efforts in techniques for generating,
querying and maintaining data cubes in both relational OLAP (ROLAP) and
multidimensional OLAP (MOLAP) environments. However, the ever growing
data volume can make these approaches very costly unless we compromise by
discarding certain dimensions and limit the time granularity of accessible data.

Efficiency observations lead to the development of *column-oriented databases* and *nearline storages*, to two architectures related to our two-phase solution.

Column-oriented database systems such as the *C-store* [28] are read-optimized databases designed for relatively few concurrent users asking sophisticated queries by storing relational data in columns rather than in rows as in the conventional "row-store" approach. Similar to our second phase, the column-wise storage enables sophisticated compression methods [4] and evaluate queries on compressed data as far as it is possible. While we also compress data column-wise, we store them as a row store as an additional benefit over column stores to avoid the use of join indices that would slow data mining down. Nevertheless the possibility of keeping the data in column-wise separate files as well as multiple views under different sorting and partitioning is possible in our second phase although our data management philosophy stays closer to data streams than to common database principles.

Our concept shares some properties with **nearline data warehouses** like Sybase IQ and Sand/DNA Access that extend existing data warehouses by utilizing compression highly integrated to the host data warehouse. The term "nearline storage" [18] is used for an intermediate type of storage that lays between on-line and off-line storage as a golden mean, avoiding both cheap but slow tape-resident storages [10] and expensive huge on-line storages.

When comparing column-wise and nearline storages with our solution, first of all we stress that our second phase primarily supports data mining and relies on the existing first phase as a fully functional database system. Data mining enabled database system architectures can be classified by the strength of the coupling between data mining algorithms and the DBMS systems [25]:

Tight coupling. Data mining is *integrated* into the DBMS using only the existing query processing methods. When used for data mining, this solution has known efficiency limitations [25,26].

Semi-tight coupling. The existing DBMS system is extended with data mining primitives of different complexity and in turn provides an extension of the SQL query language. This corresponds to an *interfaced* connection between a second phase or nearline data storage where preprocessing, cleaning and basic analysis can be left to the existing DBMS. The advantage is easy development but the drawback is the lack of optimization for immense data volumes moved through the interface.

Loose coupling. Data are read from the DBMS and directly loaded into a separate DM system. While both our and other typical existing data mining solutions are loosely-coupled and use locally stored copies, in our approach we introduce an *external* data storage that replicates some of the DBMS functionalities similar to a nearline solution. With a clear increase in development costs, this is the only solution that allows an external storage optimized for data mining.

Finally we mention the desired common aim in the fields of knowledge discovery and inductive databases to find a satisfactory formalism for data modeling and mining [8]. A part of existing approaches concentrates on a relatively high level of abstraction but restricted to the particular type of knowledge to extract (like association rules, classification etc). Typical solutions of this type are DMQL [14], MSQL [17] and OLE DB [22]. Since our algorithms are tightly coupled to the second phase storage, we are able to extend SQL (e.g. [30,31], [13]) similar to other tightly coupled solutions; we are currently limited on the SQL side due to development costs.

2   The Proposed Architecture

Figure 1 shows the proposed two-phase architecture. While the first phase is a traditional DBMS that processes data sources and provides user interface for management and analysis, the new feature is a background second phase warehouse similar to a nearline solution but with slightly different goals. Data is imported either from the first phase or, for real time applications, directly from raw logs and stored compressed. The background storage keeps data available through streaming and data mining interfaces and also provides archival. Long term aggregates as well as custom mining reports are moved up into the traditional first phase DBMS and presented to the user over a standard interface.

The first phase is implemented using standard data warehouse technologies. The source data is extracted, transformed and loaded into the database by the ETL tools. The database is responsible for managing data cubes and metadata, such as dimension tables. First the dimensions and dimension hierarchies are refreshed, and fully detailed data cubes are built. These tables contain data only for a limited time frame. Additional cubes store the derived, subject area-specific data, which are updated after the main cubes. These smaller cubes contain data with no time restrictions. (They can be implemented as independent data marts

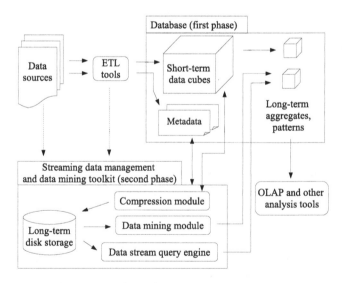

Fig. 1. Two-phase data warehouse architecture

as well [3].) Reporting and analysis is done by tools connecting to the data warehouse.

A goal of the second phase is to optimize data mining access to very large data sets. This is achieved by compressed storage optimized for high throughput by large compression rates, relative slower but rare compression and frequent very fast decompression. We employ our semantic compression column by column [24] described in more detail in Section 4.3. While similar to column stores in the use of compression, a main difference is that we only compress data in columns but we store in rows in order to serve data mining algorithms without the need of join indices over the data.

We primarily use the second phase data over a streaming interface without ever storing large uncompressed data chunks. Sequential access to all or certain relatively large blocks of the data fits well with a variety of data mining and machine learning algorithms. Frequent itemset mining as well as partitioning clustering algorithms such as k-means algorithms are designed to use a few passes of full scans over the data [15]. A given model can be applied to classify data; certain models such as Naive Bayes or decision trees can also easily be trained by sequential passes. Finally database sketches or synopses can be efficiently built for further processing [7].

The second phase data consists of one or more basic fact tables with all frequently used attributes joined. Access is restricted *read-only sequential* with the exception of inserting fresh data. While the architecture does not prohibit indices similar to column stores, the only index type we use is a very coarse block index suitable for example for selecting data from different time periods. Queries hence use full or partial table scans and joins are implemented only for small tables by internal memory indices; notice that in our high throughput architecture full table scans are relative inexpensive operations.

In conclusion our two-phase architecture uses a traditional DBMS to handle authentication both to OLAP queries and to predefined data mining output generated from the second phase data. The DBMS contains detailed dimension tables with no restriction on its scheme (snowflake or even more complex). By cost considerations the first phase is restricted in its time window or granularity; for historic data only aggregates are preserved. The second phase, on the other hand, acts both as a nearline solution to store archive data as well as a data source for tightly integrated mining algorithms. The second phase is restricted to a star schema with one or more basic fact tables that are read only except for the addition of new data and are optimized for full table scans with possibly only very coarse or no indices implemented.

3   A Case Study

We illuminate key concepts of two-phase data warehouses by the case study of the largest Hungarian web portal (www.origo.hu). We give an overview next; details, specialties of this implementation and measurements are presented in Section 4. The portal has from 7 to 9 million successful page requests per day, which ends up in around 35 GB of raw web server log files each day that should be kept accessible for periods of years both for analysis as well as for legal obligation and security policies. Since the cost of a huge log data warehouse is not affordable, they used to build data marts on aggregated data while archive the raw data on tapes that is very difficult to access and analyze.

Our solution is built on top of their existing Oracle 9i database that we also use for presenting reports to the users through an easy-to-use web-based interface. The web server log data enter the DBMS system through our ETL tools; in addition these tools collect data from the editorial systems as well. The web server produces logs in a rich format to facilitate user behavior analysis including date, time, user agent, page hit (URL), content, referrer page, HTTP method, HTTP protocol, cookie and IP address of the visitor. The raw data is filtered, completed (with domain names for IP addresses for example) before sent to the data warehouse component. The main page-hit data cube is partitioned by date: each day has a new partition. We also build hierarchies on top of the dimensions including domains for the IP addresses and page groups based on the structure of the site.

The most granular page hit data cube can store data only for a limited time period, in our case approximately five months. The most granular data is aggregated into smaller, subject oriented data cubes for the purposes of content optimization, marketing and web-design that do not run into capacity problems. Additional structures store patterns found by scheduled data mining processes. All the cubes share the dimension tables and metadata.

The data warehouse has a refresh period of one day, new data arrives overnight. First we make the database consistent by building the main table. At this point the second phase data is generated: the compression module reads out and compresses the most detailed data. After compression additional data mining tasks are performed, and the results are written back into the database for analysis. Second-phase modules connect to the database through standard Oracle C++ APIs.

To ensure that the second-phase data is always consistent to the database, they share all the data warehouse dimensions and metadata. However, the dimension data is stored also in the second phase as dictionaries, to handle changes of the schema and slowly changing dimensions. Archive, rolled-out detailed data of the star schema is always properly accessible from the second-phase. The second-phase modules are built on the relational-like data model which fits the snowflake schema using the same surrogate keys of dimensions as the database.

4   The Second Phase Component

In this section we describe the design issues and the architecture of our second phase solution, a single modular suite of software written entirely from scratch in C++ language that spans the tasks of compression, high-throughput data access and data mining by providing a data mining query language. The motivations behind these features and some interesting consequences are also discussed here.

The data mining engine of the second phase is designed and developed for handling and processing of very large datasets using a data stream approach. It combines an abstraction of data source, run-time modularity and configurability with keeping performance and resource management issues in hand. This enables a versatile platform for data mining and data analysis that allows an ordinary desktop or workstation-range computer to perform queries including data mining operations on very large datasets that are difficult to handle by boxed DBMS or statistical systems.

4.1   Modular Framework and Query Language

All the second-phase tasks are performed by a set of over 200 independent modules for data manipulation (filters, transforms, aggregation, grouping, sorting etc.) and modeling (clustering, classification, frequent pattern mining) instantiated at runtime. In this approach the plan of the knowledge discovery process is given by the sequence and the detailed parameter setting of the algorithms to apply. Module configuration can be given in a query language that specifies the required modules, their settings and virtually unrestricted interconnection over a standard interface.

An important question in the usage of a data mining solution is the user interface for designing and constructing the different data mining models. Our first solution was a simple configuration file edited by hand, which required considerable technical background to understand and develop. However, it took a relatively small effort to create a graphical user interface with more advanced functionality. Using this application building and modifying the configurations

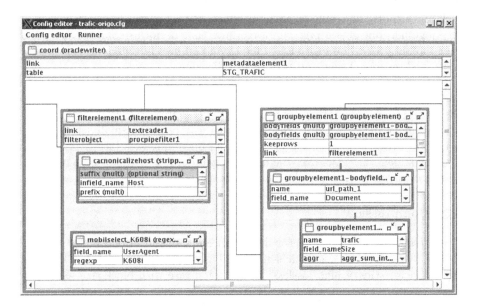

Fig. 2. Screenshot of the configuration UI

are quick and easy, thus one can realize the desired interactive process for developing data mining solutions. A similar open system approach for DM API is the Mining Mart [21].

Figure 2 depicts the configuration UI in use. As the simplest example of a data aggregation query we decompress and feed the output into a filter performing a WHERE clause (bottom left block) that filters users of handheld devices. The next module groups the records and calculates aggregated traffic fields. Finally, the resulting data may be loaded into the first-phase DBMS for further use (top). In a more advanced example we may feed aggregates into a data mining algorithm such as pattern discovery, clustering or classification. Finally, the result of the data mining task can be post-processed to select relevant or interesting patterns, or perform advanced visualization computations, and the result is again loaded into the main DBMS for display or further use.

The query language of our second-phase data warehouse is relatively low level and highly implementation-dependent. Application developers need to submit an execution plan as a query, formulated by the sequence of elementary operations to apply on the input data sources. This gives an absolute control over what is being done and how – which has both advantages and disadvantages over very high level query languages, such as SQL. We claim that some of the disadvantages are indeed desired in case of the immense data volumes of second-phase data.

4.2   The Data Stream Interface

The modules adhere the streaming data source interface both for input and output with a limited number of exceptions that use external memory sorting. Modules take next input, perform some transformation or data manipulation task and export the result on their interface. By connecting several such modules together, one gets a *pipeline* of modules that performs complex operations over the data as it flows through while never completely buffered. This ensures controlled resource usage and processing efficiency.

Data streaming allows second-phase data to be decompressed on-the-fly for queries while never stored, not even temporarily. The query engine has to process the stream of records as they come from the decompressor; records are discarded from memory once they are processed. This way only the small set of records being currently processed exist in the memory uncompressed. Intuitively it is like drawing a magnifier glass over the miniaturized data: only the records under the glass are currently visible and occupy resources.

4.3   Compression

Compressed input is a key factor in the efficiency of the second phase solution. In the case study we used our semantics-based compression scheme [24] with the characteristics of high lossless[1] compression rate with block size selected to

---

[1] A lossy compression might be adequate for certain applications, but analyzing this option is beyond the scope of this paper.

balance between supporting coarse indices and utilizing inter-block data correlation. While compression rate is very important, compression speed is not a high priority. We optimize for decompression speed as it will be a considerably more frequent operation than compression.

The compression module follows the modular concept and employs hand tunable *semantic methods* specialized for the type and content of data in the table to be compressed. The compression interface takes a sequence of values on its input and produces a bitstream, allowing arbitrary invertible transformations to be applied before the actual compression algorithm. Instead of a universal compression algorithm we provide a choice of several algorithms specialized for different data.

Transformations prior to compression may improve the rate, as shown in the following example. The timestamp field in the web server log has a close to uniform distribution over the entire period. However, if we sort the records in increasing order of timestamps and apply the delta transformation that outputs the difference between successive values, then the resulting sequence will contain only 0 and 1 (for each second jump exactly one 1 and all the remaining downloads will have 0) and extremely rarely some larger number. This is very well compressable even with a simple and fast entropy coder like Huffman.

Different compressed blocks may share *metadata* such as compression models, histograms or data distribution information. For example each day of data is compressed in a separate partition of the second-phase table. One such partition contains models built from scratch for the entire partition, and several data blocks using these models, which are individually decompressable.

When querying we utilize the ordering created by the compression module and the natural order of blocks/partitions (usually according to time) as an index for selecting which blocks to decompress and which blocks to skip entirely in accordance with the filter conditions of the current query.

4.4   The Data Model

In the second phase storage and query execution engine we use a special data model which we developed by keeping the needs of data mining applications and efficiency reasons in mind. This model is a common generalization of the relational data model and the sparse matrix data model. A relation is a set of n-tuples (records). The sparse format of a binary matrix is the following: for each row of the matrix, we take the set of nonzero entries as a list of their column identifiers.

In our model we group the n attributes of the classic relational model into k *header* attributes and $n - k$ *body* attributes. Those records, which have the same values in all the header attributes constitute a *row* and are collected together. The values of the header attributes are stored, processed and transmitted only once for each row, independently of the number of records belonging to that row. Essentially this is one level of grouping pushed into the data model.

A basic relation can be represented easily in our model by taking $k = n$ or $k = 0$, i.e., all attributes are header attributes (one row for each record) or there are no header attributes (in which case there will be a single row). A sparse matrix can be represented by taking a single header attribute, the row identifier and a single body attribute, the column identifier.

The advantages of this model, and how it is suited to data mining applications are best demonstrated through the example of user transactions such as Web page downloads, phone calls, sent messages or other service usage logs such as credit card transactions. In these databases the goal is to discover user behavior patterns or identify outlying users (such as credit card fraud). In our data model the attributes describing the users can be selected as header attributes, and attributes of the actual transaction as body attributes with a single row for each user grouping together the actions of a specific user for pattern or feature extraction. Although there may be up to billions of transactions in the dataset, the number of distinct users is usually considerably smaller (up to tens of millions). Since user data is stored and processed only once in our system, this conserves a huge amount of space and computation time. For example, joining another table on a user attribute has a cost proportional to the number of users and not the number of records in the relation. It also becomes feasible to even store the most frequently accessed user metadata by joining table(s) directly in the table of the main dataset.

5   Measurements

In the following we show the effectiveness of the two-phase architecture by some selected measurements. We compare the database and the second phase store according to space requirements and query performance. Unfortunately we are unable to use the TPC-H benchmark [2] due to the specialties of the web usage analysis and the second-phase storage. Instead, as in [19] we measure basic data warehouse implementation independent details.

Table 1 shows the space requirements of one month (31 days) web log data in the different phases. The DB table notion covers the main fact table of the most granular page hit data, without the dimension and hierarchy tables. The second-phase storage contains the basic dimension attributes as well. Oracle's data segment compression technique [23] achieves around 13 % storage saving, as a result of the very sparse dataset. Our compression method reduces storage down to 4.2 % for the basic fact table.

Figure 3 shows execution times for some basic queries of Table 2, observed on the same server. We chose queries that do not use dimension tables and require

Table 1. Space requirements of the page hit data cube (one month)

Storing method	Size on disk
Compressed (bzip) raw log files	180.7 GB
Compressed (bzip), preprocessed log files	17.1 GB
Standard DB table	44.9 GB
Compressed DB table	39.1 GB
Second-phase compressed storage	1.9 GB

Table 2. Reference queries

Query	SQL
Q1	select sum(PAGE_ID) from FACT_PAGE_IMPRESSION where DATE_KEY between 20060101 and 20060131
Q2	select count(*) from FACT_PAGE_IMPRESSION where DATE_KEY between 20060101 and 20060131 and HTTP_STATUS_CODE = 200
Q3	select count(distinct USER_ID) from FACT_PAGE_IMPRESSION where DATE_KEY between 20060116 and 20060122

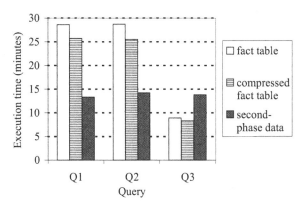

Fig. 3. Execution times for the reference queries

full table scans (we use no daily block index that would speed up our execution of Q3) of the fact table that store the required foreign keys. An appropriate tuning of the database requires careful implementation and documentation beyond the scope of this paper.

Querying second-phase data has near constant performance. The reason of the quite high Q3 execution time is the following: the granularity (partition size) of the compressed data is one month. In case of a query for one week of data we have to process a whole month to produce the result, in contrast to the database engine, where the query can be optimized to read only the appropriate fact table partitions for the selected date range. However, the granularity of the compressed data can be chosen arbitrarily, with the possibly increasing penalty of the storage overhead of the dimension tables.

We demonstrate the strength of our architecture for data mining tasks on Figure 4 (the experiment extends [26]). The four depicted algorithm incorporate four different philosophy for solving the task of frequent itemset mining in databases.

FP-TDG2 uses only relational database facilities to compute frequent itemsets, namely tables, indices and SQL operations.

NFP-CACHE is a tiny cache-mine system, reading the input data from the database, caching it on the local filesystem, computing the results by an

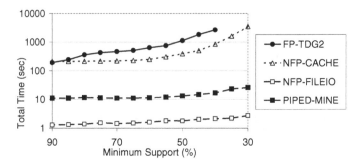

Fig. 4. Frequent itemset mining on the ACCIDENTS dataset

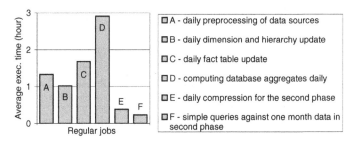

Fig. 5. Comparing average execution times of regular weblog processing jobs

efficient C++ standalone application (nonord-fp [1]), and writing back the results to the database.

NFP-FILEIO serves as a baseline on the figure, representing the nonord-fp algorithm using efficient file I/O libraries, getting the input data from files and writing the output into files too, without any database connection.

PIPED-MINE stores the input data compressed on local disk, computes and writes the result to the database using our second-phase toolkit.

The experiments were were performed on a PC server with a 3 GHz Intel Pentium processor, 2 GB memory, RAID 5 with IDE disks, Debian Linux operating system and Oracle9i Release 2 DBMS (see [26] for details). The dataset is a public dataset, having 340,183 transactions and 468 different items [1].

The SQL-based FP-TDG2 performs poor mainly because the structures and operations provided by the database are not suitable enough for implementations of data mining algorithms. The main part of the execution times of NFP-CACHE comes from reading the input data from the database and writing back the results. As the result set growths, the execution times are becoming therefore also larger. PIPED-MINE employs a similar implementation of frequent itemset mining algorithm as NFP algorithms. The time saving comes partly from using the compressed data as input, and partly from using a faster database connection API.

Figure 5 illustrates the execution times of the main regular jobs in our experimental system. We see the DBMS daily aggregation as the main bottleneck; another reason for using our architecture is that monthly or weekly aggregates cannot even be computed in tolerable time. We observe that the second phase offers a good basis computing these aggregates as well as for running data mining tasks.

6   Conclusions

We propose a two phase data warehouse architecture by adding a second phase data source to a traditional DBMS. The philosophy of the second phase lays between data streams, nearline databases and column-oriented databases: we provide very fast streaming access for full table scans of long-term fine granularity historical data stored column-wise compressed. While our data mining algorithms are loosely coupled to the DBMS, they are tightly coupled with the second phase data source and thus overcome the high cost of reading from DBMS. Our architecture promises effective long-term archival, computation and data mining at low costs as demonstrated by the example of a large scale Internet content provider server log warehouse.

References

1. Frequent itemset mining implementations repository
   `http://fimi.cs.helsinki.fi/`
2. TPC benchmark h standard specification revision 2.3.0.
   `http://www.tpc.org/tpch/spec/tpch2.3.0.pdf`
3. Designing data marts for data warehouses. ACM Trans. Softw. Eng. Methodol., vol. 10(4), pp. 452–483 (2001)
4. Abadi, D.J., Madden, S.R., Ferreira, M.C.: Integrating compression and execution in column-oriented database systems. In: SIGMOD '06: Proceedings of the ACM SIGMOD International Conference on Management of Data. ACM (2006)
5. Adamic, L.A., Lukose, R.M., Puniyani, A.R., Huberman, B.A.: Search in power-law networks. Physical Review E, vol. 64 (2001)
6. Ansari, A., Essegaier, S., Kohli, R.: Internet recommendation systems. Journal of Marketing Research 37(3), 363–375 (2000)
7. Babcock, B., Babu, S., Datar, M., Motwani, R., Widom, J.: Models and issues in data stream systems. In: PODS '02: Proceedings of the twenty-first ACM SIGMOD-SIGACT-SIGART symposium on Principles of database systems, pp. 1–16. ACM Press, New York, NY, USA (2002)
8. Boulicaut, J.-F., Masson, C.: Data mining query languages. In: The Data Mining and Knowledge Discovery Handbook, pp. 715–727 (2005)
9. Castells, M.: Rise of the Network Society: The Information Age: Economy, Society and Culture. Blackwell Publishers, Inc., Cambridge, MA, USA (1996)
10. Chatziantoniou, D., Johnson, T.: Decision support queries on a tape-resident data warehouse. Inf. Syst. 30(2), 133–149 (2005)
11. Chaudhuri, S., Dayal, U.: An overview of data warehousing and OLAP technology. SIGMOD Rec. 26(1), 65–74 (1997)
12. Dezső, Z., Almaas, E., Lukács, A., Barabási, A.-L.: Fifteen minutes of fame: The dynamics of information access on the web (2005)
13. Gray, J., Chaudhuri, S., Bosworth, A., Layman, A., Reichart, D., Venkatrao, M., Pellow, F., Pirahesh, H.: Data cube: A relational aggregation operator generalizing group-by, cross-tab, and sub-totals. Data Min. Knowl. Discov. 1(1), 29–53 (1997)

14. Han, J., Fu, Y., Wang, W., Koperski, K., Zaiane, O.: DMQL: A data mining query language for relational databases. In: DMKD'96 (June 1996)
15. Han, J., Kamber, M.: Data Mining: Concepts and Techniques. Morgan Kaufmann, San Francisco (2000)
16. Harinarayan, V., Rajaraman, A., Ullman, J.D.: Implementing data cubes efficiently. In: SIGMOD '96: Proceedings of the 1996 ACM SIGMOD international conference on Management of data, pp. 205–216. ACM Press, New York, NY, USA (1996)
17. Imielinski, T., Virmani, A.: MSQL: A query language for database mining. Data. Mining and Knowledge Discovery 3, 373–408 (1999)
18. Inmon, B.: The role of nearline storage in the data warehouse: Extending your growing warehouse to infinity. White paper
19. Joshi, K.P., Joshi, A., Yesha, Y.: On using a warehouse to analyze web logs. Distrib. Parallel Databases 13(2), 161–180 (2003)
20. Mena, J.: Data Mining Your Website. Butterworth-Heinemann, Newton, MA, USA (1999)
21. Morik, K., Scholz, M.: The mining mart approach to knowledge discovery in databases. In: Zhong, N., Liu, J. (eds.) Intelligent Technologies for Information Analysis, pp. 47–65. Springer, Heidelberg (2004) ISBN 3-540-40677-8
22. Netz, A., Chaudhuri, S., Fayyad, U.M., Bernhardt, J.: Integrating data mining with SQL databases: OLE DB for data mining. In: Proceedings of 17th International Conference on Data Engineering (2001)
23. Pöss, M., Potapov, D.: Data compression in oracle. In: VLDB 2003: Proceedings of 29th International Conference on Very Large Data Bases, pp. 937–947. Morgan Kaufmann, San Francisco (2003)
24. Rácz, B., Lukács, A.: High density compression of log files. In: Data Compression Conference, p. 557 (2004)
25. Sarawagi, S., Thomas, S., Agrawal, R.: Integrating association rule mining with relational database systems: alternatives and implications. In: SIGMOD '98: Proceedings of the 1998 ACM SIGMOD international conference on Management of data, pp. 343–354. ACM Press, New York (1998)
26. Sidló, C.I., Lukács, A.: Shaping SQL-based frequent pattern mining algorithms (Revised Selected and Invited Papers). In: Knowledge Discovery in Inductive Databases: 4th International Workshop, KDID 2005, pp. 188–201. Springer, Heidelberg (2005)
27. Srivastava, J., Cooley, R., Deshpande, M., Tan, P.-N.: Web usage mining: discovery and applications of usage patterns from web data. SIGKDD Explor. Newsl. 1(2), 12–23 (2000)
28. Stonebraker, M., Abadi, D.J., Batkin, A., Chen, X., Cherniack, M., Ferreira, M., Lau, E., Lin, A., Madden, S., O'Neil, E., O'Neil, P., Rasin, A., Tran, N., Zdonik, S.: C-store: a column-oriented dbms. In: VLDB '05: Proceedings of the 31st international conference on Very large data bases, pp. 553–564. VLDB Endowment (2005)
29. Sweiger, M., Langston, J., Lombard, H., Madsen, M.R.: Clickstream Data Warehousing. John Wiley & Sons, Inc., New York, NY, USA (2002)
30. Wang, H., Zaniolo, C.: Database system extensions for decision support: the AXL approach. In: ACM SIGMOD Workshop on Research Issues in Data Mining and Knowledge Discovery, pp. 11–20 (2000)
31. Wang, H., Zaniolo, C.: Atlas: A native extension of SQL for data mining. In: SDM (2003)
32. Zaiane, O.R., Xin, M., Han, J.: Discovering web access patterns and trends by applying OLAP and data mining technology on web logs. In: ADL '98: Proceedings of the Advances in Digital Libraries Conference, p. 19. IEEE Computer Society, Washington, DC, USA (1998)

Document-Centric OLAP in the Schema-Chaos World

Yannis Sismanis, Berthold Reinwald, and Hamid Pirahesh

IBM Almaden Research Center
{syannis,reinwald,pirahesh}@us.ibm.com

Abstract. Gaining business insights such as measuring the effectiveness of a product campaign requires the integration of a multitude of different data sources. Such data sources include in-house applications (like CRM, ERP), partner databases (like loyalty card data from retailers), and syndicated data sources (like credit reports from Experian). However, different data sources represent the same semantic attributes in different ways. E.g., two XML schemas for purchase orders may represent price as /SAP46Order/Product/Price or /PeopleSoft/Item/Sold/ Cost, respectively. The different paths to the same semantic information depend on the schema, making it difficult to index the data and for query languages such as XQuery to process aggregation queries. Shredding the XML documents is not feasible due to the vast number of different schemas and the complexity of the XML documents. The only known approach today is to ETL every single document into a common schema, and then use XQuery on the transformed data to perform aggregation. Such a solution does not scale well with the number of schemas or their natural evoluation. This paper presents a robust solution to document-centric OLAP over highly-heterogeneous data. The solution is based on the exploitation of text-indexing that provides the necessary flexibility and well-established techniques for aggregation (like star-joins and bitmap processing). We present the overall architecture and the experimental performance results from our implementation.

Keywords: Metadata, Acrhitectures, Data Warehouse Evolution, Performance and scalability, Schema-Chaos.

Submission category: Regular Paper.

1 Introduction

Modern business data analysis requires input data from in-house applications, business partners, syndicated data providers, etc. Business acquisitions, mergers, and partnerships add to the mix of data sources. The plethora of different schemas —even if the data is consistent in semantics—, makes it impossible to index the data and very difficult for query languages such as XQuery to aggregate the data. The only known approach today is to map every single document into a canonical schema, ETL the data, and then use indexing and SQL or XQuery on the canonical schema to perform aggregation. However, the mapping approach is mostly manual, and it does not scale well with the number of different sources. Traditional data warehouses have already demonstrated that the capital cost of providing a unified view of the data, while hiding the diversity of the underlying operational systems, is extremely high.

C. Bussler et al. (Eds.): BIRTE 2006, LNCS 4365, pp. 77–91, 2007.

```
<SAP46Order>
  <date> 23 Nov 2005 </date>
  <customer>                          <PeopleSoft>
    <id>8334</id>                       <item>
    <name>Sally Kwan</name>              <date> 12 Sep 2005 </date>
    <address>                            <customer>C345</customer>
      S. Oak St.                         <sold>
      San Fransisco, CA 95100              <id>P3445</id>            <SAP46Product>
    </address>                             <quantity>1</quantity>      <id>KLE</id>
  </customer>                              <cost>100</cost>            <category>Office</category>
                                         </sold>                      <name>Desk</name>
  <product>                            </item>                      </SAP46Product>
    <id>KLE</id>
    <quantity>4</quantity>             <item>                       <SAP46Product>
    <price>56</price>                    <date> 10 Nov 2005 </date>   <id>FGE</id>
  </product>                            <customer>C121</customer>     <category>Glass</category>
                                        <sold>                       <name>Window</name>
  <product>                              <id>P4332</id>            </SAP46Product>
    <id>FGE</id>                          <quantity>2</quantity>
    <quantity>6</quantity>               <cost>50</cost>
    <price>30</price>                   </sold>
  </product>                           </item>
</SAP46Order>                        </PeopleSoft>

        (a)                          (b)                              (c)
```

Fig. 1. Example of SAP Order, PeopleSoft Order & SAP Product

Consider the two purchase orders in Figures 1(a) and 1(b). A typical example of an OLAP query is to get the total amount of office supplies sales in 2005 grouped by the state of the home address of the customer. If the data is already mapped to a common schema —like that in Figure 2(a)—, then the query can be specified using SQL (or XQuery) as shown in Figure 2(b). In reality, queries are more complicated, for example when joins between orders and lineitems are required. However, the execution of such a query does not only require that the data has been mapped to a common target schema, but the problem is exacerbated by the fact that certain information does not appear embedded in the order documents but needs to be "fetched" from other documents or data sources. In the example, the requested product category might originate from the UNSPSC[1], the United Nations Standard for product categorizations. The evolving needs and the required flexibility of modern business intelligence require "merging" together an increasingly large corpus of data sources which very quickly obsoletes any common target schema. Today, users might be happy with the UNSPSC categorization, but tomorrow another product hierarchy might appear, and the target schema needs to be updated and all the documents remapped.

Data warehouses classify data as *dimensional* (or *reference*) data and *fact* (or *transactional*) data. Dimensional data typically includes customer information (like customer address, income range, and age), or product information (like product id and year of production), while fact information (like an order or a complaint) joins different dimensional data (in this case customers and products). Facts include additional transactional information (like the date when the order was placed) or measures (like quantity or price for each ordered product). Fact data is bigger than dimensional data by orders of magnitude. An OLAP query is typically processed as follows: (a) A part of the dimensional entities is selected by applying predicates on the dimensional data (like product.category='Office Supplies' in our example). (b) A "slice" of the facts is

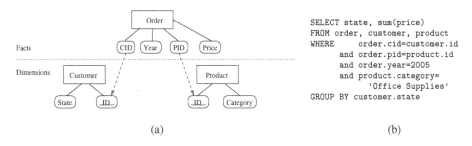

Fig. 2. Unified Warehouse Schema & Typical OLAP Query

selected using predicates on transactional data (in our example, using the predicate order.year=2005). (c) The dimensional entities are joined with the facts (in our example, the predicates order.cid=customer.id and order.pid=product.id). (d) Finally, the resulting tuples are aggregated on the requested hierarchical levels, and the results are returned.

In this paper, we present a robust approach to the problem of aggregating repositories of highly-heterogeneous data. Our main goal is to circumvent the intractable problem — from a pragmatic point of view— of defining, maintaining, and most importantly *using* hundreds or even thousands of different XML schemas (and probably different indexes defined for each one) over the underlying data. Our approach exploits text-indexing and well-established relational techniques for aggregation (including star-joins and bitmap processing). More specifically, we target 90% of the queries in the document-centric OLAP context by performing processing in the following stages: *Apply a "red" filter* that is based on text-indexing techniques and quickly filters out the majority of irrelevant documents or document fragments. *Apply a "blue" filter* that removes the false positives of the red filter by more thoroughly checking the validity of the selected documents. *Apply a unified join* that allows joining together dimensional information with fact information using just two composite indexes.

Our solution greatly simplifies the management of the underlying documents without requiring explicit mapping of their content to a unified common target schema. It exploits recent, innovative techniques for data-driven discovery of primary/foreign relationships and similarity of data attributes[2]. We strongly believe that the simplicity and flexibility of our approach will provide the query robustness that business applications demand.

In particular, we make the following contributions: We introduce MAVIS (MAterialized VIews for Schema chaos), a novel approach for handling schema-chaotic information, by leveraging existing reliable and optimized technology we demonstrate that it is possible to handle efficiently the document-centric/schema-chaos world today. We provide techniques for aggregating information in the document-centric/schema-chaotic world. We demonstrate in detail the applicability and robustness of our approach and finally we present the experimental results of our implementation.

Recently, there have been great advances in master data management (MDM) by commercial products like IBM WebSphere Product Center (WPC) [3] or WebSphere Customer Center (WCC) ([4]). Furthermore, syndicated data providers offer invaluable information to derive business insights, and in-house data (like sales, orders and complaints) represents the core of an enterprise. Our approach fits nicely in this model, managing to bring together and process both "cleansed" dimensional information along with proprietary fact data.

The remainder of the paper is organized as follows: Section 2 shows the overall system architecture. Section 3 describes in detail all the components of our approach. The experimental evaluation of our implementation is demonstrated in Section 4 using both real and synthetic datasets. Section 5 discusses the related work, and our conclusions are summarized in Section 6.

2   System Architecture

In this section we describe the overview of the architecture of our systems and introduce the basic concepts of our approach.

The process of coming with a common schema and maintaining it, requires considerable resources and time for applications that deal with thousands of schemas and millions of documents. In this document-centric OLAP scenario (*schema-chaos* world), our goal is to provide aggregate results without having to define explicitly a target schema and map all underlying documents to that schema.

In Figure 3, we depict a *data-driven* data warehouse system. Data from operational (OLTP) systems like ERP, CRM, etc. are *automatically* connected (matched) ([2],[5]) to data in a Master Data Management (MDM) repository. The MDM repository contains and maintains cleansed "dimensional" information about customers, products, etc. The enterprise software industry has acknowledged the need for MDM using, for example, [3] for product master data management, or [4] for customer master data management. Such cleansed MDM data with well defined semantics and meaningful slice-dice queries provides meaningful results to Business Intelligence experts. However, the transactional data is represented in a plethora of different (and continuously evolving) schemas in an attempt to capture the nature of the underlying evolving applications. We refer to this situation as *schema-chaos* world. Different data sources represent the same semantic attribute in different ways. For example, two XML schemas can represent price as /SAP46Order/Product/Price or /PeopleSoft/Item/Sold/Cost. The two syntactically different paths lead to the same semantic information , making it difficult to index the data, and for query languages such as XQuery to process aggregation queries. It is not practical to shred the XML documents due to the vast number of different schemas and the complexity of the XML documents. The only known approach is to ETL every single document using a common target schema, and then use XQuery on the transformed data to perform aggregation. However, such a solution does not scale well with the number of schemas.

In our system, the matcher component automatically links documents from the underlying OLTP systems to the data in MDM repository. For example, for the SAP order document in Figure 1(a), the matcher component links the order documents with the information about 'Sally Kwan' in the customer MDM repository and with the information about the 'Window' product in the product MDM repository.

Other interesting (from the OLAP perspective) attributes like price or discount, that do not explicitly appear in the MDM repositories are classified and annotated using approaches like [6] and [2].

The MAVIS (MAterialized VIews for Schema chaos) component we introduce in this paper, provides the framework for performing OLAP analysis in the schema-chaos world. More specifically it allows the efficient execution of slice/dice & group-by OLAP queries with a performance comparable to that of an optimized warehouse.

For querying purposes, the user or the application can navigate the objects and specify constraints. For the query example in Figure 2(b), the user could select the objects order, customer, and product, and set the constraints "2005" for the order date, the constraint "Office Supplies" for the product, pick the customer's state as the grouping attribute, and aggregate over the order price.

Our system currently provides the following: (a)Simplified architecture for executing the majority of OLAP queries, compared to SQL or XQuery. (b)Existing systems that provide elaborate analytical models and user interfaces can work unchanged using an automated translation from SQL queries to MAVIS queries. (c)All the content in the underlying schema-chaotic documents can be used for slice/dice, and not only the greatest common denominator that existing mapping techniques provide. (d)Leverages existing optimized techniques helping the transition from fixed-schema or semistructured-schema technology to fully schema-chaotic systems.

3   MAVIS (MAterialized VIews for Schema-chaos)

In this section, we describe in detail our approach, called MAVIS, to perform document-centric OLAP in the schema-chaos world. We describe in detail the MAVIS entities and indexes, how to populate them, and how to use them for OLAP queries.

3.1   MAVIS Definition

MAVIS targets the management, storage & indexing of both fact documents (like orders, complaints or reviews) and reference data. MAVIS has a collection of entities, and a set of indexes. The entities provide an abstraction of the information stored in the underlying data sources. Along with the indexes, it is possible to apply local predicates with high precision and perform joins very efficiently.

MAVIS Entity. For every single document in the repository, a variable number of MAVIS entities is created. The number of entities is a function of the number of repeating objects inside a document. Figure 4 depicts the general structure of a MAVIS entity, and Figure 5 shows the corresponding MAVIS entities for the order document in Figure 1(a). MAVIS entities have the following properties:

The Class-ID uniquely identifies the high-level business object of the document, i.e. whether it is an order, a complaint, a review, a customer, a product. Documents with the same business object are semantically clustered together. The classification based on class allows MAVIS to avoid the problem of "mixing" information between different clusters, even if the information is structurally equivalent. For example, both orders and complaints reference the same customer and product information, but when we are interested in sales we do not mix complaint documents into the aggregation process.

The Schema-ID uniquely identifies the schema of the underlying document. For example, for orders with a schema like the one in Figure 1(a), an ID of 'SAP46Order' is

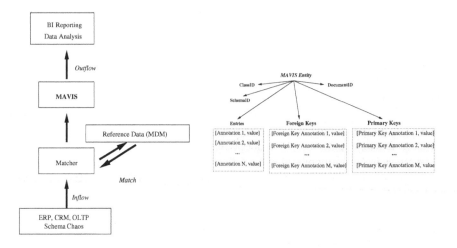

Fig. 3. Automated Warehouse Architecture   **Fig. 4.** A MAVIS Entity

assigned, while for orders with a schema like the one in Figure 1(b), an ID of 'People-Soft' is assigned. Every time a document with a new schema is processed, we create a new unique id for that schema.

The Document-ID uniquely identifies the exact document that the MAVIS entity corresponds to. The Document-ID allows MAVIS to access the original document, whenever it is required. In Figure 5, we use Document-ID 'D1' to refer to the document in Figure 1(a).

The set of MAVIS entries consists of pairs (annotation tag, values) that annotate the values which appear in the leaves of the document. These annotations allow MAVIS to apply local predicates and describe the content of the document in a fixed "structured" way. For example, customer names are represented using the tag 'CustomerName', product names are represented with the tag 'ProductName', etc. Such annotations are possible using annotation technologies like [6].

The set of MAVIS primary keys consists of pairs (primary key tag, value) that characterize the primary keys in the document. These characterizations (along with MAVIS foreign keys) make it possible to index and join facts with reference information. This happens for all the documents in MAVIS regardless of their underlying schema. For example, primary keys of customer information are represented by the primary key tag 'CustomerKey', primary keys to product information are represented by the primary key tag 'ProductKey', etc.

The set of MAVIS foreign keys consists of pairs (foreign key tag, value) that characterize the foreign keys in the document. The primary and foreign key characterizations make it possible to index and join with reference information. This happens for all the documents in MAVIS regardless of their underlying schema. For example, foreign keys to customer information are represented by the foreign key tag 'CustomerKey', keys to product information are represented by the foreign key tag 'ProductKey', etc. The automatic discovery and the characterization of keys can be automated using approaches like [7],[2] or [8].

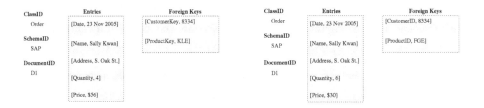

Fig. 5. The MAVIS entities for the SAP Order in Figure 1(a)

Each document may correspond to more than one MAVIS entities. The exact number depends on the number of repeatable objects inside the document. In our example, the repeatable object product appears twice in a document, so there are two MAVIS entities for the order document in Figure 1(a). The flexibility of the MAVIS entity allows us to store all the information of an underlying document factoring out the complex, hierarchical structure of the document (which can still be used by annotators or data profiling tools).

We use the MAVIS entity to store both fact and reference information. The main difference between fact and reference information is, that fact data has much richer foreign key information. Reference data use foreign keys mostly to define hierarchies, while facts combine many reference data by means of foreign keys (thus forming dimensions, that can be used for analysis). Although our system uses additional reference information that MDM systems provide, we also choose to handle any *additional* information that appears in the transactional data, so that more interesting slice & dice queries can be performed.

MAVIS Indexes. MAVIS uses the following indexes to allow for local predicate processing and indexing: *The Red Index* allows for fast keyword search over the entire corpus of documents. For example, for the two orders in Figures 1(a) and 1(b), the keyword '2005' qualifies both SAP and PeopleSoft documents, while the keyword 'San Franscisco' qualifies only the SAP order. As it is always the case with text indexing, the red index produces false positives. In order to filter the false positives an exact processing (called the *Blue Filter*) is applied. The Blue Filter is discussed in more detail in Section 3.3. *The Foreign Index* is a composite index that covers all the MAVIS foreign keys and the ClassID. For example, for the MAVIS entities in Figure 5, there are two MAVIS foreign keys `CustomerKey` and `ProductKey`. The Foreign Index in this case is a composite index on ⟨ClassID, Foreign CustomerKey, Foreign ProductKey⟩. The ClassID uniquely identifies a high-level business object as described in Section 3.1. *The Primary Index* is a composite index that covers all the MAVIS primary keys and the ClassID.

3.2 Populating MAVIS

In this section we describe how we can populate the MAVIS entities with documents from a large number of different schemas.

The population algorithm takes as input the corpus of highly-heterogeneous documents and creates the MAVIS entities and reference indexes. The algorithm parses one-by-one all the documents in the corpus and automatically profiles the contents of the document. The annotation enriches the system's understanding of the data (for example, it annotates that a given leaf is a date, or a person's name), while profiling identifies similarities among nodes and primary/foreign key dependencies.

After the processing , the document is "enriched" with additional metadata, including: (a)The repeating objects in the document. For example, the object product in the SAP46Order in Figure 1(a) or the item in the PeopleSoft Order in Figure 1(b). (b)The foreign keys that reference other information. For example, /SAP46Order/customer/id and /PeopleSoft/item/customer are foreign keys to reference customer information. (c)The primary keys that uniquely identify such information. For example /SAP46 Order/orderid uniquely identifies order information. Primary key (just like foreign key) discovery is data-driven, but can also be user-specified. (d)For example, /SAP46Order/ date and /PeopleSoft/item/date are dates, /SAP46Order/customer/name is a person's name, etc. This process is data-driven like the key discovery process. (e)The overall class of the document is identified (like order, complaint or customer). For example, in our case the documents in Figure 1(a) and Figure 1(b) are classified as orders.

MAVIS depends and builds on data-discovery and data-profiling technologies, and is orthogonal to the advances that happen in these areas. Specialized annotators can be written using a generalized framework (like [6]) and relationships between objects can be discovered using techniques like [2], [9] or [8]. Finally, the enriched object is indexed on the red-filter. The annotations make it possible to use higher-level keywords to search for documents, although those keywords never appeared in the original documents. For example, consider the case where we are looking for orders by female customers and that there is no sex attribute in the order that explicitly specifies the sex of the customer. An annotator that can identify, whether a token in the document is a female name, can be used easily to annotate accordingly.

We create one MAVIS entity for each repeating object in the document by repeating the static, non-repeating information that appears in the document. This "flattening" step simplifies the structural-chaos that different document schemas choose to organize their information. This approach does not limit the generality of our approach, and it is necessary to process the tree-like structure that semi-structure documents have using existing OLAP technology.

3.3   Querying MAVIS

In this section, we describe how MAVIS entities, the red filter and the reference indexes can be used to execute aggregation queries.

Since there is no explicit unified target schema, existing languages like SQL or XQuery cannot directly be used to express an OLAP query in MAVIS. However, OLAP queries typically follow the same pattern. Certain Reference data are selected using predicates on attributes like customer income range, product categorizations, or store locations. These predicates only affect the reference (dimensional) data. A "slice" of the fact data is selected using predicates on attributes like order date, product price, or quantity. Using MAVIS we do not have an explicit target schema, where those attributes are mapped to. However, we use annotation tags to achieve the same result. For example, although the price information is structured differently from one order

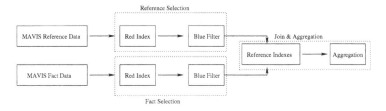

Fig. 6. MAVIS OLAP Processing

schema to another, in MAVIS it is annotated as 'price' and stored in the MAVIS entries. Finally, the slice of the fact data is joined with the reference data and the aggregation is performed.

Figure 6 shows the processing steps. They correspond to the OLAP query pattern described above. The user selects the high-level business objects, specifies constraints on related attributes, chooses the grouping attributes and the aggregation to perform.

We explain the whole process using the query in Figure 2(b). The user selects the interesting high-level objects, orders, customers, and products, specifies the constraint "2005" for year, "Office Supplies" for product, grouping attribute is customer's state, and finally the sum of the order's price as the aggregation. The steps "Reference Selection" and "Fact Selection", i.e. the application of local predicates to reference and fact data respectively, is executed using a *Red-Blue* filter approach which consists of two parts. The first part (red-filtering) is approximate and efficient. It prunes irrelevant to the query documents (or document fragments) using the text index. It has perfect recall (i.e. it doesn't miss any relevant documents) but also has a low precision since it may return a large number of false positives. The second part (blue-filtering) filters the false-positives using exact processing this time over the results that the red-filter returns.

Finally the joining of the reference data with the facts happens using the reference indexes and the grouping along with the aggregation is performed.

In this work, we focus on how the typical OLAP query can be executed on top of the flexible MAVIS organization under reasonable performance expectations. Our implementation currently translates SQL-like queries that require the user to have knowledge of the annotation types/schematics. The problem of using a "simpler" query paradigm specifically for MAVIS is future work.

3.4 Prototype Implementation Using *Rental Columns*

Although the MAVIS framework is generic and can be implemented on top of relational or semi-structured database management systems, we chose to implement it on top of a relational database management system. Such systems are very mature providing very efficient implementations of all the operations that MAVIS requires. Our goal is not to design a "faster" system but rather a "flexible" one that can scale w.r.t. to the plethora of different and evolving schemas and that can also perform under reasonable expectations.

MAVIS entities are mapped to tuples of a single table using the novel concept of "rental columns". The red index is implemented using text indexing, and the

Table 1. MAVIS Implementation using Rental Columns

			Entry Rental					Foreign Rental					Primary Rental		
Class	Schema	Doc	Map$_1$	Value$_1$	Map$_2$	Value$_2$	...	Foreign$_1$	FValue$_1$	Foreign$_2$	FValue$_2$	...	Primary$_1$	PValue$_1$	...
Order	SAP	D1	Date	23 Nov 2005	Name	Sally	...	CustKey	8334	ProdKey	KLE	...			...
Order	SAP	D1	Date	23 Nov 2005	Name	Sally	...	CustKey	8334	ProdKey	FGE	...			...
Order	People	D2	Date	12 Sep 2005			...	CustKey	C345	ProdKey	P3445	...			...
Order	People	D2	Date	10 Nov 2005			...	CustKey	C121	ProdKey	P4332	...			...
Product	SAP	D3			Category	Office	...					...	ProdKey	KLE	...
Product	SAP	D3			Category	Glass	...					...	ProdKey	FGE	...

reference indexes are implemented using the composite indexing support of the underlying DBMS provided.

In our prototype implementation, we represent one MAVIS entity in one tuple. The variable number of entries, primary and foreign keys in a MAVIS entity, contradicts the static nature of a relational schema. We introduce the concept of "rental columns". Conceptually, a rental column consists of two columns: the first column contains the annotation, and the second column contains the MAVIS attribute value. We introduce three types of rental columns that correspond one-to-one to the MAVIS attributes. More specifically, we have:

Entry Rental Columns store the different MAVIS entries of a MAVIS entity. There are three types of entry rental columns, *String, TimeStamp, Numeric* depending on the basic type of the corresponding MAVIS entry.

Primary Key Rental Columns store the MAVIS primary keys, that appear in a MAVIS entity. All the keys are converted to a string datatype in order to avoid the need of having many different kinds of primary key rental columns. Since primary keys are only used for equi-joins in MAVIS the conversion does not hurt the generality of the solution.

Foreign Key Rental Columns store the MAVIS foreign keys of a MAVIS entity. As for the primary keys, the foreign key rental columns have a string datatype and the corresponding data in the underlying documents are converted to strings, without affecting the generality of the solution.

We chose a fixed number of rental columns in our prototype implementation to accommodate the maximum number of attributes in a MAVIS entity. Table 1 shows the representation of the MAVIS entities in Figure 5. Columns `Class`, `Schema` and `Doc` correspond to the ClassID, SchemaID and DocumentID of the MAVIS entity.

The rental columns $(Map_i, Value_j)$ map to the corresponding MAVIS entries. For example, the pair $(Map_1, Value_1)$ corresponds to the date MAVIS entry for the SAP Order in Figure 1(a), and has a type of timestamp. $(Map_2, Value_2)$ corresponds to the customer name and has a type of string. The rental columns $(Foreign_i, Value_j)$ correspond to the discovered foreign keys in the MAVIS entities. In our SAP order example, we see that $(Foreign_1, Value_1)$ corresponds to a customer key, while $(Foreign_2, Value_2)$ corresponds to a product key. Similarly for the PeopleSoft order in Figure 1(b), the rental column $(Map_1, Value_1)$ contains the Date of the Order, the rental column $(Map_2, Value_2)$ contains the Name of the customer and $(Map_3, Value_3)$ column contains the price of the ordered product. Customer and product key are stored in $(Foreign_1, Value_4)$ and $(Foreign_2, Value_5)$ respectively.

Rental columns are well-suited with column-oriented DBMS's (like for example [10]). Traditional tuple-oriented DBMS's may "suffer" from the possible large number of NULLS that need to be stored.[1] However even then, we believe that the flexibility of our approach outweighs the storage overhead.

The red index was implemented using the text indexing support that the RDBMS supports. The underlying documents are text indexed. At query time, the result of the text index query part is a set of document ID's, that match the specified keywords.

The blue filter was implemented using a rewrite technique that maps the local predicates to a large CASE statement in SQL. For our toy example, the select statement that was generated for the blue filter for orders and products are:

```
CREATE VIEW FilteredOrders AS
SELECT Class, Schema, Doc,
       CASE
            when Map1='Date' then Value1
            when Map2='Date' then Value2
            when Map3='Date' then Value3
            ...
       END as Date,...
FROM MAVIS
WHERE Date contains '2005' and Class=Order
```

```
CREATE VIEW FilteredProducts AS
SELECT Class, Schema, Doc,
       CASE
            when Map1='Category' then Value1
            when Map2='Category' then Value2
            when Map3='Category' then Value3
            ...
       END as Category,...
FROM MAVIS
WHERE Class=Product
      and Category contains 'Office Supplies'
```

which -conceptually- go over all the rental columns one-by-one looking for the rental column where the order Date was stored. Modern DBMS however, optimize the execution of such CASE statements, minimizing the required processing.

The join between the fact and the dimensional data is implemented by generating a SQL statement like the one depicted in Figure 7. FilteredOrders and Filtered Products are the results that we get after applying the local predicates on the facts and the dimensional data respectively. Both, FilteredOrders and Filtered Products are essentially projections of one MAVIS table. The primary and foreign keys are stored in the MAVIS table but are potentially scattered around in different rental columns. The WHERE clause joins the two projections regardless of the rental columns where the primary/foreign keys appear. In this example, we assume that the primary key might be stored in two different rental columns $(Primary_1, Value_1)$ or $(Primary_2, Value_2)$ and that the foreign key might be stored in two other rental columns. That's the reason, why we have four combinations for the join between orders and products. Exactly the same reason holds for the join between orders and customers.

In the general case with F rental columns for foreign keys and P rental columns for primary keys, the join between the facts and one dimension will require a conjunctive clause of size $F \cdot K$. If we use the symbol d to represent the number of dimensions, then the complete join between the facts and all the dimensions will require exactly $d \cdot F \cdot K$ terms.

The join statement in Figure 7 looks pretty complex, considering that it only addresses two primary rental columns and two rental columns. Indeed the generated queries are expected to be relatively big and in our implementation we had to properly tweak the optimizer so that it doesn't abort the optimization of the query. More specifically we had to force an optimal plan, in the sense that: (a)The MAVIS primary index and the MAVIS foreign index are used since they provide full coverage for the

---

[1] Recent versions of commercial RDBMS optimize the storage of NULLs and not suffer from that problem.

```
CREATE VIEW JoinResult AS
SELECT Fact.Price, Cust.State
FROM FilteredOrders as Fact, FilteredProduct as Prod, MAVIS as Cust
WHERE
        (*Join Orders and Products*)
        ((Fact.Foreign1='ProdKey' and Prod.Primary1='ProdKey' and Fact.FValue1=Prod.PValue1) or
        (Fact.Foreign2='ProdKey' and Prod.Primary1='ProdKey' and Fact.FValue2=Prod.PValue1) or
        (Fact.Foreign1='ProdKey' and Prod.Primary2='ProdKey' and Fact.FValue1=Prod.PValue2) or
        (Fact.Foreign2='ProdKey' and Prod.Primary2='ProdKey' and Fact.FValue2=Prod.PValue2))
        and
        (*Join Orders and Customers*)
        ((Fact.Foreign1='CustKey' and Cust.Primary1='CustKey' and Fact.FValue1=Cust.PValue1) or
        (Fact.Foreign2='CustKey' and Cust.Primary1='CustKey' and Fact.FValue2=Cust.PValue1) or
        (Fact.Foreign1='CustKey' and Cust.Primary2='CustKey' and Fact.FValue1=Cust.PValue2) or
        (Fact.Foreign2='CustKey' and Cust.Primary2='CustKey' and Fact.FValue2=Cust.PValue2))
```

Fig. 7. MAVIS Join between Orders, Products and Customers

where clause, and, (b)Using bitmap indexes to represent the MAVIS primary and foreign index, the system performs a *star-join*, that minimizes the I/O by fetching only the necessary tuples for the facts.

The above observations are the main reasons why the performance of the MAVIS approach is surprisingly very close to the performance of an optimized and well-designed warehouse, as we will demonstrate in the subsequent experimental section.

4   Experiments

In this section we describe the experimental results from our initial implementation of MAVIS using an industrial strength RDBMS as backbone. All the experiments were run on a Pentium 4 Machine running at 2GHz, with 1GB of main memory and 120GB of disk space.

4.1   Performance Evaluation

In order to provide a controlled environment for evaluation, we used a synthetically generated dataset consisting of four dimensions that models a typical warehouse with orders/lineitems, products, customers and suppliers. All dimensions have hierarchies associated with them.

The well-designed relational data warehouse provides the baseline performance. We defined indexes on the primary and the foreign keys in the relational warehouse. No materialized views were defined. In Figure 8(a), we depict the performance of MAVIS compared with a well-designed relational implementation of the data. The y-axis shows the execution time for a three way join query. The performance of MAVIS is surprisingly close to the performance of the well-designed warehouse. The bottleneck in processing typical OLAP queries is the cost of joining the dimensional/hierarchical tables with the facts. In MAVIS the query optimizer picked a plan that corresponds to a star join query and hence, produced comparable performance numbers. The additional overhead has to do with the bigger size of the two composite indexes that are used in MAVIS.

We scaled the size of the warehouse by scaling the number of tuples of the fact table as depicted in Figure 8(b) where x represents the *scale* factor in thousands. A scale

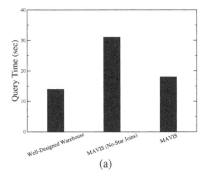

Relation	Size(tuples)
Product	$1000 + x$
LineItem	$100x$
Orders	$50x$
Customers	x
Suppliers	x

(a) (b)

Fig. 8. Typical MAVIS Performance & Experimental Parameters

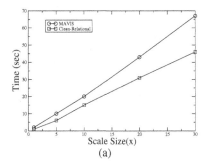

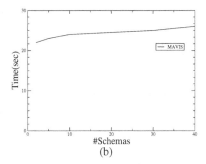

(a) (b)

Fig. 9. Performance v.s. Size & #Schemas

factor of 30 corresponds to 30,000 customers and 1,500,000 orders. In Figure 9(a) we show the behavior of MAVIS in comparison to the well-designed relational warehouse for various scale factors.

In Figure 9(b) we scale the number of schemas in order to evaluate the behavior of MAVIS for very heterogeneous repositories. We see that MAVIS scales almost linearly with the number of schemas making it appropriate for the schema-chaos world.

The use of rental columns for MAVIS affects negatively the required storage, since it actually increases the tuple size. In our implementation, we minimized the overhead of a rental column by using varchar(s), which require minimal storage when empty. When compared to the optimized relational OLAP system we typically required about two times more storage. However, this storage overhead is being offset by two crucial factors: the flexibility, adaptation and ability to work in schema-chaotic environments and the fact that the storage MAVIS requires is much smaller than that required to store the actual semi-structured documents we are interested in analyzing.

5   Related Work

In this section, we describe related work to our approach from several different perspectives.

The problem of schema matching, or ontology alignment, has received significant attention from the database and the Artificial Intelligence community. A comparison and discussion of the different approaches is presented in [14] and [15]. Schema matching finds expressions that relate data in multiple data sources, and uses the discovered expressions to map the data from one schema to another. [16] provides a survey of schema matching approaches. A very ambitious approach that leverages knowledge from different schemas and mappings in order to discover matches between with new, unseen schemas is described in [9]. An equally ambitious approach that attempts to automatically integrate continuously changing and evolving schemas is described in [2]. Such data-driven techniques are of great importance to our approach as they provide the basic framework to automatically understand the underlying data. In [17] the notion of "dataspace" is introduced to address the problem of managing a large number of diverse and often interrelated data sources within organizations. Recently, a lot of annotation techniques have been developed and their importance has been recognized by frameworks such as [6]. Although, annotations help the mechanical understanding of content, they do not help with the interactions or relationships between documents. Read-optimized DBMSs that use "vertical" data storage instead of the traditional "horizontal" storage, have been currently shown to outperform popular commercial systems. Examples of such systems include C-Store[10], Sybase IQ[18,19], Addamark[20], KDB[21], Bubba[22] and Monet[23]. The performance benefits of such systems, mainly stems from the fact that any I/O brings only data that are 100% relevant to a given query, unlike traditional DBMS where a relatively small percentage of each tuple is used.

6   Conclusions

We have described a scalable and robust solution for executing OLAP queries in the document-centric, schema-chaotic world. The same semantic information appears in different places in different document schemas, making indexing almost impossible, and for query languages such as XQuery very difficult to express the aggregation query. MAVIS is a flexible solution that combines text-indexing with well-established techniques for aggregation like star-joins and bitmap processing. We demonstrated the robustness and performance of our implementation. Our solution can work on top of existing OLAP installations and can be used to bridge the transition from the fixed-schema and semi-structure world to a schema-chaotic world. We have demonstrated that existing reliable and optimized technology can be used to handle the performance aspects of the very demanding schema-chaos world. The experimental evaluation from our current implementation shows a small performance degradation when compared to an optimized relational design, but in exchange it provides much better flexibility and adaptation to new schemas.

References

1. United Nations. United Nations Standard Product Characterization. In:
   http://www.unspsc.org
2. Brown, P., Haas, P., Myllymaki, J., Pirahesh, H., Reinwald, B., Sismanis, Y.: Data Management in a Connected World, chapter Toward Automated Large-Scale Information Integration and Discovery. Springer, Heidelberg (2005)

3. IBM. WebSphere Product Center. In:
   `http://www.ibm.com/software/integration/wpc`
4. IBM. WebSphere Customer Center. In:
   `http://www.ibm.com/software/integration/wcc`
5. IBM. DB2 Entity Analytic Solutions. In:
   `http://www-306.ibm.com/software/data/db2/eas`
6. IBM. An Open, Industrial-Strength Platform for Unstructured Information Analysis and Search. In: `http://www.research.ibm.com/UIMA`
7. IBM. WebSphere ProfileStage. In:
   `http://ibm.ascential.com/products/profilestage.html`
8. Sismanis, Y., Brown, P., Haas, P.J., Reinwald, B.: GORDIAN: Efficient and Scalable Discovery of Composite Keys. In: VLDB (2006)
9. Madhavan, J., Bernstein, P., Rahm, E.: Corpus based schema mapping. In: ICDE (2005)
10. Stonebraker, M., Abadi, D.J., Batkin, A., Chen, X., Cherniack, M., Ferreira, M., Lau, E., Lin, A., Madden, S., O'Neil, E.J., O'Neil, P.E., Rasin, A., Tran, N., Zdonik, S.B.: C-Store: A Column-oriented DBMS. In: VLDB, pp. 553–564 (2005)
11. Gray, J., Chaudhuri, S., Bosworth, A., Layman, A., Reichart, D., Venkatrao, M., Pellow, F., Pirahesh, H.: Data cube: A relational aggregation operator generalizing group-by, cross-tab, and sub-totals. J. Data Mining and Knowledge Discovery 1(1), 29–53 (1997)
12. Beyer, K.S., Chamberlin, D., Colby, L.S., Ozcan, F., Pirahesh, H., Xu, Y.: Extending XQuery for analytics. In: SIGMOD (2005)
13. Widom, J.: Research problems in data warehousing. In: 4th International Conference on Information and Knowledge Management, pp. 25–30, Baltimore, Maryland (1995)
14. Madhavan, J., Bernstein, P., Rahm, E.: Generic Schema Matching with Cupid. In: VLDB (2001)
15. Doan, A., Domingos, P., Halevy, A.: Reconciling Schemas of Disparate Data Sources: A Machine-Learning Approach. In: SIGMOD, pp. 509–520 (2001)
16. Rahm, E., Bernstein, P.: A survey of approaches to automated schema mapping. VLDB Journal 10, 334–350 (2001)
17. Franklin, M., Halevy, A., Maier, D.: From Databases to Dataspaces: A New Abstraction for Information Management. In: SIGMOD Record (December 2005)
18. French, C.D.: "One Size Fits All" Database Architectures Do Not Work for DDS. In: Carey, M.J., Schneider, D.A. (eds.) SIGMOD, pp. 449–450 (1995)
19. Sybase. Sybase IQ. In: `http://www.sybase.com/bi`
20. SenSage. Addamark. In: `http://www.addamark.com/product/sls.htm`
21. Kxsystems. Kdb. In: `http://www.kx.com/products/database.php`
22. Copeland, G.P., Alexander, W., Boughter, E.E., Keller, T.W.: Data Placement in Bubba. In: Boral, H., Larson, P. (eds.) SIGMOD, pp. 99–108 (1988)
23. Boncz, P.A., Zukowski, M., Nes, N.: Monetdb/x100: Hyper-pipelining query execution. In: CIDR, pp. 225–237 (2005)
24. Pedersen, D., Riis, K., Pedersen, T.B.: XML-Extended OLAP querying. In: SSDBM, pp. 195–206 (2002)
25. Pedersen, D., Pedersen, J., Pedersen, T.B.: Integrating XML Data in the TARGIT OLAP System. In: ICDE, pp. 778–781 (2004)

Callisto: Mergers Without Pain

Huong Morris[1,*], Hui Liao[2], Sriram Padmanabhan[2], Sriram Srinivasan[2],
Eugene Kawamoto[3,**], Phay Lau[4,**], Jing Shan[5,**], and Ryan Wisnesky[6,**]

IBM T. J. Watson Research, 19 Skyline Drive, Hawthorne,
New York, 10532, USA
[1] IBM Research
thm@us.ibm.com
[2] IBM Data Management
{huiliao,srp,sriram}@us.ibm.com
[3] University of California, Berkeley
kawamoto@haas.berkeley.edu
[4] San Jose State University
ptaclau@gmail.com
[5] Northeastern University
jshan@ccs.neu.edu
[6] Stanford University
wisnesky@stanford.edu

Abstract. As value networks evolve, we observe the phenomenon of businesses consolidating through mergers and businesses disaggregating and then virtually "re-merging" dynamically to respond to new opportunities. But these constituent businesses were not built in any standard way, and neither were their IT systems. An example in the industrial sector is the need to merge product and parts catalogs, and selectively share customer data. Companies that merge can spend a year integrating their catalogs, by which its time for the next deal. As such, business object integration has become a key aspect of today's enterprise. In this paper we describe an innovation where, by integrating product data management (PDM) systems that manage business objects into Extract-Transform-Load (ETL) technology, we can provide a novel cross-industry solution which can be used in a variety of industries.

Keywords: Business Intelligence, Data warehouse, Master Data Integration, Business Objects Integration, ETL Technologies, Enterprise Information Integration.

1 Introduction

As business systems have consistently expanded throughout the enterprise, the need for multiple systems with different architectures to inter-operate becomes ever more

---

[*] This work was carried out when the author was at the IBM Almaden Research Center, California, USA.
[**] This work was carried out when the authors were at the IBM Almaden Research Center as Extreme Blue interns.

C. Bussler et al. (Eds.): BIRTE 2006, LNCS 4365, pp. 92–105, 2007.

important. To make this happen, enterprises are turning to higher level software, such as the solutions provided by SAP, Oracle's PeopleSoft, Siebel, and the IBM Web-sphere Product Center, to manage their *business objects* directly. Existing work in this area mainly focuses on how to design business objects in business systems and how to use them in business processes [3, 4, 10, and 11]. The goal of efficient management of distributed information has become progressively more difficult because of increasing heterogeneity and rapid churn. As cited in [5], the major trends of Enterprise Information Integration (EII) and Enterprise Application Integration (EAI) are overlapping and creating a further integration problem.

Every important entity in a business can be represented as a business object. Business objects are then composed into schema models that capture the semantics of business concepts and are directly useful for business processes. They represent the key concepts that a business needs to operate such as people, services, and whatever is sold. Business objects are used directly by business developers to implement business functions. Examples of commercially available product data management (PDM) systems that manage business objects are already mentioned above. However, because of their intrinsic complexity and the fact that they come from different vendors, such products do not interoperate with each other. Most PDM systems represent business objects in terms of a master data management (MDM) system and store them in a backend data store using a relational database. Any techniques for transformation must be able to access these backend data stores. But naïve access to these objects may have unintended consequences, caused by the semantics of the data and the relationships and constraints required of the data. As a result, conventional approaches to integration may not provide an adequate solution.

Our project, Callisto, originated as an IBM Extreme Blue project http:// www.ibm.com/extremeblue aimed to study master data integration requirements and develop a prototype information integration system that leverages current data management technology. We will illustrate the approach with meaningful examples drawn from the retail industry. In this paper, we start with business entities that are represented by hierarchical or multidimensional objects that are in turn supported by products such as SAP, IBM WPC, etc. We will show how they can be managed or analysed by application toolsets such as IBM DWE, Microsoft SQL Server Integration Services (SSIS), Oracle Workflow Builder, etc. that understand relational data and business intelligence. By combining these two product sets in this novel way we can provide an integration framework to do management, mining and analytics on disparate master data systems.

2 Why Bring Business Objects into ETL Tools?

Accessing disparate business objects can be complex due to business objects being compound versions of the data embedded inside many databases and unstructured data sources. Depending on how they are represented and derived, they can suffer from problems of inconsistency and misinterpretation. Business functions are about managing business objects and, while based on typical and existing system functions, they therefore suffer the same fate. Such a separation of business concepts and system implementation in theory enables a business developer to construct business components without detailed knowledge of underlying software technologies, such as specific programming languages, communication protocols and database systems, etc. Traditionally, each business process is built as an application system, which encapsulates the specific task. When business objects are embedded in applications, it is dangerous to inter-operate without a deep understanding of the semantics of each of the applications, and this understanding often requires an understanding of the implementation. This makes such business process integration difficult [5].

Integration is usually tackled using one of four main techniques: transformation tools such as Extraction-Transformation-Loading (ETL), replication, database gateways, and virtual data federation. ETL tools are pieces of software responsible for the extraction of data from several sources, cleansing the data, and customized insertion of the data into a data warehouse.

Today's commercially available ETL products are exemplified by the IBM SQL Warehousing (SQW) component within the IBM Data Warehouse Edition (DWE) product, the Oracle Workflow Builder (OWB) within the Oracle Warehouse Management product, and the Microsoft SQL Server Integration Services (SSIS) within the SQL Server 2005 product. These products are able to support data provisioning processes that exhibit complex data flow. Examples of previous ETL work that has focused on the modelling and managing of the ETL processes can be found in [3].

The user of ETL tools can focus on the semantic mapping from a data source to a data target and then let the ETL tool take care of the underlying transformation details. But current ETL technology only supports the lower level software data (e.g. data inside a DBMS). In short, there is an "impedance mismatch" between business-object-aware software (e.g. SAP, IBM WPC) and business intelligence toolsets (e.g. IBM DWE) which provide real time decision support systems for an enterprise. To keep the business objects encapsulated and consistent, and to make business objects transformation easier and smoother, there is an opportunity to use these two toolsets in a more synergetic way. That is the main idea of Callisto.

3   Callisto: Motivation and Challenges

In this section, we describe more of the motivation behind our Callisto project and show some of the challenges that face a business object integration project using ETL technology.

3.1   WPC Business Objects

The Websphere Product Center (WPC) is a product information management (PIM) system that provides a centralized repository for an enterprise's master data. Like most other business objects systems, e.g. SAP, Oracle PeopleSoft, this information is maintained in a relational database in the back end, but is presented to the user as business objects in a way that is rich enough to support a realistic business environment such as may be found in a retail business: *Items* belong to *Categories*, and Categories are organized into *Hierarchies*. Hierarchies are an especially useful feature of the WPC, and are a good example of how business objects simplify user interaction: a user can organize and view the categories in different hierarchies and can create different catalogs for the same item set. A complete overview of WPC schema model will be given later in section 5.2.

We chose to use the Websphere Product Center as our proof of concept project to test the idea of using ETL tools to accelerate integration. Consider the following scenarios:

1. *Business intelligence:* Because the WPC stores valuable master data, we would like to be able to use this information for analysis. For instance, combining transactional data with categorical information from the WPC could allow for analysis of optimal item categorizations. ETL technology is advantageous for this type of scenario because it provides a way to link into business intelligence tools: once information is exposed to the ETL through Callisto, the ETL itself can then be used to manipulate the data to place it into a data warehouse for analysis.

2. *Trading partner collaboration:* Trading partners wishing to collaborate need access to the other partner's information, but if one partner is using WPC and the other partner a relational database, there is no easy way to transfer information between the two systems. By using Callisto, the business using the WPC can expose its business objects selectively, and in a way the other business can use, and the ETL itself can be used to massage this relational data so that it can be exchanged easily.

3. *Global data synchronization:* It is common for businesses to use a single WPC instance as a master information repository and also have redundant information stored in relational systems throughout the enterprise. To synchronize the WPC and such systems, it is necessary to expose the business objects in an ETL tool so that they can be mapped to schemas suitable for use by the other systems (and vice versa).

4. *Catalog construction:* Catalog construction (including catalog merging) is similar to data synchronization in the sense that the initial construction of a WPC instance requires the use of other various types of datastores. To speed up the deployment of a new catalog, Callisto could be used to extract, rather than synchronize, information from various data sources.

3.2 Integration Challenges

Current ETL technology supports relational formats, such as relational database tables, and some file system formats, such as CSV files, etc. To represent business objects inside of the ETL, we must find a way to describe business objects in a relational format without resorting to examining how the business objects are implemented and stored. In essence, we must create custom ETL *operators* that expose the required information. This is not an easy task because business objects are often semistructured, as in the case of WPC. The following are some key challenges:

1. The relational presentation of a business object must be as rich as the original object. That is, information about the business object should not be lost when the object is represented in a relational way. In addition, the information presented in the relational view must be presented in a way that is useful.

2. In many business-oriented systems, there is no clear boundary between data and metadata. An ETL system requires operators to expose metadata while a dataflow is designed, and to manipulate the data during runtime.
3. Different business objects of the same type may not share common properties, so that there is not necessarily a common relational representation for different instances of a type of business object. For instance, a retail Category business object may be represented as a table with columns for 'name' and 'price', but another Category object may require 'UPC' and 'description'. However, both are called Category objects, and so we cannot always decide on relational representations for an entire class of such objects.
4. Business objects and their relational views must relate to each other in a consistent, complete, and useful way. For instance, it is common for one business object to reference another; say, for a person object to reference a department object, thus capturing the relationship that the person is employed by the department. Thus, when multiple business objects are represented in multiple relational tables, if one objects references another, that information must be suitably and consistently encoded wherever it is represented in the relational tables.

4   Illustrative Scenarios and Use Cases

In this section, we describe several use cases that make clear the requirements for integration of WPC business objects using an ETL toolset. A procedure to execute each use case is also given here for illustration. Note that the solution for each use case is very similar to any regular ETL based solution. The difference is that instead of using typical ETL operators such as *join, union, etc.* Callisto's solution uses its own customized operators for WPC business objects. Some of the value will become clearer in later sections when we describe the Callisto internal design and run time engine.

4.1   Use Case 1

Our first scenario will focus on master data integration; a typical customer pain-point of most master data management systems. WPC catalog building is a semi-automatic process that can require a substantial amount of skill and manpower to deploy. This process could be more complex and involved when there is a need for master data integration. In this scenario Callisto's aim is to see whether the process integration of new data into the WPC master catalog can be simplified.

Situation: In a fictitious example, WorldMart, the world's largest retail chain, plans to expand its product portfolio by acquiring HomeMart. The acquisition needs to be completed by integrating WorldMart's product catalog with HomeMart's various data sources.

System Environment: WorldMart uses the IBM Websphere Product Center to centrally manage its product catalog information. HomeMart's product, suppliers, stores, and pricing information are scattered throughout different systems and suppliers' databases.

Limitation: WorldMart's upper management has required that the integration of HomeMart's product information into WorldMart be completed in three months. However WorldMart's systems group estimates that this could take much longer if they have to use 'import' and 'export' functions, such as those found in WPC, for different HomeMart's product data silos. Instead we will develop *'Item Import'* and *'Item Export'* ETL operators that will be defined in more detail in the next section.

Solution using Callisto

1. Define data source: HomeMart's product information using Callisto's operator *'Item Export'*
2. Define target source: WorldMart's WPC product catalog using Callisto's operator *"Item Import"*.
3. Connect date source and target using metadata mapping.
4. Complete and dynamically execute Callisto dataflow.
5. Load Data into WorldMart's Master Catalog.

4.2   Use Case 2

Our second scenario shows how Callisto can allow BI queries to be entered against the master data that is found in WPC. Traditionally, BI tools were limited to analyzing transactional data only and business systems such as WPC do not support business intelligence.

Situation: A fictitious online bookseller, Book4Sale.com, found that the sales of its Harry Potter books grew two-fold when it changed the category from "Children" to "Fantasy". Changing categories can dramatically boost sales. Book4Sale.com would like to analyze the past trends of its sales to determine the optimal category for its products.

System Environment: The bookseller uses the IBM Websphere Product Center to centrally manage its products and categories. WPC manages Book4Sale catalog but it does not have the ability of a Business Intelligence tool such as reporting and analysis for evaluating product trends.

Limitation: Conventional data export techniques are too slow to react to the high volume of daily catalog changes. Failing to spot a bad branding or categorization can lead to a huge loss. In addition, peak sales trends may be missed by slow, conventional techniques.

Solution using Callisto

1. Define data source using Callisto's operator *'Item Sources'*
2. Add the ETL existing operator *"Current Time'*
3. Define BI using Callisto's operator *'SCD'* (a.k.a. *'Slow Changing Dimension'*).
4. Complete and execute Callisto dataflow
5. Load Master Data into ETL toolset like SQW.
6. Analyze Results using any reporting and analysis experiment, we use IBM Alphablox and data mining tools.

5 Callisto Architecture and Implementation

5.1 Architecture

Callisto, as depicted in Figure 1, is essentially implemented as a set of plug-ins around an ETL system. Our implementation used Eclipse plug-ins to the IBM Data warehouse Edition (DWE) toolset called SQL Warehousing (SQW)[1]. Callisto extracts and loads information into the WPC using the scripting mechanism and a JSP interface. Callisto also transforms information to and from the hierarchical format that the WPC uses by examining a model of WPC business objects. Finally, Callisto presents and receives relational representations of WPC information from the ETL tools set. The ETL tools set provide support for transforming relational information and connectivity to various relational systems, thus allowing WPC information to be integrated into the ETL tools set along with other BI and transformational operators.

We developed a set of *'customized'* WPC operators within the SQW design studio, which represent the business objects for Import and Export functions in WPC:

1. **Item Export:** Export a category of items from the WPC. The items contain the values of their attributes as columns in a table.
2. **Item Import:** Import a category of items into the WPC, with attribute information.
3. **Hierarchy Export:** Export a hierarchy from the WPC, where parent-child relationships are maintained using paths and parent/child columns.
4. **Hierarchy Import:** Import a hierarchy into the WPC, while maintaining parent/child relationships.

Users may use the Callisto operators in the same way that they would use typical ETL operators within the SQW toolset. As such, the DWE and Callisto infrastructure provides a unified framework to do mining and analytics on WPC master data that otherwise would not be easily possible.

Callisto operates by analogy with existing DWE toolset. For both use cases in above section 4.1 and 4.2, Callisto first examines a WPC instance and reads relevant catalog schema information. This information is used to dynamically populate an Eclipse Modeling Framework (EMF) model of the WPC instance. Thus, the model provides information that categories are related, hierarchies have these categories, etc. This model is the foundation of the rest of Callisto.

With a model in hand, user can drag and drop the Callisto operators into an ETL dataflow. Depending upon the operator chosen, the user must select different aspects of the WPC instance in order to create the operator. For instance, in Use case 1, when using Item Export, a user would browse a WPC instance and select a particular category of items to export from HomeMart.

---

[1] Like most commercially available ETL toolset, SQW provides a framework called the *Data Flow*. The data flow is an extensible framework that allows users to build data extraction, transformation and load sequences as a flow of *'Operators'*. The SQW also allows the addition of *Custom operator libraries,* where developers can provide operators to represent their own customized processing in the form of *plugins.* [15].

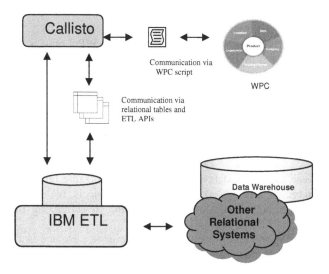

Fig. 1. Callisto Architecture

Callisto provides a code generator for each operator, which generates script that performs the required WPC operation. For example, a *Hierarchy Export* operator causes the generation of a WPC script that involves exporting the whole hierarchy being exported from the source catalog to the target catalog without user's intervention. In Use Case 1, user can select the whole *'Home'* hierarchy within the HomeMart catalog to be export to the target *'Household'* hierarchy in the WorldMart catalog.

Finally, Callisto provides a runtime so that data flows using Callisto operators can be executed. This runtime uses a script-generation technique to create scripts to communicate with a WPC instance, sending or receiving information form as required.

5.2 Callisto MDM Schema Model

Websphere Product Center (WPC) is a product information repository. The "core objects" in the WPC are catalogs, items, attributes, category trees (a.k.a. hierarchies) and categories (a.k.a. hierarchy nodes). *Attributes* hold values or group other attributes. Attributes are defined through specifications (a.k.a. specs).

Items make up the primary data element in WPC. They are typically represented as SKUs, individual products etc. Catalogs are the containers for items. An item belongs to one an only one catalog. Each catalog has one primary specification that defines the attributes that all the items in that catalog share.

Category trees are hierarchical arrangements of categories. This provides users with different "views" into the same set of data. Hierarchies are built and stored separately from items and catalogs. This enables the same hierarchy to be deployed in multiple catalogs, and also allows items in a catalog to be viewed in multiple hierarchies.

Items are mapped to categories. Categories defined specific attributes for the items mapped to them through secondary specifications.

5.3   Callisto UML Data Model

In Callisto, we use IBM Rational Rose [14] to model WPC objects. This UML tool
defines data models in a higher abstracted level using a set of well-defined graphical
tools. Figure 2 shows the Callisto data model.

Each WPC object is modeled as a standard class. And their containment relationships are modeled as aggregation relationships in the Rose model.

The Eclipse Modeling Framework (EMF) [2] is a Java framework for generating
tools and other applications based simple class models. After modeling the above two
steps, these models are exported as EMF 'ecore' (Eclipse modeling framework core)
models.

EMF uses these 'ecore' models and generates customizable Java code that can then
be used to manage the life cycle of these business objects, including their relationships as well as provides means of serializing and de-serializing these objects as
XML/XMI files.

Note that our UML model of business objects is incomplete and is a simplification;
however, it is sufficient and simple for us to use in this prototype. The code generated from the UML and EMF artifacts are what we refer to as the 'WPC model'.

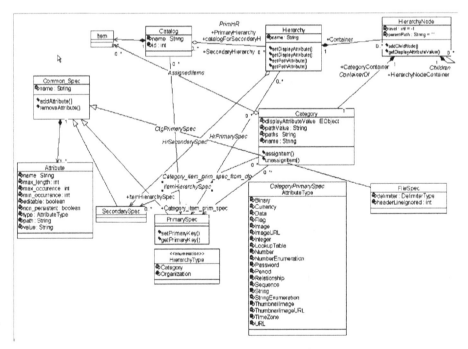

Fig. 2. Callisto MDM Data Model

5.4   Callisto Implementation

Callisto has both a design time and runtime component. We will first describe the
runtime in Figure 3.

Figure 3 shows a cloud representing the sources of data that the ETL runtime is capable of connecting to. This can be essentially any form of data, as the runtime is capable of invoking arbitrary Java classes at run time. So as long as an adapter Java class is created, the runtime can connect to anything. The runtime itself currently has adapters for databases that use JDBC, along with a few other special data sources and sinks.

The ETL Data flow code generator creates an execution plan that is woven together from the generated code of the operators connected in the Data flow designer. The Callisto operator code generators generate WPC scripts corresponding to the operator properties that the user set. The ETL runtime takes care of moving the data around in *Virtual Tables* for the runtime code to use.

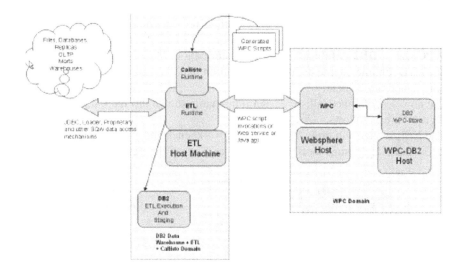

Fig. 3. Callisto runtime interactions

The Callisto component generates WPC scripting code to perform its work; the ETL runtime uses a Java runner [1] to invoke the Callisto runtime Java class which executes the WPC code (and using the generated script as input) remotely against the WPC instance. The ETL runtime can run any executable, including a Java class. WPC script generation is performed at code generation time and these serialized scripts are directly referenced by the generated code. For instance, to export items, Callisto generates a script that pulls all items from a category. Then at runtime, this script is executed via an *'execution plan'* which can be run (or scheduled) using the SQW runtime component.

The runtime component of the ETL takes care of running the execution plan and moving the data around from component to component. In a production environment, it would typically run inside of an IBM Websphere Application Server that is running other business logic applications. For our purposes, it can also be housed inside the same Eclipse instance as the design environment.

Figure 3 also shows some other elements of the Callisto runtime that are now described.

The **Data Warehouse** component represents a generic data warehouse; it may be a database like DB2 with an associated Business intelligence tool and data mining components. Regardless of its form, the data warehouse represents one possible final destination for the data extracted from WPC.

The **WPC** is a J2EE application that we are using as our source (or target of trans-formed items) of catalog data. The instances of WPC are the web applications run-ning inside of an application server. Connections to the backend WPC storage data-base will usually occur over a network. WPC information is stored as tables in DB2, however this information is "internal" and only very specific API is allowed to ma-nipulate the WPC catalog. WPC provides a web based interface to present the catalog in a hierarchical format to the end user, as well as provides an administration interface to maintain the product catalog.

WPC uses a **DB2 database** to store its information. A DB2 instance is also used by the ETL runtime engine as its SQL execution database as well as a repository for staging temporary content.

We now describe the Callisto design time that is shown in Figure 4. The elements of Figure 4 are as follows.

The **Eclipse** platform provides a graphical workbench and extendible plug in archi-tecture. The ETL design tools use Eclipse as part of the editing environment. By

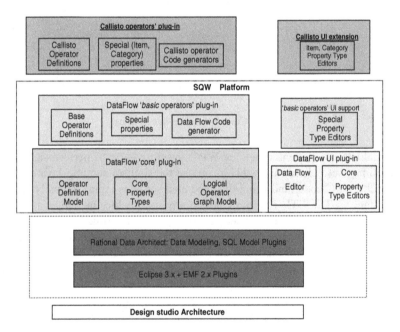

Fig. 4. Callisto design structure

registering Callisto with ETL, the ETL platform becomes aware of its existence and makes it available to the designers of a dataflow, where it can be used like any other Data flow operator.

The **ETL plug-ins** for Eclipse also contains the graphical designer and associated pieces and the Data flow code generator. Once a dataflow is developed, the Data flow code generating system compiles the operators into an Execution Plan Graph that can be executed on the ETL runtime. The ETL runtime thus will be able to invoke the Callisto Java runtime classes with input the WPC scripts that are generated by Callisto's code generators. The Callisto operators appear in the Data flow design tool as regular operators.

Figure 5 shows a screen shot that captures Callisto at run time for the second scenario where on the top right hand section shows the SQW Design Studio area. In this area, several SQW pre-defined operators (*Add Current Time* operator and *Slowly Changing Dimension* operator) and one Callisto operator, *WPC Item Source* operator, are shown. They were selected from the operators' palette at the right hand side of the Design Studio. When the *WPC Item Source* operator is defined or clicked from the palette, SWQ Design Studio, acting on behalf of Callisto, will open up an instance of Book4Sale catalog. From this catalog, which appears in the bottom right hand pane of Figure 3, user selects *Fantasy* category and can see that this category is defined by 2 attributes: *id* and *name*. When the data flow is run, this operator will connect the WPC instance and present this selected item source, namely *Fantasy*, in the WPC category

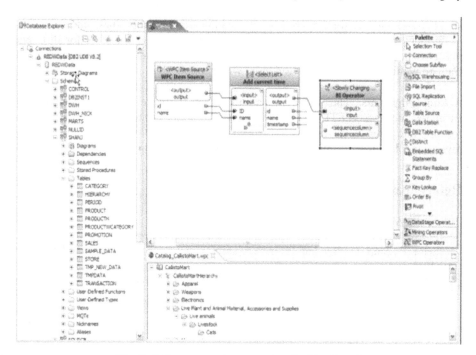

Fig. 5. Callisto screenshot at runtime for Use Case 2

as a relational table to the next SQW operator, *Current Time,* which will then add time stamps information to this selected WPC category. The last SQW operator in the second scenario is the *Slowly Changing Dimension* operator. It takes the input data from previous operators, *WPC Item Source* and *Current Time*, and merges it with existing data in the data warehouse. Once the dataflow is run and complete, the new information will be available for analysis with a reporting tool such as IBM Alphablox.

6 Conclusion

We have demonstrated that by adding some conceptually simple Java-based operators to a transformation tool business objects can be simply integrated, assembled or disassembled.

Our approach has been relatively simple and makes use of commonly available technology: we use UML and EMF modeling, which captures the key constraints between objects, to generate Java code. The Java code is used to present relational representations of selected business object instances based on the object's state. Finally, custom operators use these Java objects to present clean relational table schemas (virtual tables) to the rest of the ETL transformation framework.

While we are only able to provide initial results at this point, we believe there can be some encouragement that existing business intelligence tools can be combined in this novel way to address data residing in relational database systems and therefore simplify and improve some approaches to data integration and business intelligence.

Further experiences and development of more and richer operators for different master data system such as SAP, PeopleSoft and Siebel would make mergers with Callisto within the ETL toolset even more widely applicable.

Acknowledgments. The authors thank the IBM Software Group, especially the Business Intelligence ETL and the Websphere Product Center development groups for providing resources to this project. The authors also thank the anomymous reviewers for a thorough and constructive set of reviews of this paper.

References

1. Apache Velocity Engine http://Jakarta.apche.org/velocity
2. Eclipse Modelling Framework (EMF) http://www.Eclipse.org/emf/
3. Eeles, P., Sims, O.: Building Business Objects. Wiley Computer Publishing, Chichester (1998)
4. Gillibrand, G.: Essential business object design. Communications of the ACM 43(2), 117–119 (2000)
5. Halevy, A., Ashish, N., Bitton, D., Carey, M., Draper, D., Pollock, J., Rosenthal, A., Sikka, V.: Enterprise Information Integration: Successes, Challenges and Controversies, ACM SIGMOD, pp. 778–787 (2005)
6. Madnavan, J., Halevy, A.: Composing Mappings among Data Sources. VLDB, pp. 572–583 (2003)

7. Maier, A., Mitschang, B., Leymann, F., Wolfson, D.: On combining business process integration and ETL technologies. BTW, pp. 533–546 (2005)
8. Morris, H., Lee, S., Shan, E., Zeng, S.: An Information Integration Framework for Product Lifecycle Management of Diverse Data. ACM JCISE, vol. 4(4) (2004)
9. Simitsis, A., Vassiliadis, P., Sellis, T.: Optimizing ETL processes in data warehouses. In: Proceedings of the 21st International Conference on Data Engineering, ICDE, (2005)
10. Sims, O.: Business Objects, Delivering Cooperative Objects for Client-Server. McGraw-Hill Book Co., New York (1994)
11. Sutherland, J.: Business Objects in corporate information systems. ACM Computing Survey 27, 274–276 (1995)
12. Vassiliadis, P., Simitsis, A., Skiadopoulos, S.: Conceptual modelling for ETL processes. DOLAP, pp. 14–21(2002)
13. Websphere Product Center: Architecture and Component Overview, Version 5.1 (August 2004) http://www.ibm.com/software/integration/wpc/documentation
14. IBM Rational Rose, http://www.ibm.com/software/rational
15. DB2 Data Warehouse Edition Version 8.2 http://www-128.ibm.com/developerworks/db2/roadmap/dwe-roadmap-v8.2.html

Real-Time Acquisition of Buyer Behaviour Data – The Smart Shop Floor Scenario

Bo Yuan, Maria Orlowska, and Shazia Sadiq

School of Information Technology and Electrical Engineering
The University of Queensland, St Lucia QLD 4072
Brisbane, Australia
{boyuan,maria,shazia}@itee.uq.edu.au

Abstract. The emergence of a range of new technologies like auto-identification devices, active tags, and smart items has impacted profoundly on business software solutions such as supply chain management, logistics, and inventory control. Integration of automatic data acquisition with enterprise applications as well as potential to provide real-time analytic functionality is opening new avenues for business process automation. In this paper, we propose a novel application of these technologies in a retailing environment leading to the vision of a *smart shop floor*. We firstly present the infrastructure for the smart shop floor. We then demonstrate how the proposed infrastructure is feasible and conducive to real-time acquisition of buyer behaviour data through three selected queries. Complete algorithmic solutions to each query are presented to provide proof of concept, and further deliberations on analytic potential of the proposed infrastructure are also provided.

Topic: Data Capture in Real-time.

Category: Regular Paper.

1 Introduction

It is evident from mandates from retailing giants such as Wal-Mart and Metro, manufacturers like Proctor & Gamble, and several initiatives within public sector, that technologies built on smart identification devices and wireless communication protocols will, and have already, become an inherent aspect of business operations. These technologies are providing unprecedented potential for business process automation, changing profoundly the expectations of data scale and quality and system responsiveness.

The notion of *smart items* has been proposed [1] to provide an umbrella concept to several approaches in this regard. Essentially a smart item is a device that can provide data about itself and/or the object it is associated with, and in addition has the ability to communicate this data. Examples include RFID tags [2], and sensor devices.

The deployment environment for smart item technologies clearly requires a number of additional components such as device readers, communication networks, and back-end servers. Many challenges relating to reader accuracy, noise management, variety of tag data standards (e.g. GTIN – Global Trade Identification Number,

C. Bussler et al. (Eds.): BIRTE 2006, LNCS 4365, pp. 106–117, 2007.
© Springer-Verlag Berlin Heidelberg 2007

SSCC- Serial Shipping Container Code, GRAI – Global Returnable Asset Identifier and more recently EPCGlobal [4]) impact on the integration of smart item generated data with enterprise applications.

Business solution providers have made tremendous progress in the last few years to integrate smart item technologies within enterprise application frameworks, see for example SAP Auto-ID Infrastructure [3]. Most of these developments have focused on streamlining the processes that involve packing, receiving, distribution of goods, and related services on stock management and logistics.

In this paper, we propose to extend these developments into a retailing environment, wherein a smart item infrastructure is combined with a *smart shop floor*. The smart shop floor provide additional components that go beyond product/item tagging, and introduces buyer profiles and behaviour characterizations into the environment.

In the next section we will present our vision for the smart shop floor. We envisage that the proposed environment holds the potential to generate unprecedented insights into buyer behaviour in large retail markets. These insights, made possible through the proposed infrastructure, can be supported through fully automated functions. In the remaining paper, we will provide as proof of concept three possible queries (insights) that can be provided using the proposed infrastructure. Complete algorithmic solutions are provided for each of the queries. We will conclude the paper by providing further deliberations on analytic potential of the proposed setup thereby identifying a number of interesting extensions to this work.

2 Smart Shop Floor

The motivation of smart shop floor is to increase the quality of service in retailing environments by providing shoppers personalized, valuable shopping advices and addressing common issues such as confusing price labels, long queue/waiting time at check-outs as well as the frustration of locating products. The successful deployment of the smart short floors is expected to not only offer retailers crucial advantages over competitors but also make the shopping experience more enjoyable.

The technical components in the infrastructure of such smart shop floors have been made available, as demonstrated by some prototypes currently under trial such as the U-Scan smart trolley of Fujitsu and the Metro Group Future Store Initiative (www.future-store.org). The key components related to the queries in this paper are:

- Active/Smart Trolley
    o Capture buyer profile (e.g., swipe card).
    o Read product item tags (i.e., it can recognize items being put in and maintain an ongoing shopping record).
    o Receive location data from sector indicators.

- Sector Indicators
    o Sense the existence of a trolley and send it the unique sector identification. An example is given in Figure 1 showing a regular shop floor. In practice, they could be arranged in a much more flexible manner, basically reflecting the floor's layout of the shop. The precise definition of a sector will be introduced in Section 3.1.

- Secure Wireless Network
    - o   Provide the communication between smart trolleys, sector indicators and back-end servers to collect real-time path and shopping data.

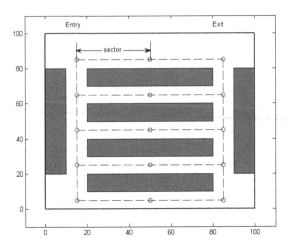

Fig. 1. A high-level illustration of a smart shop floor set-up with 18 sectors. It shows the entry/exist, product shelves and the segmentation of the shop floor in terms of sectors.

3   Characterizing Buyer Behaviour

Understanding buyer behaviour is one of the most complex endeavours in business development and marketing. Indeed it is a question that goes well beyond what computational techniques can offer. In the context of this discussion, we limit the notion of buyer behaviour to *shopping profile* within a well defined shop floor space and within a given shopping session. The shopping profile is characterized by three aspects:

1.   The Buyer – Buyer properties such as age, gender, postcode, credit limit etc.

2.   The Products – Product data and purchase list within a given session.

3.   The Navigation – Navigation path in relation to defined sectors in the shop floor space in a given session.

Based on the smart shop floor infrastructure proposed in the previous section, the data relating to all aspects of the shopping profile can be acquired in real-time. Subsequently, there are a number of queries that can be conducted to characterize various aspects of buyer behaviour through the shopping profiles. In this section, we present three typical queries and the corresponding solutions as example and proof of concept for the proposed infrastructure. These are:

- **Query 1.** To discover the path of a given length (defined by the number of sectors) shared by the largest portion of buyers.

- **Query 2.** To find out the path with as many sectors as possible, subject to a pre-defined threshold of support.

- **Query 3.** To find out sectors where buyers visit frequently but seldom purchase any products in these sectors.

3.1 Shop Floor Specification

The basic element in the proposed three queries is called "sector". Note that in most realistic shop floors, product shelves are naturally divided into sectors according to the types of products. The reasons of conducting queries based on sectors instead of precise physical locations are listed as follows:

o   The data of physical locations do not have intuitive meaning and can become totally meaningless if the layout of the shop floor is changed.

o   The data of physical locations need more storage space and usually require the process of data cleaning.

In the proposed shop floor described in Section 2, sector indicators are deployed along the product shelves. Each time a smart trolley passes by a sector, it will communicate with the corresponding sector indicator, which will send back its unique identification to the trolley. An ongoing list of sectors visited by a buyer is maintained in the trolley, which can be transferred to back-end servers in real-time via the secure wireless network in the shop. In general, sector indicators can be used to capture the general information of shopping paths, by processing only a limited amount of data. Certainly, the level of precision of the path information can be easily controlled by varying the number of sector indicators as well as their specific locations.

For the purpose of algorithmic analysis, let $S=\{s_1, s_2, ..., s_n\}$ be a set of literals representing sectors. Define G as an undirected graph on the sectors (i.e., each vertex represents a unique sector). An edge in G connecting s_i and s_j indicates the neighbourhood of the two sectors (i.e., a buyer can move directly from one sector to another). A *path* is an ordered list of sectors (i.e., minimum one sector), which must satisfy the relationship among sectors as defined in G (see Figure 2 for an example). In other words, a path is created by starting from a certain vertex in G and travelling through the graph following the edges. Here, we use the most flexible definition of paths and impose no restrictions on the possible forms of paths, which means that paths can be of different lengths and a certain sector can occur multiple times in a path.

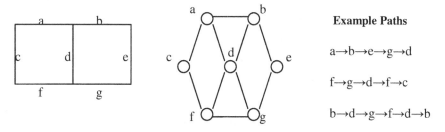

Fig. 2. A shop floor (left), its graphical notation (middle) and some example paths (right)

3.2 Finding the Most Popular Common Path with a Given Length

The objective of this query is to discover the path of a given length (defined by the number of sectors) shared by the largest portion of buyers.

3.2.1 Algorithm Framework

Given a database D of paths defined as above (i.e., each record is created by a buyer's single visit to the shop), the question is how to find out the most frequent path shared by buyers. Here, we assume that the length of the path is given in advance. In classical data mining algorithms for shopping basket problems such as algorithm *Apriori* [5] and its extensions and variations [6, 7], all candidates have to be enumerated in advance. During the scan of the database, there is a need to sequentially check which candidates are supported by each record. Suppose that there are totally P sectors in the shop floor with each sector directly connected to K other sectors. It is easy to see that the number of all possible candidate paths with N sectors is $P \cdot K^{N-1}$, which is usually quite large given realistic values of N, K and P. For example, in the shop floor shown in Figure 1, there are 18 sectors each of which is connected to 2 to 4 other sectors. In this case, there are hundreds of thousands candidate paths for N=10. Furthermore, it is also time-consuming to check whether these candidates are supported by a certain record in the database.

The approach proposed here is able to handle the query through a single scan of the database without the need to generate candidates in advance, thanks to the special features of the path mining problem. The basic idea is to sequentially process each record and use a sliding window to generate all candidate paths that it supports on the fly. In other words, only candidate paths supported by at least one record will be generated and there is no need to explicitly check whether a candidate is supported by a certain record. Our technique is different from traditional sequence mining algorithms in that the number of candidate paths supported by a record is very limited, which is due to the fact that sectors in a candidate path must be directly connected. It is easy to see that a path record containing M sectors supports at most M-N+1 unique candidate paths with N sectors. For example, a record with eight sectors {a b c d e f g h} supports the following four candidate paths with five sectors:

$$\{a \ b \ c \ d \ e\}, \{b \ c \ d \ e \ f\}, \{c \ d \ e \ f \ g\}, \{d \ e \ f \ g \ h\}$$

The general procedure of the proposed algorithm is given below:

Step 1: Select a new record from the database. If all records have been processed, go to Step 5.

Step 2: Find out all N-sector candidate paths supported by this record.

Step 3: For each candidate path generated in Step 2 that has not been met before, assign a new *id* to it.

Step 4: Increase the counters of the above candidate paths. Go to Step 1.

Step 5: Return the *id* of the counter with the maximum value.

3.2.2 Data Structure

In order to implement the above algorithm, a data structure is required to store candidate paths together with their unique *ids*. Each time a candidate path is found in a record, if it has been seen before, its *id* will be retrieved. Otherwise, it will be added into the data structure and a new *id* is created. For this purpose, a tree structure *T* is adopted where each node corresponds to a sector and *ids* are stored in the leave nodes.

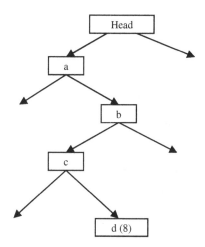

Fig. 3. An example of the tree structure storing candidate paths with four sectors

An example of *T* is shown in Figure 3 where the path {a b c d} is stored in the tree and assigned an *id* 8. For convenience, all *ids* are integer numbers starting from 1 sequentially. The depth of the tree is equal to the number of sectors in the candidate paths and the number of branches below each node is determined by the number of sectors connected to it in *G*, which is usually between 2 and 4 in a typical shop floor. Note that in order to retrieve the *id* of a candidate path, only N steps are required. Inserting a new candidate path requires the same number of operations.

The second data structure is an array *C* of counters recording the frequency of each candidate path. Each time a new candidate path (with a new *id*) is generated, a new counter is created, increasing the size of *C* by one. Since we are only interested in the number of records that support a certain candidate path, instead of the number of times that it appears in the database, only counters corresponding to candidate paths found for the first time in a record will be updated.

3.2.3 Time Complexity

Suppose that the average length of records in the database is M. On average, there are (M-N+1) candidate paths to be generated in each record, with possible duplicates. For a database with K records, there are (M-N+1)·K candidate paths to be processed. As shown in the last section, for each candidate path, retrieving or creating its *id* requires searching through *T* for N steps. Other operations such as increasing the values of counters require constant time. The overall time complexity of the proposed algorithm is given by: O ((M-N+1)·N·K)≈O(M·N·K) for M>>N.

Note that once the *id* of the most frequent path is identified, this path can be then retrieved through a depth-first search through *T*. Alternatively, all candidate paths found during the scan of the database could be stored together with their *id*s so that the most frequent path can be directly retrieved once its *id* is known.

3.2.4 Examples

To better understand how the proposed algorithm works, suppose that the first record in the database contains eight sectors: {a b c d e b c d}. There are six candidate paths with three sectors supported by this record (Table 1).

Table 1. A demo of the algorithm working on the first record {a b c d e b c d} with N=3

No.	Candidate	ID	Counters
1	{a b c}	1	[1]
2	{b c d}	2	[1, 1]
3	{c d e}	3	[1,1,1]
4	{d e b}	4	[1,1,1,1]
5	{e b c}	5	[1,1,1,1,1]
6	{b c d}	2	[1,1,1,1,1]

In Table 1, the first five candidates have never been found before. As a result, each of them is inserted into *T* and assigned a unique *id* and new counters are created for each of them. However, for the last candidate {b c d}, it is already available in *T* and its previously assigned *id* is returned and no new counter is created. Also, since this *id* has already been counted in the same record, the existing value of the corresponding counter is kept unchanged.

Next, the algorithm moves to the second record. Suppose that the first candidate in the second record is {c d e}, which is not a new candidate (No.3 in Table 1) and no new *id* is assigned to it. However, since it is the first time that this candidate is found in the second record, its counter will be increased by one and the values of counters are [1, 1, 2, 1, 1] now. Similarly, if the second candidate is {d e b}, the fourth element in the counter array *C* will also be increased by one (i.e., *C* is [1, 1, 2, 2, 1]).

3.2.5 Simulations

A test database was randomly generated with 5000 path records, each containing 50 sectors. The layout of the shop floor is based on Figure 1, which consists of 18 sectors with each sector directly connected to 2 to 4 other sectors.

The first experiment was aimed at showing the running time of the algorithm with regard to the number of records in the database with K=500, 1000, 2000, 3000, 4000 and 5000. The second experiment was conducted to show the running time of the algorithm with regard to the length of the candidate path with N=5, 6, 7, 8, 9 and 10.

Experiments were conducted on a PIII 800MHz PC with Matlab 7. Experimental results shown in Figure 4 suggest that the algorithm scaled approximately linearly.

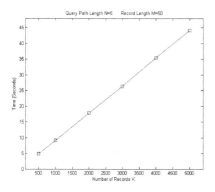 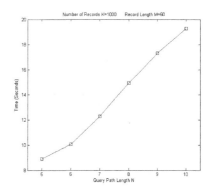

Fig. 4. The scalability of the proposed algorithm with regard to the number of records (left) and the length of the candidate paths (right)

3.3   Finding the Longest Common Path with a Given Support

The objective of this query is to find out the path with as many sectors as possible, subject to a predefined threshold of support.

3.3.1   Problem Analysis
Since the length of candidate paths are not known in advance, the solution to this query is to iteratively apply the algorithm proposed in Section 3.2 with sequentially increasing N values (i.e., N=1,2, ...) until the support of the most popular candidate path falls below the threshold. However, the major difficulty is that the cost of the algorithm will increase as the value of N grows due to its $O(M·N·K)$ time complexity. In the meantime, the storage space required may also increase greatly.

An important fact is that the support of a path is no more than the minimum support of any of its sub-paths (i.e., one or more sequentially connected sectors contained in the original path). In other words, if it is known that a certain sub-path does not have the minimum support from the database, it is always true that any longer path that contains this sub-path will not have the minimum support either.

This feature makes it possible to do some pruning of the search space based on the information gained in earlier passes. Consequently, the computational cost of handling longer candidate paths may be substantially reduced.

Note that the number of candidate paths of length N to be processed in a record with M sectors is M-N+1. The key point here is how to reduce this number so that only a much smaller set of candidate paths will need to be processed.

For example, consider a record with eight sectors:

$$\{a\ b\ c\ d\ e\ f\ g\ h\}$$

It is easy to see that it supports totally six candidate paths with three sectors:

$$\{a\ b\ c\},\ \{b\ c\ d\},\ \{c\ d\ e\},\ \{d\ e\ f\},\ \{e\ f\ g\},\ \{f\ g\ h\}$$

Suppose, based on previous passes, it is known that sectors d and f do not meet the minimum support requirement. As a result, any candidate path containing one or both of them is deemed to be infrequent. In this case, five out of six candidates are such examples and only the first candidate {a b c} needs to be processed.

3.3.2 Algorithm Framework

According to the above analysis, the algorithm for finding the longest common path with a given support works as follows:

Step 1: N=1

Step 2: Scan the database to find out the support of all N-sector candidate paths that are not deemed to be infrequent.

Step 3: If no candidate paths have the minimum support, STOP.

Step 4: Update the database D by marking infrequent candidate paths.

Step 5: N=N+1, go to Step 2.

In this framework, the algorithm starts by scanning the database once to check the support of each single sector (N=1) following the procedure described in Section 3.2. All sectors that are found infrequent are marked, which is used to prune the search space. In the next pass, the algorithm only tries to find out the support of all candidate paths with two sectors (N=2) that are not deemed to be infrequent. This process is repeated until no more candidate paths meet the support threshold.

3.3.3 Algorithm Details

In order to mark infrequent candidates in the database, we need the location information of each candidate in the database, which is stored in three arrays during the scan. The first array stores the *id* of each candidate path while the second and third arrays store the No. of record where this candidate is found as well as the position of the candidate in the record. Note that we sequentially store the information of all candidate paths and the maximum length of the above three arrays is (M-N+1)·K.

Suppose that {a b c d e f g h} is the 8th record in the database and the candidate path {c d e} is assigned an *id* 5. In this case, the values of the corresponding elements in the three arrays are {5}, {8} and {3} respectively, due to the fact that {c d e} has an *id* 5 and is the third candidate path in the 8th record.

After each pass, in order to mark sectors in infrequent candidates, we go through the array with *id*s and check the support of each *id* in its counter $C(id)$. If it is below the support threshold, its location information stored in the other two arrays will be retrieved to locate this candidate path in the database.

A data structure called *mask* is maintained with the same dimensions as the original database. Each element in *mask* corresponds to a sector in the database. Initially, all elements are set to 0 (i.e., all sectors are available). At the end of the Nth pass, when a candidate path is found infrequent, the element in *mask* corresponding to the first sector in this candidate path is set to N indicating that the path of length N starting with this sector is infrequent (i.e., longer paths are also infrequent).

Recall that in Section 3.2, each of the first M-N+1 sectors in a record of length M is used as the head sector of a candidate path with N sectors. With the information in *mask*, it is now possible to reduce the number of candidate paths to be generated by excluding those that are known to be infrequent. Each time a head sector is selected, the elements in *mask* corresponding to it as well as N-1 consecutive sectors are checked sequentially. For $1 \leq i \leq N$, if the value x of the element in *mask* corresponding to the ith sector in the candidate path is greater than zero but no more than N-i+1, it can be determined that this candidate path is infrequent because it contains at least one infrequent sub-path of length x. Note that the element corresponding to the head sector of such a candidate path should also be set to N if its original value is 0.

For example, suppose that a record is:

$$\{a\ b\ c\ d\ e\ f\ g\ h\}$$

The group of elements corresponding to this record in *mask* have initial values:

$$\{0\ 0\ 0\ 0\ 0\ 0\ 0\ 0\}$$

After the first pass with N=1, suppose that only d is found to be infrequent. The values of the elements are updated to:

$$\{0\ 0\ 0\ 1\ 0\ 0\ 0\ 0\}$$

In the second pass with N=2, the algorithm will not generate the candidates {c d} and {d e} because both of them contain d, which is an infrequent sub-path of length one, and are known to be infrequent. The element corresponding to c in *mask* is set to 2 indicating that the path of length two starting with c is infrequent. In the meantime, if candidate path {f g} is also found to be infrequent at the end of the second pass, the element corresponding to f in *mask* will be set to 2. The values of the elements in *mask* at the end of the second pass are updated to:

$$\{0\ 0\ 2\ 1\ 0\ 2\ 0\ 0\}$$

As a result, in the third pass with N=3, instead of having six candidate paths in play, only a single candidate path {a b c} will be generated while others can all be determined to be infrequent based on the existing information in *mask*.

In general, the number of nonzero elements in *mask* is expected to increase after each pass, which will make it more likely for a candidate path to be infrequent. In a word, *mask* is used to avoid generating candidate paths that are already known to be infrequent and thus saves a large amount of computational effort.

3.4 Finding Sectors Below a Given Purchase Level

The objective of this query is to find out sectors where buyers visit frequently but seldom purchase any products in these sectors.

3.4.1 Problem Analysis

The purchase level of a sector is defined as the ratio between the number of records in which at least a product in that sector is purchased and the number of records in which this sector is visited. A sector with low purchase level means that most customers visiting it are not interested in products in that sector. The reason that it is visited may be simply due to the fact that it is close to the entry/exit of the shop or it is on the way to other sectors with popular products.

Note that we are only interested in knowing that during each single visit to the shop whether a buyer visited a certain sector and whether this buyer purchased any products from that sector. In practice, a buyer may visit a sector multiple times and purchase nothing or multiple products during a single visit to the sector or in different times.

In addition to the database containing records of paths, we assume that there is a database with records of transactions (i.e., lists of products purchased). Also, it is assumed that there is a table specifying the relationship between products and sectors.

A condition is that any product is only available in a specific sector (i.e., given any product *id*, there is a unique corresponding sector *id*).

3.4.2 Algorithm Details

The basic idea is to transform the transaction database into a sector database using the product-sector table so that each record in the new database is a set of sectors where shopping activities happened. Note that, unlike the path database, sectors in this new database are likely to be disconnected from each other.

The general procedure of the algorithm is as follows:

Step 1: Apply the algorithm in Section 3.2 on the path database (N=1) to find out the frequency of each sector.

Step 2: Transform the transaction database into a database of sectors using the product-sector table.

Step 3: Apply the algorithm in Section 3.2 on the sector database (N=1) to find out the frequency of each sector with purchasing activity.

Step 4: Calculate the purchase level of each sector.

In the above algorithm, Step 1 is used to find out the frequency of each sector being visited while Step 3 is used to find out the frequency of each sector appearing in the transaction records. Note that the tree structure T generated in Step 1 is used in Step 3 to make sure that sectors are associated with consistent *id*s. In Step 4, the purchase level of each sector is calculated by the ratio between its frequency in the transaction records and its frequency in the path records.

4   Conclusions

In this paper, a smart shop floor setup was proposed to capture real-time buyer behaviour data. We are particularly interested in discovering patterns embedded in the shopping paths of buyers, defined in terms of product shelf sectors. For this purpose, three queries have been identified together with detailed algorithmic solutions. In the meantime, there are some other queries that can be conducted on the data collected from the proposed smart shop floor. For example, it would be interesting to analyse the relationship among sectors to find out the set of sectors that are often visited during the same shopping trip. It may also be of interest to see, if a buyer visited a certain sector, which other sectors this buyer is likely to visit. These queries belong to classical data mining tasks such as mining association rules and sequences, which could be tackled by existing techniques [8, 9].

Furthermore, real-time path planning function can be incorporated into the smart trolley to guide shoppers through the shop floor, according to their specific shopping lists. Also, more advanced queries can be supported by introducing additional functionality into the proposed infrastructure. For example, sector indicators can be designed to transfer time stamp information in addition to the sector identification to the smart trolley. By doing so, it is possible to conduct time-related queries such as finding the sectors where buyers spend most of their time.

References

[1] Alexander, K., Gillian, T., Gramling, K., Kindy, M., Moogimane, D., Schultz, M., Woods, M.: IBM Business Consulting Services – Focus on the Supply Chain: Applying Auto-ID within the Distribution Center. Auto-ID Center, White paper IBM-AUTOID-BC-002 (September 2003)

[2] Finkenzeller, K., RFID,: Handbook: Fundamentals and Applications in Contactless Smart Cards and Identification, 2nd edn. John Wiley & Sons, New York (2003)

[3] Bornhovd, C., Lin, T., Haller, H., Schaper, J.: Integrating Automatic Data Acquisition with Business Processes – Experiences with SAP's Auto-ID Infrastructure. In: Proceedings of the 30th VLDB Conference, Toronto, Canada (2004)

[4] EPCGlobal: EPC Tag Data Standards Version 1.1 Rev. 1.24, EPCGlobal, Standards Specification (April 2004) http://www.epcglobalinc.org

[5] Agrawal, R., Srikant, R.: Fast Algorithms for Mining Association Rules. In: The 20th International Conference on Very Large Data Bases, pp. 487–499 (1994)

[6] Agrawal, R., Srikant, R.: Mining Sequential Patterns. In: The 11th International Conference on Data Engineering, pp. 3–14 (1995)

[7] Srikant, R., Agrawal, R.: Mining Sequential Patterns: Generalizations and Performance Improvements. In: The 5th International Conference on Extending Database Technology, pp. 3–17 (1996)

[8] Luo, C., Chung, S.: A Scalable Algorithm for Mining Maximal Frequent Sequences Using Sampling. In: The 16th International Conference on Tools with Artificial Intelligence, pp. 156–165 (2004)

[9] Maimon, O., Rokach, L.: The Data Mining and Knowledge Discovery Handbook. Springer, Heidelberg (2005)

Business Process Learning for Real Time Enterprises

Rodion Podorozhny[1], Anne Ngu[1], and Dimitrios Georgakopoulos[2]

[1] Texas State University, Computer Science Dept., 601 University Dr.,
78666 San Marcos, TX, USA
{rp31,hn12}@txstate.edu
[2] Telcordia, 106 E. Sixth Street, Littlefield Building #415,
Austin, TX 78701, USA
dimitris@research.telcordia.com

Abstract. Existing approaches for business process mining cannot satisfy Real-Time Enterprise (RTE) goals, such as time-based competition. To support RTE requirements we propose a Process Learning System (PLS) that is capable of learning business processes from a few observed traces and do this in a time-frame that is close to the actual time for completing the process. Unlike existing approaches PLS employs a rich process model that facilitates "guessing" business processes, utilizes domain-specific knowledge captured by activity and resource ontologies, ensures that learned processes comply with specified business rules, and optimizes them to reduce required cost and time. In this paper we focus on the architecture of PLS, and describe the functionality and algorithms employed by key PLS components. We use examples from initial experiments involving learning of processes that assemble complex products from specialized parts.

1 Introduction

The notion of the real-time enterprise (RTE) is rooted in an emerging business strategy that is currently being pursued by the business community. As with Business Process Re-engineering (BPR) in the early 90's, RTE aims to squeeze time and associated costs out of business processes. However, RTE's broader goal is to provide the means for time-based competition. This calls for enterprises to deliver products and services faster than their competitors, as well as to customize these as needed to satisfy the specific needs of each specific customer or business transaction. Becoming an RTE involves providing solutions to the following problems:

1. Discovering the *actual* business processes being used in doing business. These may include significant differences from the business processes instituted by and/or believed to be in use by the enterprise's management team (e.g., due to implementation approach or legacy IT problems), or the actual processes may be uncertain or unknown (e.g., due to a merger or outsourcing).

2. Capturing specific RTE objectives by *business rules* formulated in terms of business activities, important artifacts, such as products and other resources, at the strategic level of enterprise management or at the highest tactical levels. Such business rules should be used to guide business process adaptation, optimization, and automation to achieve specific RTE objectives.

C. Bussler et al. (Eds.): BIRTE 2006, LNCS 4365, pp. 118–132, 2007.

3. Performing *dynamic* business process adaptation, optimization and automation within prescribed time and cost. Comply with business rules when adapting and optimizing existing processes and/or developing new ones.

In this paper we propose a *Process Learning System* (PLS) that uses domain knowledge and business rules to automatically discover and optimize business processes and do this in a timely manner (i.e., learn a process in the same time-frame as it takes to execute a process instance). Existing solutions for automatically discovering and optimizing business processes are either too expensive, or require too much time. Furthermore, in many cases they cannot discover a complete process. In particular, traditional BPR approaches for capturing business processes typically involve conducting stakeholder interviews and compiling comprehensive process documentation. These activities require teams of people to work for months at a high cost. Business process mining [1, 2, 8, 10] is an alternative approach for process discovery that involves the analysis of traces produced by executed instances of the process. Assuming that a sufficient number and kind of traces are available, process mining can be automated and it is inexpensive. However, to discover a complete business process, process mining requires a very large number of traces to be available (e.g., several thousands of traces for a process containing a few dozens of activities [2]). In addition, the available traces must provide a complete coverage of the process [1] (i.e., they must include sufficient number of traces for all paths, not only the most frequent paths). These requirements are difficult (or impossible) to satisfy even in traditional enterprises. In situations where a sufficient number of traces can be eventually collected, the collection effort requires significant planning and it may take months or years to complete. Therefore, process mining is not appropriate for RTEs.

The Process Learning System (PLS) we propose in this paper requires only a few traces to learn a business process. Instead of attempting to discover the actual process that was executed to create the traces, PLS learns a business process that is compatible with the known execution traces and is optimized by utilizing available domain knowledge provided by *activity* and *resource ontologies*, as well as specified *business rules*. This paper focuses on the novel PLS architecture and its key components. Since the PLS prototype is currently under development, in this paper we report some initial results and use examples based on them. The automation of learned business processes is outside the scope of PLS and this paper. This can be accomplished by employing traditional workflow or EAI platforms (e.g., [14, 15, 16]), or an RTE-ready platform that supports dynamic process adaptation at any time [13].

The remainder of this paper is organized as follows: Sections 2 discusses our process learning approach, including the needed ontologies and models for capturing business rules and processes. Section 3 introduces the PLS architecture. Section 4 describes key PLS algorithms. Section 5 discusses related work. Our conclusions and PLS status are in Section 6.

2 Process Learning Approach

Our goal in this paper is to learn a *rich* process model based on a *few* traces of process execution instances. At a theoretical level, this problem seems to require us to learn an accepting computation abstraction specification (e.g., a Turing machine) for a language based on a few sentences of that language. This goal seems to be impossible in the absence of additional information.

Our approach for overcoming this theoretical limitation is based on the following two hypotheses about our ability to *generalize* (i.e., be able to include control flow, resource flow, and resource utilization dependencies that were not present in) the known execution traces of the process. First, the available domain knowledge (e.g., the descriptions of the well-formedness constraints of the products produced/services provided by the process, related bills of materials, business rules, etc.) is sufficient for accomplishing process generalization. Second, simulations of possible process alternatives can determine whether or not they produce well-formed products/services, complete bills of materials, and satisfy business rules.

Assuming that these two key hypotheses hold, the process learning (i.e., synthesizing and generalizing) approach we advocate in this paper involves the following:

- Employing a *rich* process model that captures important/comprehensive information about processes that will facilitate in "guessing" them;
- Utilizing available domain knowledge, including domain specific activity and resource *ontologies*, as well as relevant *business rules* to validate or prune alternative processes under consideration; and,
- Learning validated processes that are compatible with known traces.

In this paper we consider possible that an observed trace itself provides a low quality product. Nevertheless, if the observed trace is feasible in the "guessed" process model then it validates the model. Otherwise, the trace is considered to be a counter-example; the process model is considered incorrect and thus it must be modified to satisfy the observed trace, or be eliminated from consideration.

In the following sections we describe the models, ontologies, and rules utilized in this process learning approach. In particular, in Section 2.1 we describe the domain-specific activity and resource ontologies we utilize. Section 2.2 discusses the rich process model we employ to learn a business process from a few traces. In section 2.3, we discuss specification of business rules and how we determine process compliance with them. The architecture of the proposed Process Learning System and the functionality of its components are described in Section 3.

2.1 Resource and Activity Ontologies

A *resource ontology* describes domain specific resource types and their IS-A and PART-OF relationships. In this paper, we use the term *artifact type* to refer to an input or output resource type to a basic activity or a process. To refer to the final output artifacts types of a process model, we use the term *product type*. Correspondingly, we define input and output artifact instances. In addition to artifact instances and activities a process instance may utilize additional resources, such as roles/actors, tools, and programs that are not specified as activity/process input or output.

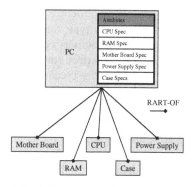

Fig. 1. Resource ontology fragment

Figure 1 depicts a fragment of the resource ontology that contains a PC product attributed with CPU speed, RAM total size, RAM access speed, motherboard specification via the kinds and number of slots it has, video processor card specifications including speed and bus type, the power supply specifications via the delivered power, the case specifications via the kind of motherboard and power supply it accepts, the number of fans, the color of the case cover. This artifact ontology captures constraints on well-formedness of the PC that describe the facts that the motherboard must match the case, CPU, RAM, and video card must be compatible with the motherboard, etc.

The ontology also includes corresponding artifact types for various kinds of CPUs, RAMs and other computer components. Many of the attributes of a compound artifact instance can only be filled if a corresponding component instance is connected to the compound artifact instance. For example an activity cannot write a CPU specification into a PC artifact instance directly, instead it can only attach the CPU component instance and only then the CPU speed will be copied to the attribute of the PC artifact instance. Such restrictions in the resource ontology allow PLS to apply graph similarity algorithms [3] that compare composite artifact instances.

In addition to a resource ontology, PLS utilizes domain specific *activity ontology*. This ontology defines domain-specific activity types used to specify business rules and to learn business processes. In addition to activity types, the activity ontology captures IS-A relationships between such types. This relationships facilitates the mapping of high level business rules (i.e., rules involving activities at a strategic business level or at a high tactical level) to the lower level (i.e., tactical or implementation) activities in a learned business process.

The use of the activity and resource ontologies in business process modeling and business rule specification are discussed further in the Sections 2.2 and 2.3, respectively. In the rest of this paper we assume that the activity types of all activities in a learned process model are included in the activity ontology. Furthermore, we assume that the input and output of a learned process model is an assembly of artifacts whose type, as well as the types of its parts, are described in the resource ontology. Finally, the input (output) of any learned process model is assumed to partially match the input (output) of an activity type in the activity ontology.

2.2 Process Model and Traces

PLS utilizes a rich process model and assumes that execution traces are produced using this model. By *process model* we refer to a process specification or a process "program" that can be instantiated by a process enactment engine. The following aspects characterize PLS's process model:

- Set of typed activity variables to be filled with activity identifiers.
- Each activity is characterized by an identifier, its activity type, and typed resource variables to be filled with resource identifiers. The activity types are defined in the activity ontology and describe the activity interface (the input and output resource types of the activity), as well as the activity precondition and post condition.
- Specification of control flow dependencies between activity types.
- Resource utilization dependencies specify the needs of activity types for resource types including people roles, programs, and tools. Resource types are defined in the resource ontology.
- Predictors that provide distributions for cost and duration of individual activities, as well as assessment of quality of output artifacts of an activity type.

The PLS process model is richer than the workflow reference model proposed by Workflow Management Coalition (WfMC) [17]. In particular, PLS's process model has the same expressive power as WfMC's in terms of activity, control flow, data flow and resource utilization specification. In addition to these, PLS's process model includes activity post/pre conditions and predictor/quality functions.

An *execution trace* observed by PLS is a process instantiation that results in a single execution path through a process model. An execution trace typically contains a timestamp-ordered set of elements, where each element describes an activity state change as defined by WfMC (e.g., started, completed, etc.), the activity ID and type, the input and output resource/artifact instances for this particular state of the activity, and the timestamp of the activity state change.

Both the process model and the execution trace refer to activity and resource types defined in the corresponding ontologies. Unlike a process model, an execution trace includes activity and resource variables that have been filled up during instantiation with specific activity and resource identifiers. Since an execution trace covers only a single execution path, a trace typically refers only to the types of activities and resources that were encountered in its path (this is typically a subset of the types referenced in the process model). From an execution trace we can extract a sequence of process state transformations, accurate estimations for each transformation, resources used in each transformation, explanation of choices in control flow, activities and resource assignments.

2.3 Business Rules

Business rules in PLS are domain-specific constraints in the execution of activities and the utilization of resources. Business rules are specified on activity types defined in the PLS activity ontology. The types of business rules supported by PLS include:

- *Coordination business rules* ensure that the (child) activities of a process are coordinated appropriately with other (child) activities. For example, a coordination business rule for a PC assembly process might state that the AttachCPU activity cannot be performed after the AttachCaseCover activity.
- *Resource utilization business rules* constrain how or which resources can be used at a given point. For instance, a role resolution business rule might constrain the person that performs the AttachCPU activity to be a technician of a certain level.

In PLS, a business rule is defined by a *business rule locus* and a *business rule effect*. The locus of a business rule P is a precondition that determines the types of potential parent processes to which P should be evaluated, while the effect of P is a post condition that determines whether a business rule P has been satisfied or not. Both business rule locus and effect are defined by constraints that are specified using PLS's business rule specification language.

Coordination business rules define constraints on relationships between the activity types, while resources utilization business rules typically involve the definition of constraints on utilization relationships between activity types and resource types. For example, the effect of a coordination business rule typically defines constraints on temporal relationship (e.g., before, after) between activity types. PLS provides a comprehensive business rule language, but its details are outside the scope of this paper.

3 Process Learning System Architecture

PLS utilizes the process model we described in Section 2 to extract process related information from process traces, ontologies, and business rules, and utilizes these in synthesizing, transforming, and learning processes. PLS employees various learning methods, since the effectiveness of each particular method depends on the process aspect that need to be leaned, as well as the domain and business knowledge available. To accommodate these, PLS's architecture permits great flexibility in the choice of activity types involved in the process synthesis, the tools used for performing the synthesis, and the order of their application. To achieve these we propose using a process specification and execution system for managing the process synthesis process itself. In other words, we propose using a process system to learn a process.

The architecture of the process learning system is depicted in Figure 2. Rounded corner rectangles denote provided components, shaded rectangles illustrate domain-specific components, directed arcs indicate data flow, unshaded rectangles associated with the arcs describe the actual data involved, while the cylinder denotes persistent storage. Below we will describe these and the architecture rationale. PLS learns processes by performing two major processing steps, namely process learning and trace compliance testing. These steps are discussed next. The algorithm used for PLS's Process Generator is discussed further in Section 4.

Process Learning: The *Process Generator* forms an initial process (in a process specification language that complies with the PLS process model) based on the domain knowledge (process product, business rules, known execution traces, resource utilization) and refines some aspects of the initial process based on the execution traces (observations).

Next the Process Enactor, Domain-specific Simulator, Process Miner, and Domain Planner synergistically subject the initial process to dynamic analysis and refinement. The interaction of these architecture elements is as follows: the *Process Enactor* receives an initial process and, provided the cost, duration and quality of activities can be estimated, submits the process to the *Domain Planner*.

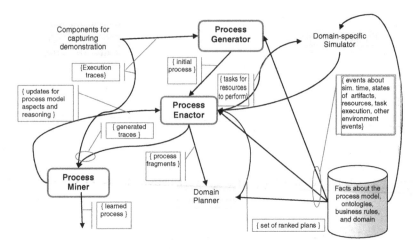

Fig. 2. Architecture of a Process Learning System

Next, the *Simulator* starts modeling the execution of the activities by the simulated resources, which affect the state of simulated artifact instances. The Simulator notifies the Process Enactor of various events such as completion of activities by resources, time ticks, contingencies due to the simulated environment, and contingencies due to artifact instances' states.

Let us suppose that the learning system architecture in Figure 2 is used for learning a process of assembling a Personal Computer (PC) from computer parts. The Process Generator produces an initial process that specifies the control flow constraints gleaned from domain knowledge and execution traces. It is not guaranteed that this process produces a well-formed product artifact. The process itself can be traversed via various paths from a start node to a final activity node (assuming several possible start or final nodes) provided there is branching in the process. The Domain Planner selects a subset from the set of all possible traversal paths in the process such that the paths in this subset satisfy some criterion, for instance the fact that each path in that subset has a cost of execution lower than a certain threshold. If the set of computer parts has a corresponding set of activities in the ontology then the Domain Planner can suggest the choice of parts by suggesting its subset of paths. For instance, there can be activities BuyHighEndMotherboard, BuyMediumMotherboard, BuyCheap-Motherboard. In an actual process these will correspond to available motherboards currently available. Each activity is further described by a cost, duration, and quality triple. In the case of these three activities their triples will be affected by quantifications of cost and quality of the respective motherboards. A path traversed through a process is quantified by a "goodness" metric which is a cumulative value based on the cost, duration, quality of the activities that are visited by the path. Therefore, the Domain Planner, given a "cost reduction" criterion, is likely to suggest paths that include the BuyCheapMotherboard.

Once a path has been selected by the Domain Planner, dynamic analysis is performed to determine its feasibility. For the sake of an example let us assume an incorrect process was produced. A path that was chosen by the Domain Planner prescribes such a sequence of activities: AttachCpuToMotherboard, AttachFanToCpu,

ApplyThermalCompound. The Process Enactor dutifully notifies agent resources to perform these activities. The Simulator models the effects of application of these activities to resources (including artifact instances) according to the artifact well-formedness constraints. Thus, after an agent initiates the ApplyThermalCompound activity the Simulator will report a failed termination of that activity if the artifact ontology captures the fact that the thermal compound cannot be added to a mother-board with a processor attached. By analogy to software development, among other things, the Simulator performs the role of a testing oracle that derives correct test cases from the artifact ontology and compares the actual behavior of an activity against its expected behavior. By the same analogy, if the resource ontology does not capture the well-formedness artifact constraints relevant for the process, the Simulator will OK a process that will fail validation in real world. It is important to emphasize that while a process is supposed to be correct by construction we cannot guarantee that because of incomplete domain knowledge. In a way, the initial process is an edu-cated guess produced in a systematic manner that still has to be verified against the modeled artifact well-formedness constraints and then validated by a real world dy-namic analysis (checking both the correctness of the process and adequacy of the modeled well-formedness constraints). Another benefit of the Simulator is checking the accuracy of activity duration estimates. An activity is not finished until the Simu-lator registers either a success or a failure of the artifact instance manipulation pro-vided by the activity. The Process Enactor reacts to the events from the Simulator or events generated by the Process Enactor itself (e.g. time-out of activity completion).

The simulation and learning of a single process instance continues until either all the activities are finished and/or final artifacts/products are produced or predefined time runs out or it is determined that there are insufficient resources to produce final artifacts. On completion of enactment of one process instance from the initial gener-ated process, the Process Miner component might use their machine learning tech-niques (supervised neural networks, reinforcement learning and evolutionary compu-tation) to learn the optimal policy (e.g. control flow decisions and resource utilization) for executing the process in the simulated environment. The information from the available execution traces (actual, not simulated) is given higher preference over data obtained from simulation during the learning.

Our PC assembly example demonstrates a specific method for learning an initial process in the case of very limited number of traces and abundant information about artifact types' structure. By taking a process-based approach to learning business processes, our architecture can also leverage other process mining approaches [1] [2] [8] once sufficient number of execution traces is collected for PLS.

Trace compliance test: At the final step, the known actual execution traces are used as test cases to verify the process learned from the domain knowledge and simulation. Thus in this final step we check the compliance of the process behavior to real world execution traces.

4 Process Generator Algorithm

The Process Generator produces an initial process by utilizing PLS domain-specific ontologies, business rules, and execution traces. An outline of the algorithm that can generate the initial process is described in the following paragraphs.

Cleaning execution traces from noise: First, the Process Generator checks for consistency of the observed precedence relationships in the execution traces using a control flow graph representing provided business rules. Such consistency checking is performed by bisimulation [3] [4]. The main tasks of this algorithm are shown in Figure 3. The output of the consistency checking that is a set of business rules violations by the execution traces. Next, execution traces are modified to remove the violations. For this task to be effective the business rules must be consistent with each other. The output of this stage of process generation is a set of cleaned execution traces that do not include such violations.

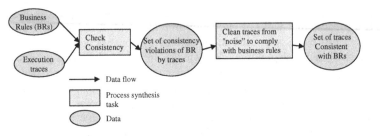

Fig. 3. Main tasks in bisimulation algorithm

Identification of possible final and start activities of a process: Next, by comparing the specification of the artifact *tree* for the process product (in its simplest form this is just a bill of materials) and the output artifacts of the activities types in the

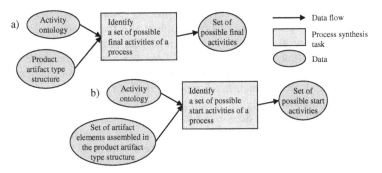

Fig. 4. Main tasks in identifying start and final activities

activity ontology, we determine the subset of activities types in the ontology that can produce the product artifact type. Here the provided activity ontology is used to find those leaf activities whose post-conditions satisfy the well-formedness requirements of the product artifact type. This task forms the set of possible final leaf activities. The set of possible start leaf activities is formed similarly except that the algorithm matches the specification of the input artifact type *subtree* to the input artifact parameters of the activity types in the ontology. The tasks of identification of final and start activities are shown in Figures 4(a) and 4(b).

Creation of an initial process control flow graph: This is the next stage of the process generation algorithm and is depicted in Figure 5.

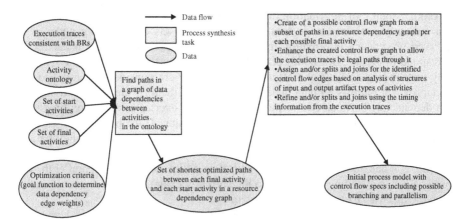

Fig. 5. Main tasks in synthesizing process control flow

Using a modified single source shortest path Dijkstra's algorithm [6] we find all shortest paths between each of elements of the set of possible final leaf activities and that of the possible start leaf activities in the resource/data dependency graph. The input and output parameters of activities define the data dependency graph between the activities. The input data to this step include the activity ontology, sets of start and final activities of a process to be learned, optimization criteria, and the cleaned execution traces. The optimization criteria are expressed as a goal function that combines relative preferences between cost, duration, and quality of process output. The activity ontology is assumed to have activities attributed with cost, duration and quality. The weights of edges used by this modified algorithm are determined by this goal function. The output of this step is a set of shortest paths in the data dependency graph in regard to the weights.

In the next step, this set of paths in the data dependency graph derived from the activity ontology is used to produce a set of paths corresponding to control flow. The execution traces are used to enhance the control flow paths so that they would allow the actually observed traces. Thus a process derived from the domain knowledge is combined with the information from the observed traces.

Branching and parallelism between activities are identified using various information sources. One source of information that can help creating sets of nodes that can execute in parallel is the "shape" of artifact types. The predecessor nodes inside such a set can run in parallel to those in another set. The predecessor nodes of a currently examined node in the data dependency graph are those whose output types (partially) match input types of the currently examined node. Since artifact types and instances are represented as trees it is possible to recognize their shapes.

If the output artifact types' trees of candidate predecessors are different in shape (as trees, considering the types of nodes) then those candidates are possibly parallel activities. If the artifact types' tree shapes are the same then they are possibly branching alternatives (different ways to produce the same). Thus the algorithm provides a possible control flow graph based on the data dependency that includes branching and parallelism. This is only possible due to an assumption about representation of artifact types and their instances.

Another source of information that can help breaking the set of predecessor nodes of a currently examined node into possible parallel sets of branching nodes is the observed precedence information from traces. If two or more activity instances that correspond to predecessor nodes of a currently examined node appeared at least partially overlapping in their execution times then they are considered parallel to each other provided there is no data dependency between them. If the algorithm detects a data dependency between two or more activities that overlap in execution time in the traces then a flag is raised asking for manual resolution. If the possibility of manual resolution is turned off then the Process Generator deems such activities non-parallel, i.e. data dependency information is trusted more than the observed precedence relationship. If it has been identified that a pair of activities can be run in parallel then the control flow arcs leading from them to the currently examined node are connected by an *and*. Otherwise they are connected by an *or*.

A special and important case can appear if there are loops in the data dependency graph of activities. The suggested algorithm will reject a path along which the same node has been visited more than once. Such a solution ensures that the algorithm is not "stuck". The downside is that we cannot account for iteration.

Description of example input and output of the algorithm: In Figure 6 we see a depiction of sample information that is expected to be available to the Process Generator. The lower plane contains the leaf process activities with the precedence

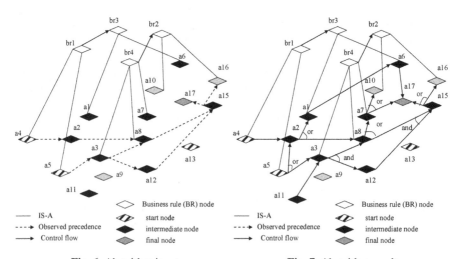

Fig. 6. Algorithm input   **Fig. 7.** Algorithm result

relations that were observed between their instances in the actual execution traces before learning started. The highest plane contains the activity types referenced by business rules, with IS-A relationships to the leaf process activities. Business rule constraints are defined between the activity types at highest plane. For instance, for the PC assembly process, the br1 activity type can correspond to the AttachMotherboard activity type. The a4 and a5 activities would correspond to the AttachIntelMotherboard and AttachAMDMotherboard activities. The br3 activity type can correspond to the AttachRAMStick activity. The a1 and a6 activities would correspond to the AttachSingleRAMStick activity.

In Figure 7 we see a possible result of the algorithm. The control flow has been learned from the data dependency graph and observed precedence. The and/or connectors are used to show possible parallel and alternative control flow. The a17 activity can correspond to AttachFrontPanel. Its predecessors by data dependency graph are a6, a7, a15 that correspond to AttachWhiteCaseCover, AttachBlackCaseCover, AttachSilverCaseCover. Since the output artifact types of a6, a7, a15 are of the same tree shape then the a6, a7, a15 are considered to be alternatives and the corresponding control flow arcs are *or*-joined.

Let us assume that the a8 activity corresponds to AttachTrayToCase and it produces an artifact type that corresponds to a computer without a case cover. Let us also assume the a12 activity corresponds to BuySilverCover and that input to the a15 (AttachSilverCaseCover) is composed of artifact of the CaseCover type and an artifact that corresponds to an uncovered, but otherwise assembled computer (described by a tree as in Figure 1). Then the output of the BuySilverCover is a subset of the input of AttachSilverCaseCover and the output of the AttachTrayToCase is a subset of the input of AttachSilverCaseCover. But the tree shapes of output artifact types of BuySilverCover and AttachTrayToCase are not the same, thus these are possibly parallel steps such that the execution of both is needed for the input AttachSilverCaseCover. The control flow arcs created by the algorithm from the AttachTrayToCase (a8) to AttachSilverCaseCover (a15) and from the BuySilverCover (a12) to AttachSilverCaseCover (a15) are joined by an *and*. In addition, the precedence information from a trace indicates that AttachTrayToCase (a8) and BuySilverCover (a12) were observed to execute in parallel.

The asymptotic upper bound of the Dijkstra algorithm is of the order of $|V|^2$ where V is the set of vertices in the data dependence graph between activities. Thus the asymptotic upper bound due to the multiple executions of Dijkstra's algorithm is $|V|^4$. There are polynomial algorithms for bisimulation [4] in the size of the compared graphs. Thus we expect our algorithm to be efficient (polynomial in the size of the data dependency graph of leaf activities and the size of the trees representing the artifact types and instances) and capable of providing real time process improvement.

5 Related Work

Business process mining is a relatively new research area as compared to areas such as business processing simulation, modeling, design, execution and verification.

Datta [8] proposed both probabilistic and algorithmic approaches for the automatic discovery of business processes from a number of process execution traces. He compared the discovery of business process from execution traces to the problem of *grammar discovery* from examples of sentences in a regular language. However, using *grammar discovery*, there is a simplistic assumption that business processes are fully characterized by a partial ordering of activities. Clearly, conditional, parallel or concurrent activities are also important attributes of any business processes. These control flows cannot be discovered using *grammar discovery* technique. The work by Cook and Wolf [7] on discovering software engineering processes uses a similar mix of statistical and algorithmic approaches. The generated process is also strictly sequential.

van der Aalst [1] proposed an Alpha mining algorithm for discovering processes that can be expressed in free-choice Petri-net. This means control flows like sequential, parallelism, branching and iteration need to be discovered. It is an improvement over Datta's approach, however there is the assumption that the workflow log will contain *complete* execution paths of the process. All the tasks that potentially directly follow each other must have the corresponding traces in the workflow log. The proposed mining algorithm cannot mine advanced control flow such as implicit dependencies between tasks or hierarchical task structures. More robust mining algorithms have been implemented recently in the ProM Framework [18]. However, none of them make use of process domain knowledge.

Agrawal, Gunopulos and Leymann [2] generalized the algorithm for mining sequential patterns to mining process graph. This approach requires a significant number and variety of traces to be collected. The learning algorithm did not make use of any process domain knowledge or product artifact well-formedness constraints. For a process graph of fifty vertices, 10000 execution traces is needed to find a *conformal* graph, which still does not represent a complete process. The learning algorithm cannot guarantee that the process generated is a generalization of all the observed execution traces. Our generation of the process does not depend on the availability of a large number of execution traces. Instead, we make use of process domain knowledge to generate a process that can be fine-tuned with even a single trace.

There are many commercial process mining tools [9] [10] [11] proposed in the context of Business Process Intelligence (BPI). No new mining or learning algorithms are proposed in BPI tools. The main contribution is the ability to leverage generic mining tools such as SAS Enterprise Miner for advanced analysis on process data. The main goal of BPI tool is to support real-time monitoring, analysis and management of running business processes such that Service Level Agreements (SLAs) can be met. Process execution data are extracted, clustered to predict the performance of the current or future executing processes. There is no attempt to generate a process from concrete execution traces.

6   Conclusions and Future Work

In this paper we proposed a Process Learning System (PLS) architecture and outlined the functionality of some of its key components. PLS is capable of learning business processes from a few observed traces and from domain-specific information provided in the form of activity and resource ontologies, as well as from business rules. Initial experiments have indicated that the proposed PLS will be capable to synthesize and learn business processes that are both compatible with known instances and optimized to reduce time and cost, comply with business rules, and produce well-formed products and services. PLS provides the novel capability of learning un-captured (e.g., new or improved) processes in time to meet Real Time Enterprise objectives.

We are in the process of developing and testing a prototype PLS. PLS's Process Enactor and Domain-Specific Simulator Components are based on ATLAS [14] – an existing process management system. The initial Domain Specific Planner performs cost and time optimization to select between process alternatives, while the Process Miner component will be utilizing existing algorithms that are enhanced to take advantage of domain specific knowledge and the rich modeling capabilities of PLS's process model. Initial experiments involved learning processes for assembling physical products out of parts.

References

[1] van der Aalst, W.M.P, Weijters, A.J.M.M., Maruster, L.: Workflow Mining: Discovering Process Models from Event Logs. IEEE Transactions on Knowledge and Data Engineering, vol. 16(9) (2004)

[2] Agrawal, R., Gunopulos, D., Leymann, F.: Mining Process Models from Workflow Logs. Sixth International Conference on Extending Database Technology (1998)

[3] Clarke, Draghicescu, Kurshan: A unified approach for showing language containment and equivalence between various types of w-automata. In: Proc. of the 15th Colloquium on Trees in Algebra and Programming. LNCS, vol. 407, Springer, Heidelberg (1990)

[4] Clarke, Grumberg, Peled,: Model Checking. MIT press. ISBN 0-262-03270-8

[5] Cormen, Leiserson, Rivest,: Introduction to algorithms, 2nd edn. ISBN 0-07-013151-1

[6] Cook, J.E., Wolf, A.L.: Discovering Models of Software Processes from Event-Based Data. ACM Trans. on Software Engineering and Methodology, vol. 7(3) (1998)

[7] Anindya, D.: Automating the Discovery of AS-IS Business process Models: Probabilistic and Algorithmic Approaches. Information Systems Research, vol. 9(3)(1998)

[8] Grigori, D., Casati, F., Dayal, U., Chan, M.C.: Improving Business Process Quality through Exception Understanding, Prediction and Prevention. In: Proceedings of the 27th Int.Conf. on Very Large Database Conference, Rome, Italy (2001)

[9] Castellanos, M., Casati, F., Dayal, U., Shan, M.-C.: A Comprehensive and Automated Approach to Intelligent Business Process Execution Analysis. Distributed and Parallel Databases 16(3), 239–273, special issue on Data Warehousing, OLAP and Data Mining Technology (2004)

[10] Sayal, M., Casati, F., Dayal, U., Chan, M.C.: Business Process Cockpit. In: Proc. of the 28th International Conference on Very Large Database Conference, Hong Kong, China (2002)

[11] Srikant, R., Agrawal, R.: Mining Generalized Association Rules. In: Proceedings of the 21st International Conference on Very Large Database, Zurich, Switzerland, pp. 407–419 (1995)

[12] Georgakopoulos, D., Nodine, M., Baker, D., Cichocki, A.: Awareness Enabled Coordination for Large Scale Collaboration Management. International Symposium on Collaborative Technologies and Systems (May 2006)

[13] ATLAS, Telcordia Technologies http://www.argreenhouse.com/ATLAS/
[14] SAP: NetWeaver http://www.sap.com
[15] BEA: WebLogic Integrator (2006) http://www.bea.com/
[16] Workflow Management Coalition (1998) http://www.wfmc.org
[17] ProM Framework (2006) http://is.tm.tue.nl/research/processmining

An Integrated Approach to Process-Driven Business Performance Monitoring and Analysis for Real-Time Enterprises

Jonghun Park, Cheolkyu Jee, Kwanho Kim, Seung-Kyun Han, Duksoon Im, Wan Lee, and Noyoon Kim

Digital Interactions Lab., Seoul National University, Seoul, 151-744, Korea
jonghun@snu.ac.kr

Abstract. Business process management systems (BPMSs) are increasingly gaining momentum as a software platform on which to define, execute, and track enterprise-wide business processes. BPMSs promise to facilitate automation, integration, and optimization of business processes in order to support decision making, increase operational efficiency, and lower the cost of doing business. In spite of the growing popularity, however, realization of the grand vision BPMSs ultimately seek to achieve calls for renewed focus on the holistic approach to continuous process improvement instead of on the process automation alone. In this paper, we present a framework, named xPIA (eXecutable Process Innovation Accelerator), which can effectively facilitate the continuous process improvement through enhancing monitoring capabilities for business data that can significantly affect process performances. In addition to the basic process-related data such as activity start and finish times, the proposed framework allows for monitoring other important business contents as well as events from various sources, including business process definitions, forms and documents, database management systems, enterprise applications, and web services. The presented results outline the key concepts and architectures of xPIA to realize such functionalities on top of contemporary BPMSs while at the same time addressing the implementation issues.

1 Introduction

Design, analysis, execution, and improvement of business processes have been widely regarded as a major challenge for big and medium-sized organizations across all industries. Over the past decades, information technology has continued to evolve in an effort to control and improve key business processes. In particular, BPM (Business Process Management) is recently becoming the prominent paradigm for realizing business process optimization through providing effective and efficient means for integrating, coordinating, and streamlining enterprises vital resources, namely people, IT applications, and processes.

BPM is a framework of applications that effectively tracks and orchestrates business processes. It not only allows a business process to be executed more

C. Bussler et al. (Eds.): BIRTE 2006, LNCS 4365, pp. 133–142, 2007.

efficiently, but also provides the tools that allow businesses to measure performance and identify opportunities for improvement. As a result, many existing workflow and EAI (Enterprise Application Integration) vendors have rapidly positioned their systems as BPMSs (Business Process Management Systems), and claim that their platforms can provide solutions for measuring and analyzing the effectiveness of business processes [1,2].

At present, however, current generation of BPMSs so far have accounted mainly for the issues of automatically managing the processes, leaving the problem of continuous process improvement (CPI) largely unexplored [3,4]. Implementation of CPI usually entails the need to collect diverse information from various sources of enterprise IT systems, including not only the BPMS itself but also the systems external to BPMS such as ERP, content management systems, and databases [5]. Hence, business data that can be collected from BPMSs are currently far from being sufficient from the viewpoint of process improvements.

On the other hand, in response to the needs for obtaining and analyzing business performance data, IT industry has fielded a wide range of technologies that address parts of the real-time data access and analysis problem, including business activity monitoring (BAM) and corporate performance management (CPM) systems [6,7,8]. These technologies provide a useful, but still inadequate framework for assembling enterprise data into timely and effective information. The user is still faced with manual data input that inhibits real-time use of relevant business performance information.

Specifically, with an objective of real-time monitoring and alerting, BAM systems collect business performance data from various sources of enterprise IT systems and present them in forms of dashboards and various charts. In addition, they help managers take corrective actions through alerting mechanisms whenever there are collective signals or performance indicators that deviate from some pre-specified limits. Yet, currently most of BAM systems are operated independently of business processes in execution, making the process-oriented performance data collection rather difficult.

Taking a different approach to gathering and analyzing business performance data, CPM systems such as ARIS PPM (Process Performance Monitoring) [9] and FileNet Process Analyzer [10], aim at optimizing business processes through utilizing various OLAP analysis functionalities. In an attempt to compute KPIs (Key Performance Indicators), they are designed to extract data from legacy information systems as well as logs of a variety of systems. In spite of their wide acceptance, thay lack the satisfactory support for process-oriented view of business performance analysis mainly because the performance data are collected according to the rules that are not driven by the events specific to business process specifications.

Therefore, there are still several issues to be addressed further in order for BPMSs to realize its full potential. Motivated by the above remarks, this paper presents a new BPMS-enabled framework for continuous process improvement, named xPIA (eXecutable Process Innovation Accelerator), that attempts to addresses these shortcomings of current generation of BPMSs. The main objective of the proposed framework is the development of an accelerator module which facilitates the automated gathering of performance data of business processes by effectively integrating with BPMS.

In xPIA, all the necessary data that pertain to process performance improvement are identified in the context of a specific business process model, and they are collected according to the rules that are defined in terms of the events which are generated during business process execution. The proposed framework is expected to provide more meaningful data for process improvement than the current BPMSs do, while at the same time it overcomes the limitations of current BAM and CPM solutions by allowing the performance data to be organized around the business processes so that CPI activities become more effective.

The paper is organized as follows: In Section 2, we present the proposed framework through defining the architecture and the functionalities of xPIA. Section 3 discusses in detail the proposed concepts and shows some screenshots of xPIA. Finally Section 4 concludes the paper.

2   Proposed Framework: xPIA

The quality of a business process depends on not only the basic performance measures such as execution time and cost incurred by the individual activities that constitute the process, but also other factors such as (i) the people (and organizations) who perform the activities, (ii) the time each activity is carried out, (iii) where the process is instantiated, and so on [11]. For instance, the customer satisfaction level for an automotive insurance claim handling process can be affected by several factors which may include the person responsible for the claim handling, the car type involved in the accident, and the place the accident took place.

Accordingly, in order to construct a useful statistical model that describes cause and effect relationships between the process quality and the factors affecting the quality, it is necessary to record such factors along with the quality of the business process observed. We will refer to these factors as performance elements (PEs) afterwards. Subsequently, a thorough statistical analysis of the model may yield a new business rule like "John is the best person for handling the BMW accident that took place in the Harvard university campus."

Not all performance element data are available from the execution logs of the current generation BPMSs mainly due to the fact that they are managed by the systems external to the BPMS. To address this problem, the xPIA defines a PEM (Performance Element Mapper) module that attempts to provide capability to collect data from various sources of enterprise information systems in a process-centric manner. The target systems PEM currently have access for data acquisition include business process definitions, documents and forms generated and routed by the process, process execution logs, organization data such as LDAP directory, databases, enterprise applications that can be accessed via EAI platform, and finally web resources such as XML web services and html resources. They are depicted in Fig. 1.

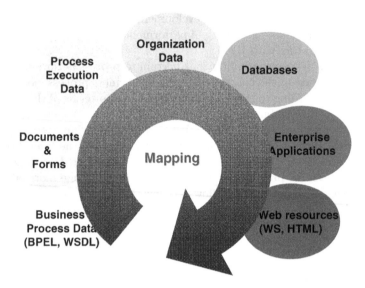

Fig. 1. Target systems of PEM

PEM allows users to define the performance element data to be collected and the event structure that dictates the rules by which the actual data collection is carried out for a specific data of interest. Specifically, the event structure consists of (i) scope that defines the life time of the data collection (ii) trigger that indicates when the data are collected, and (iii) condition that needs to be satisfied for the data collection to proceed. In particular, the trigger is defined in terms of the events that can be generated by BPMS during process execution. For instance, it is used to extract a piece of data from a DBMS whenever an instance of a specific type of business process finishes.

The output of PEM is stored as an SRD (Sampling Rule Definition) file which specifies the performance element data to be extracted as well as the data collection rule in the form of an XML document. An SRD file is composed of four primary XML tags that represent (i) the set of performance element data to be collected, (ii) the access information such as URL of a target system, protocol, login data, and XQuery (or SQL) expressions, (iii) the type and structure of data, and finally (iv) the event structure.

Having introduced the PEM module, we now present the run-time architecture of xPIA. Based upon a multi-component suite of application modules, xPIA has been designed to provide a comprehensive business performance monitoring solution that can be seamlessly integrated into an existing BPM system. It embraces two major components: BPS (Business Performance Sampler) and xPIA monitor.

The basic functionality of BPS is to collect the values of performance elements from various sources of enterprise information systems (including BPMS) according to the rules defined in the SRD file while processes are executed by BPMS engine. During the execution of BPS, the business performance data are recorded in the database, and then made available for further analysis to a range of solutions such as BSC, BAM, BI, statistical analysis, and 6 sigma systems [12]. Hence, BPS is located in a middle layer between enterprise systems and performance analysis tools, supporting automated collection of business quality measures and their related performance elements. On the other hand, xPIA monitor provides an environment in which a user can manage and monitor the behavior of BPS. The run-time architecture described above is shown in Fig. 2.

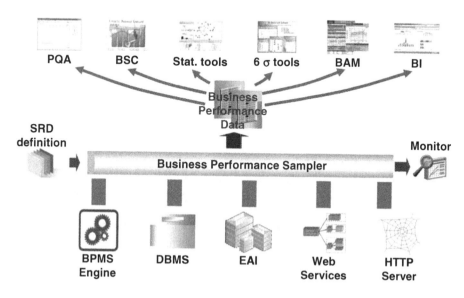

Fig. 2. Run-time architecture of xPIA

Figure 3 shows internal architecture of BPS. Upon receiving a new SRD file, BPS identifies performance elements to be sampled and passes the technical details necessary for data collection to the sampling scheduler which is responsible for constructing and maintaining a schedule of sampling tasks. Each sampling task represents a set of activities consisting of retrieving the current values of appropriate PEs either by parsing the event messages delivered to BPS or by accessing the target systems specified in the SRD file, and then recording them into the business performance database. Depending on the type of a trigger defined in the SRD file, a sampling task can be either time-driven or event-driven. While time-driven sampling tasks are scheduled deterministically by the sampling scheduler, event-driven tasks are dynamically created and scheduled on the fly whenever an event message that satisfies a trigger and its condition is received by event listener. Therefore, the sampling scheduler maintains a priority queue for managing the schedules to cope with this dynamic scheduling requirements.

Given a set of performance elements, $X_1, X_2, \ldots, X_n$, it is often required that their values are collected as a bundle for the purpose of statistical analysis. However, in many cases, some performance elements among $X_1, X_2, \ldots, X_n$ may

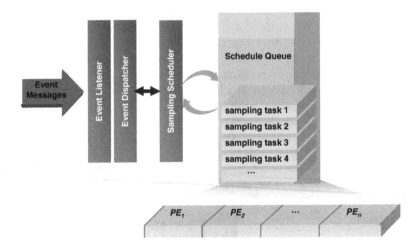

Fig. 3. Internal architecture of BPS

have different frequency requirements for data collections, and there may be no data that jointly satisfy the common data collection frequency (i.e., the least common multiple).

In order to record such a set of data into the BPS database consistently and efficiently, we define a data schema of the form $(X_1, X_2, \ldots, X_n, \Delta)$, where $\Delta = d_1 d_2 \ldots d_n$ is a binary number of length n in which d_i, $i = 1, \ldots, n$, has a value of 1 if the value of X_i is recorded at the time when data collection of X_i is specified, and has a value of 0, otherwise. In the proposed data schema, a new record $(X_1, X_2, \ldots, X_n, \Delta)$ is inserted into the BPS database whenever a new value of any element $X_i, i = 1, \ldots, n$ is obtained at time τ according to a sampling rule definition, and the values of all the other performance elements within the scope defined in an SRD such that $X_j, j \neq i$ are replaced by their most recent values recorded since their current values were not collected at τ. From the definition, $d_i = 1$ and $d_j = 0, \forall j \neq i$, in this case. We remark that more than one performance element can be sampled at the same time since an SRD is defined in an event driven manner.

The motivation behind introducing the above data schema comes from the fact that undefined values and in particular the values of response variables that were recorded at the time when data collection was not specified should not be considered during the analysis. As an example, consider a factor analysis involving three performance elements, X_1, X_2, and X_3, in which the influence of factors X_1 and X_2 against the response variable X_3 is examined. When the sampling frequencies for X_1, X_2, and X_3 are different, a simple data schema of the form (X_1, X_2, X_3) may produce the set of records like (a', undef, c), (a'', b, c'), and (a'', b, c'') where undef indicates that the value is undefined at the time of data collection.

While one viable approach to this problem would be to introduce a separate data table for each data element, it will require an additional data field for maintaining data collection times and subsequently a lot of join operations during the analysis. In contrast, with the proposed data schema, we can maintain the size of the BPS database more succinctly when the performance element data to be collected have different sampling requirements. That is, if the BPS database had the set of records, $(a', \mathtt{undef}, c, 101)$, $(a'', b, c, 100)$, and $(a'', b, c', 111)$, following the proposed schema, it is easy to see that the only meaningful data for analysis would be the third record since the first record has an undefined value for the independent variable X_2 and the second record is obtained at the time when the sampling of the response variable X_3 was not specified.

3   xPIA in Action

In this section, we present some of screen shots of xPIA to elaborate on the proposed concept in more detail. Fig. 4 shows a user interface of PEM in which a data field of e-Form document is being mapped as a performance element. The selected business process definition is shown on the left window in Fig. 4. Through clicking a specific activity within the process, a user is provided with the associated e-Form from which a data field of interest can be chosen for sampling.

The selected performance element then needs to be associated with an event structure to define a sampling rule. As described in Section 2, an event structure is instantiated through defining the scope, trigger, and condition. For the definition of these components, xPIA provides a dialogue-based user interface which is a commonly used interaction method for defining rules [13]. In this

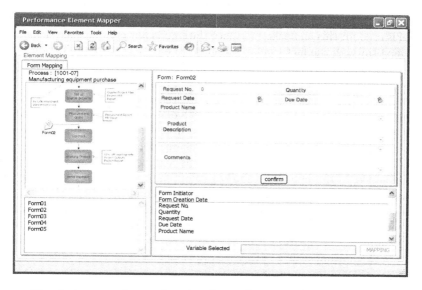

Fig. 4. An example user interface for performance element mapping

rule definition environment, rules are developed in a WYSIWYG syntactic rule editor that graphically steps users through the process of writing rules. As an example, Fig. 5 illustrates the case in which the value of the considered performance element is collected whenever the activity "ActivityName6" of process "ProcessName2" is started.

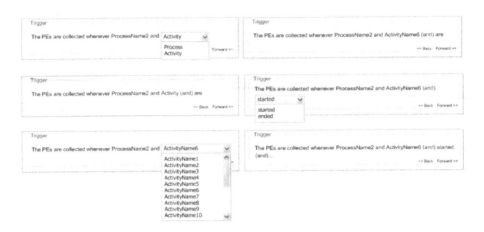

Fig. 5. Trigger definition for a selected performance element

Finally, xPIA also provides a simple performance analysis tool, named PQA (Process Quality Analyzer), that currently supports two types of analysis: factor analysis and performance prediction. The factor analysis module allows users to derive some specified number of performance elements that are critical to the performance of a business process in consideration. A simple least squares regression model is used for this analysis [14]. Once the significant performance elements are identified through the factor analysis phase, the performance prediction module can be used for cause and effect analysis as well as process optimization. As shown in Fig. 6, each performance element identified to be significant is displayed as a slide bar in this module so that a user can examine its effect of on the processs performance by varying the value of the performance element.

As an example, Fig. 6 illustrates the case in which five performance elements, namely "accident location", "car type", "claim handler", "accident hour", and "time taken for approval", are identified as significant factors for the performance named "claim handling time" of an automotive insurance claim handling process. Through examining the effect of various combinations of those five performance elements, one can derive a useful business rule such as "John is the best person for handling the BMW accident that took place in the Harvard university campus." as mentioned in Section 2. Furthermore, this module can also facilitate the optimization of process performance.

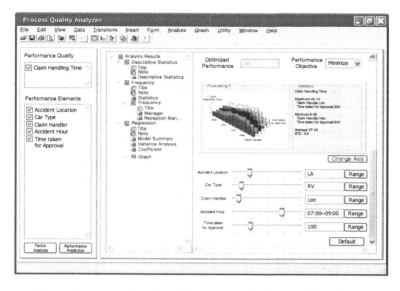

Fig. 6. A screen shot of performance prediction module of PQA

4   Conclusion

The need for automated support from BPMSs that allows organizations to improve their business processes is becoming critical. BPMS aims to automate, integrate and optimize business processes to speed up critical business decision making, increase operational efficiency, lower the cost of doing business, and improve customer services. Yet, realization of continuous improvement of business processes requires BPMSs to provide more information about the process execution results than they currently do.

Recognizing this need, in this paper, we proposed a novel framework, named xPIA, that attempts to automatically gather the business performance data from various types of enterprise information systems in addition to BPMS itself. Furthermore, compared to the current BAM and CPM solutions, xPIA provides a distinct advantage in that it can collect performance data from a business processs point of view, which can significantly facilitate the analysis for process improvement.

The proposed framework is designed as an accelerator that can be seamlessly integrated in to existing BPMS implementations. Therefore, it is anticipated that it will increase the user acceptance of BPMS through making it a vital tool for realizing the vision of continuous process improvement.

Acknowledgments. This work was supported by the Korea Research Foundation Grant funded by the Korean Government (MOEHRD) (KRF-2005-041-D00917) and also by Engineering Research Institute at Seoul National University.

References

1. Smith, H., Fingar, P.: Business Process Management: The Third Wave. Meghan-Kiffer Press (2003)
2. Dumas, M., van der Aalst, W., ter Hofstede, A.H.M.: Process-Aware Information Systems: Bridging People and Software through Process Technology. John Wiley & Sons, Chichester (2005)
3. Smith, H., Fingar, P.: Digital six sigma: Integrating continuous improvement, with continuous change, with continuous learning. White paper, BPTrends (2003) http://bptrends.com
4. Jeng, J.J., An, L., Bhaskaran, K., Chang, H., Ettl, M.: Sense-and-respond grids for adaptive enterprises. IT Professional, pp. 33–40 (September/October 2005)
5. George, M.L.: Lean Six Sigma for Service: How to Use Lean Speed and Six Sigma Quality to Improve Services and Transactions. McGraw-Hill, New York (2003)
6. Sonnen, D., Morris, H.D.: Businessfactor: Event-driven business performance management. White paper, IDC (2004)
7. Srinivasan, S., Krishna, V., Holmes, S.: Web-log-driven business activity monitoring. IEEE Computer, pp. 61–68 (March 2005)
8. Thomas, M., Redmond, R., Yoon, V., Singh, R.: A semantic approach to monitor business process performance. Communications of the ACM 48, 55–59 (2005)
9. IDS Scheer: ARIS process performance manager. Web site, IDS Scheer (2006) http://www.ids-scheer.com/
10. FileNet: Filenet process analyzer. Web site, FileNet (2006) http://www.filenet.com
11. Raisinghani, M.S., Ette, H., Pierce, R., Cannon, G., Daripaly, P.: Six sigma: Concepts, tools, and applications. Industrial Management & Data. Systems 105, 491–505 (2005)
12. Hammer, M.: Process management and the future of six sigma. MIT Sloan Management Review 43, 26–32 (2002)
13. ILOG: ILOG JRules. Web site, ILOG (2005) http://www.ilog.com
14. Neter, J., Kutner, M.H., Nachtsheim, C.J., Wasserman, W.: Applied Linear Statistical Models. 4th edn. IRWIN (1990)

Quality Contracts for Real-Time Enterprises

Alexandros Labrinidis, Huiming Qu, and Jie Xu

Advanced Data Management Technologies Laboratory
Department of Computer Science
University of Pittsburgh
Pittsburgh, PA 15260, USA
{labrinid,huiming,xujie}@cs.pitt.edu

Abstract. Real-time enterprises rely on user queries being answered in a timely fashion and using fresh data. This is relatively easy when systems are lightly loaded and both queries and updates can be finished quickly. However, this goal becomes fundamentally hard to achieve due to the high volume of queries and updates in real systems, especially in periods of flash crowds. In such cases, systems typically try to optimize for the average case, treating all users, queries, and data equally. In this paper, we argue that it is more beneficial for real-time enterprises to have the users specify how to balance such a tradeoff between Quality of Service (QoS) and Quality of Data (QoD), in other words, "instructing" the system on how to best allocate resources to maximize the overall user satisfaction. Specifically, we propose Quality Contracts (QC) which is a framework based on the micro-economic paradigm and provides an intuitive and easy to use, yet very powerful way for users to specify their preferences for QoS and QoD. Beyond presenting the QC framework, we present results of applying it in two different domains: scheduling in real-time web-databases and replica selection in distributed query processing.

1 Introduction

Globalization and the proliferation of the Web have forced most businesses to evolve into real-time enterprises; it is always daytime in some part of the world! Such real-time enterprises rely on vast amounts of collected data for business intelligence. Data is processed continuously and typically stored in data warehouses, for further analysis.

Given the real-time nature of businesses in our fast-changing world, getting answers in a timely fashion and using fresh data is of paramount importance. This is fairly easy to do in periods of light load, however, it becomes fundamentally hard to achieve in periods of high volumes of queries (e.g., multiple analysts working towards a deadline for end of the year reports) or updates (e.g., influx of sales data because of a 3-day special sale weekend)[1]. In cases of high load, systems will typically try to optimize for the average case, treating all user queries and quality metrics equally.

In this paper, we argue that it is more beneficial for real-time enterprises to have their users (business analysts in this case) supply their *preferences* on how the system should

---

[1] This scenario assumes a complete separation of operational and business analysis information systems; the situation is even worse if these are coupled together under a single system.

C. Bussler et al. (Eds.): BIRTE 2006, LNCS 4365, pp. 143–156, 2007.

balance the trade-off between Quality of Service (QoS) and Quality of Data (QoD), in other words, instruct the system on how to best allocate resources in order to maximize user satisfaction. We propose to do this by utilizing *Quality Contracts*, a framework for describing user preferences that is based on a micro-economic model. Quality Contracts (QCs) empower users to quantify QoS and QoD using their favorite metric(s) of interest and to specify their preferences (in an intuitive and integrated way) for how the system should allocate resources in periods of high load.

In order to compete successfully in today's highly dynamic environments, real-time enterprises are expected to rely on two types of querying capabilities. First, *ad hoc queries* are utilized by business analysts to explore previously collected data; such queries have been the staple of business intelligence units for decades. Secondly, *continuous queries* (CQs) are registered ahead of time and constantly monitor the incoming data feeds to detect patterns and other precursors of customer behavior. The goal in such cases is to provide actionable information as soon as possible, by continuously executing (i.e., re-evaluating) CQs with the arrival of new relevant data. Such CQs belong to a new data processing paradigm, that of Data Stream Management Systems (DSMSs) [7,17,6,4,20]. Clearly, both types of queries are crucial to improving the real-time enterprise's performance.

Although there exist multiple metrics for measuring QoS or QoD for ad-hoc and for continuous queries, they have two major shortcomings.

(1) Lack of a unified framework that can evaluate quality for both ad-hoc as well as for continuous queries: Currently, quality measures used for ad-hoc queries (in DBMSs) are different from those used for continuous queries (in DSMSs). It is not clear how these two types of quality measures relate to each other in a system that supports both kinds of queries. Many of these measures do not even have a bounded domain, which makes comparison impossible. The major problem this limitation creates is with regards to *provisioning of resources*: the system does not have a common framework to compare usage/utility of resources allocated to ad-hoc versus continuous queries. As such, the system is forced to allocate resources separately to the two types of queries with the danger of under-utilization and overloading, and all the consequences that these bring. Another problem is that of usability: users must "learn" two sets of quality metrics, one for traditional queries and one for continuous queries.

(2) Limited consideration of user preferences in evaluating QoS/QoD: The most important deficiency of the current approaches to QoS/QoD is that they do not have strong *support for user preferences*. In typical DBMSs (i.e., for ad-hoc queries), quality is simply reported as an overall system property (even if both QoS and QoD are reported as separate measures); user preferences are not even considered. There are a few exceptions to this. Work on real-time databases [12,19,2] typically considers user preferences on a single QoS metric (in this case: preference on response time by means of a deadline) while attempting to maximize QoD. Our work on database-driven web servers [16,15,14], balances the trade-off between QoS and QoD, while considering user preferences on one of the two measures: given an application-specified QoD requirement, the proposed system adapts to improve the overall QoS. Finally, as part of our preliminary work (presented in the previous section), we extended the work of [12] to consider both QoS user requirements (i.e., deadlines) and QoD user requirements (i.e., freshness threshold).

In DSMSs, user preferences are indeed considered to some degree. Looking at the Borealis project [1] (which corresponds to the state of the art), we can see that a "Diagram Administrator" can provide QoS functions that could correspond to user preferences (in the same way as in the Aurora project [5]). However, the different components of the QoS (i.e., the Vector of Metrics) are aggregated into a single, global QoS score, using *universal* weights. In other words, the same QoS components are used for all queries and the same relative importance to each QoS component is assigned for all queries via system-wide weights. This system-based approach has another negative side-effect: the benefit of the overall system can often overweigh the benefit of the individual user or query (even by just a little), who/which can be "penalized" repeatedly for the benefit of the others, thus leading to starvation.

Desired Properties. Given the previously mentioned deficiencies, we believe that an effective framework for measuring QoS and QoD must have the following primary properties:

- handle ad-hoc queries and continuous queries at the same time,
- allow the user to choose from an array of QoS/QoD metrics in order to specify quality requirements/preferences,
- allow the user to combine multiple QoS/QoD metrics and indicate the relative importance of each individual metric (as a component of the overall Quality for the user),
- allow the user to specify the relative importance of different queries,
- do all of the above in a "democratic" way: it should not be that a user can always specify his/her queries to be more important than everybody else's, thus monopolizing system resources.

In the next section, we describe the proposed Quality Contracts Framework that addresses all of the above challenges.

2   Quality Contracts Framework

We propose a unified framework for specifying QoS/QoD requirements in systems that support both ad-hoc queries and continuous queries. Our proposed framework, *Quality Contracts*, is based on the micro-economic paradigm [22,21,8]. In our framework, users are allocated virtual money, which they spend in order to execute their queries. Servers, on the other hand, execute users' queries and get virtual money in return for their service. In order to execute a query however, both the user and the server must agree on a Quality Contract (QC). The QC essentially specifies how much money the server which executes the query will get. The amount of money allocated for the query is not fixed (as was the case in [21]). Instead, the amount of money the server receives depends on how well it executes the user's query. In fact, in the general case, QCs can even include refunds; a very poorly executed query can result in the user being reimbursed instead of paying for its execution (accumulated refunds can improve the odds of the user's query executing properly later).

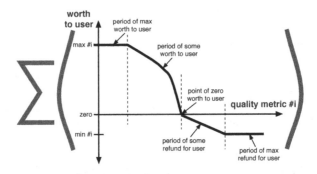

Fig. 1. General form of a Quality Contract

Under the proposed scheme, a user can specify how much money he/she thinks the server should get at various levels of quality for the posed query, whereas the server, if it accepts the query and the QC, essentially "commits" to execute the queries, or face the consequences. In this model, servers try to maximize their income, whereas users try to "stretch" their budget to run successfully as many queries as they can.

A Quality Contract (QC) is essentially a collection of graphs, like the one in Figure 1. Each graph represents a QoS/QoD requirement from the user. The X-axis corresponds to an attribute that the user wants to use in order to measure the quality of the results (e.g., response time or delay). The Y-axis corresponds to the virtual money the user is willing to pay to the server in order to execute his/her query. Notice that in order to specify more than one QC (i.e., to judge the quality of the results using more than one metric) the user must provide additional virtual money to the server. Put simply: the server can hope to receive the sum of all max amounts of the different QC graphs that a user submits along with a query. Of course, the level of money the server gets is differentiated according to the value of the quality metric for the results. There is also the possibility of the server having to issue "refunds" for queries that were not satisfactory completed. Next, we present examples of QC graphs in order to illustrate their features and advantages. For simplicity, we will use the dollar sign ($) to refer to virtual money for the remainder of this paper.

2.1 Quality Contracts Examples

Figure 2 is an example of Quality Contract (QC) for an ad-hoc query submitted by a user. This QC consists of two graphs: a QoS graph (Figure 2a) and a QoD graph (Figure 2b). We see that *QCs allow users to combine different aspects of quality.* In this example, the user has set the budget for the query to be $100; $70 are allocated for optimal QoS, whereas $30 are allocated for optimal QoD. This allocation is one important feature of the QC framework: *users can easily specify the relative importance of each component of the overall quality by allocating the query budget accordingly.*

In the next example, we have QCs for two different continuous queries, Q_1 (Figures 3a & 3b) and Q_2 (Figures 3c & 3d), issued either by the same user or by two different users. In addition to highlighting different types of QC graphs (including more complicated

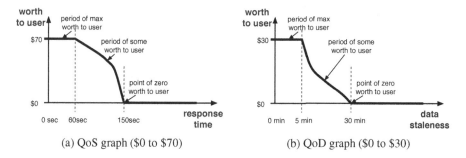

(a) QoS graph ($0 to $70)   (b) QoD graph ($0 to $30)

Fig. 2. QC example for one ad-hoc query. The QoS metric is response time, whereas the QoD metric is data staleness. Data staleness is measured as the time between the last instant when the physical world has changed and the instant when the the local storage has been updated (i.e., time since the last update on a data item access by the query).

quality metrics such as those expressed by virtual attributes), this example also illustrates another important feature of the QC framework: *users can easily specify the relative importance of each query by allocating their budgets accordingly.* In our example, Q_1 has a total budget of $100 (with the most important quality metric being QoD, allocated $80 out of $100), and Q_2 has a total budget of $150 (with the most important quality metric being QoS, allocated $120 out of $150). Finally, this relative importance can also be evaluated over different types of queries altogether (e.g., the ad-hoc query of Figure 2 can be executed at the same time as the continuous queries of Figure 3).

2.2 Quality Contracts Implementation

We envision that a system which supports Quality Contracts (QCs) will provide a wide assortment of possible types of QoS/QoD metrics to the users. Examples of such QoS metrics include response time (esp. in connection with a soft or hard deadline), delay, stretch (average, maximum), etc. Examples of QoD metrics in the presence of ad-hoc updates include time-based, lag-based, and divergence-based definitions. Additionally, examples of QoD metrics for continuous queries include drop-based (like the example in Figure 3b), or value-based (i.e., assign worth to the user based on the values of the result, as in Aurora [5]).

Payment Stream. For continuous queries, QCs can be seen as a guarantee for a *payment stream.* In other words, the min/max virtual money values on the Y-axis correspond to a *rate of payment* rather than a one-time payment amount, which is the case for ad-hoc queries.

Virtual Attributes. One important aspect of QCs that we plan to explore further is the ability to specify arbitrary quality metrics, in the form of *virtual attributes* that are computed over other attributes, possibly including statistics of the entire system. We have already seen an example of this in Figure 3c where the user specified QoS as the delay his/her queries received when compared to the average delay in the system. We expect such "comparative" QoS metrics to be rather frequent: it is probably harder for

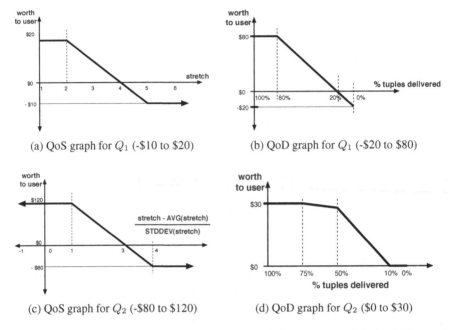

(a) QoS graph for Q_1 (-$10 to $20)

(b) QoD graph for Q_1 (-$20 to $80)

(c) QoS graph for Q_2 (-$80 to $120)

(d) QoD graph for Q_2 ($0 to $30)

Fig. 3. QC example for two continuous queries Q_1 and Q_2. The QoS metric for Q1 is stretch, or the factor by which a job is slowed down relative to the time it would have taken to execute if it where the only job in the system, where as the QoS metric for Q2 is a *virtual attribute*. Virtual attributes are computed over the entire system rather than just using the performance statistics of the individual query. In this example, the user simply wants to guarantee that his/her queries are not delayed more than average: the stretch observed for his/her queries needs to be at most one standard deviation away from the average stretch of the entire system for maximum payoff at the server ($120). The QoD metric for both Q1 and Q2 is the percentage of tuples delivered.

a user to specify exact timing requirements, but it is easier to specify that he/she wants the submitted query to be executed within the top 20% of the fastest queries in the entire system.

Parameterized QCs. Making QCs easy to configure is fundamental to their acceptance by the user community. Towards this we plan on providing *parameterized versions of QC graphs* that the users can easily instantiate. For example, we can have a parameterized QoD function based on tuples dropped (similar to Figure 3b) with four parameters: maximum worth (e.g., $80), maximum refund (e.g., -$20), percentage point beyond which QoD drops below maximum (e.g., 80%), and percentage point after which user is entitled to a refund (e.g., 20%). We can assume a piece-wise linear curve and allow the user to specify more intermediate points. We can also assume a predetermined curve and allow the user to specify even less parameters (e.g., only the maximum worth). Finally, parameterized QCs could also reduce the overhead of evaluating the QCs in the system (by essentially "compiling" their definitions).

Contract Clauses. A simple form of a parameterized QC is that of a *"contract clause"*. This is the case when the user essentially promises a "bonus" to the server when a certain quality metric is met (e.g., response time less than 30 minutes for a long analysis query), but no virtual money otherwise. The QC graph in this case is a simple step function, and the parameterized version needs two values: the maximum worth and the turnover threshold.

QC Classes. Another way to increase usability of QCs and also reduce the overhead of evaluating them is to introduce differentiated levels of service using different *"contract classes"*. In this way, users simply assign queries to a predefined class with specific characteristics (expressed by QCs) without having to specify a complicated QC. This approach is also more scalable, since it reduces the overhead of evaluating the QC for each query independently.

Overhead. We expect the overhead of evaluating different QCs to vary significantly. For example, evaluating the delay observed by tuples is fairly easy to compute (e.g., Figure 3b), whereas computing the average stretch and its standard deviation (e.g., Figure 3c) should be considerably more expensive. As such, *we propose that the cost of computing the QC is also included in the "price" that the user is supposed to pay to the server for successful execution of his/her query under the given QC*. This is a departure from current practices (where most quality metrics were very simple and therefore of similar cost), but is necessitated by the complexity of new, sophisticated quality metrics whose overhead would unfairly burden the system, but they would still be attractive to users. Given this setup, users still have a choice over a wide assortment of quality metrics for QCs, but essentially they have to pay a "commission" if they want to use a sophisticated metric.

2.3   Usability of Quality Contracts

The usability of the QCs must be address for the QC framework to be successful. Making QCs easy to configure is fundamental to their acceptance by the user community. Towards this we expect service providers to support *parameterized versions of QC graphs* (as mentioned earlier) that the users can easily instantiate. In fact, a simpler scheme is one where the service provider has already identified a certain class of QCs for each type of user (such as a pre-determined cell phone plan) and a user will simply have to turn a "knob" on whether she prefers higher QoS or higher QoD (a local plan with more minutes or a national plan with fewer minutes under the same budget). In this way, using QCs service providers can better provision their systems, provide different classes of service, and allow end users to specify their preferences with minimal effort.

Although in this paper we align QoS to response time and QoD to data freshness, the Quality Contracts framework is general enough to allow for **any quality metric**. An example of this is the concept of *virtual attributes* that was introduced earlier, where a user-defined function is used as the quality metric. Furthermore, we believe that the notion of Quality of Data can be extended in multiple ways. First of all, it can be used to measure the level of *precision* of the result (i.e., similar to data freshness, but using the values to determine the amount of deviation from the ideal, instead of time since last update). Similarly, we can use approximate data to answer questions and this can be "penalized" accordingly by the user (while it also poses a clear trade-off between response time and accuracy of results). Secondly, it can be used in systems that support *online aggregation*[10], where user queries can return results at various level of *confidence*. In such a case, QoD can be represented as a function over the confidence metric. Finally, QoD can be used to refer to *Quality of Information*, where, for example, a measure of trustworthiness of the provided information can be computed and users may express how much they are willing to "pay" for high-quality results.

2.4 Quality Contracts – Discussion

The proposed QC framework meets all the challenges set forth at the introduction. It is able to handle ad-hoc queries and continuous queries at the same time; by using virtual money as the underlying principle, different metrics can easily be compared. The proposed framework enables users to choose from a wide assortment of QoS/QoD metrics in order to specify quality requirements/preferences. QCs allow the user to combine multiple quality metrics for a single query and indicate their relative importance; the same applies for multiple queries. By employing a virtual money economy, users cannot monopolize resources (by falsely advertising their queries to be the most important), but at the same time users are safe from starvation (by accumulating virtual money when not "paying" for queries that executed below the acceptable quality level).

The proposed QC framework also introduces the following salient features. Individual users, not system administrators, are those specifying user preferences; the virtual money scheme is inherently intuitive and easy for users to grasp. To further increase usability, parameterized and class-based QCs are introduced. A wide assortment of QoS/QoD metrics (for both ad-hoc and continuous queries) is possible. The set of QoS/QoD metrics is enhanced by allowing for virtual attributes, which enable comparison of the performance to the individual query to system-wide measures. To counteract the evaluation cost of such sophisticated metrics, the overhead of computing them is include in the "price" of the query. The notion of refunds is introduced; this helps further towards eliminating starvation.

3   Transaction Scheduling Under Quality Contracts

In the first application of Quality Contracts, we considered a web-database server (for example, a stock quote information server) that answers user-submitted ad hoc queries, while it processes updates in the background. Clearly, in this environment, high volumes of queries and/or updates can wreck havoc in the allocation of resources and result in many queries having unpredictable response time and/or returning stale data. In such an environment, the QC framework provides an intuitive way to express user preferences (in terms of response time and freshness requirements for queries) and thus enable the systtem to do a "better" job at allocating resources.

3.1   QUTS Scheduling Algorithm

We proposed the Query Update Time Share (QUTS) [18] scheduling algorithm to optimize the system profit in the presence of QCs. QUTS is a two-level scheme that can dynamically adjust the query and update share of the CPU, so as to maximize the overall

Table 1. Quality Contracts Used in Performance Comparison

Varying	ps	pd	rd	uu
ps (\$)	$\{1, 2, \ldots, 10\}$	50	50	0
pd (\$)	5	$\{1, 2, \ldots, 10\}$	50	0

system profit. At the high level, it dynamically allocates CPU to either the query queue or the update queue according to a profit. At the lower level, queries and updates have their own priority queues and potentially different scheduling policies. Specifically, we adopted Profit over Relative Deadline (PRD) [9] for queries and FIFO for updates. We used multiversion concurrency control to allow for maximal concurrency.

3.2 QUTS Experimental Evaluation

We compared QUTS with two baseline algorithms (Updated-High and Global-Priority), using both real and synthetic trace data. Our experiments showed that Quality Contracts are able to capture a wide spectrum of user preferences and that QUTS consistently outperforms existing methods, under the entire spectrum of quality contracts.

Baseline Algorithms:

- **Update High (UH).** UH has a dual priority queue where update queue has higher priority than query queue [3]. Priority schemes within each queue are same with QUTS. Two Phase Lock - High Priority (2PL-HP) is used for the concurrency control, where low priority transaction is aborted and hands the lock to high priority transactions. UH guarantees the highest data freshness, but it may waste a lot time updating data that have no contribution to the system profit.

- **Global Priority (GP).** GP is a preemptive scheduling scheme with a single-priority queue. The priority scheme for updates is High QoD Profit (HDP) which uses the sum of QoD maximal profit from the relative queries. Query priority scheme is HP (High Profit) which uses the sum of QoS maximal profit and QoD maximal profit. 2PL-HP is used for concurrency control. GP automatically pushes behind the updates which may not be contributing to the data quality of the queries, but it may still lead to query starvation when a surge of "good" updates arrives.

Experimental Setup. We used query traces from a stock market information web site and update traces from NYSE to drive our experiments. As part of the experimental setup, we attach a QC t o every query before it is submitted to our system. The QC is in the form of a positive, linear, monotonically decreasing function. Such QCs can be defined by four parameters: **ps** (the QoS profit if the query is return before deadline), **rd** (relative deadline which is the difference between deadline and query arrival time), **pd** (the QoD profit if the query is return with data meet the freshness requirement), and **uu** (number of unapplied updates which measures the maximal staleness allowed). Since there are four parameters in a quality contract, we vary one and fix the others to median values to see how the performance changes. Due to the space limitations, we only show

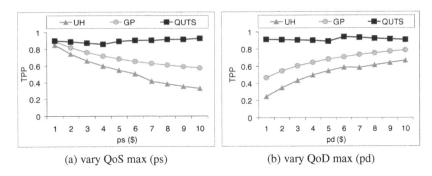

Fig. 4. QUTS performs best for all settings. UH performs worst because too many unnecessary updates execute and starve most of the queries; GP avoids those unnecessary updates. However, due to the global prioritization, starvation on queries or updates can easily occur, which jeopardizes the performance. QUTS works best because the time share scheme successfully avoids the starvation problem of GP.

two cases here (Figure 1). We measure the performance by computing how much profit has the system gained, normalized by dividing the actual gained profit over the maximal possible profit, or what we call the *Total Profit Percentage* (TPP).

Experimental Results. Figure 4(a) shows the TPP as a function of ps. QUTS performs the best among the three which almost reaches the maximum TPP. Note that the performance gap is bigger for smaller pd (when the QoS constraint is more important than the QoD constraint), which is usually of more interests in real applications. Likewise, Figure 4(b) plots TPP vs. pd. Again, QUTS outperforms all others.

4   Distributed Query Processing Using Quality Contracts

In the second application of Quality Contracts, we considered a distributed query processing environment, such as those that could be in place by a collaborative business intelligence application, where data is replicated across multiple nodes. On the one hand, data replication in this context is expected to improve reliability, expedite data discovery, and increase performance (i.e., Quality of Service, or QoS). On the other hand, however, it is also expected to have a negative impact to the Quality of the Data (QoD) that are being returned to the users. Getting results fast is crucial of course, but usually a limit to the degree of "staleness" is needed to make the results useful.

4.1   Replication-Aware Query Processing Scheme

We proposed *Replication-Aware Query Processing* (RAQP) [23], to address the problem of replica selection in the presence of user preferences for Quality of Service and Quality of Data (expressed as QCs).

Using the Quality Contracts framework as a natural and integrated way to guide the system towards efficient decisions, the RAQP scheme optimizes query execution

Table 2. Default System Parameters in Experiments

Simulation Parameter	Default Value
Core Node Number	100
Edge Node Number	1000
Unique Data Source	1000
Unique Data Number Per Data Source	U(10, 100)
Data Size	U(20, 200Mb)
# of Replicas Per Data	U(10, 30)
Bandwidth between each pair of Nodes	U(1, 50Mbps)

plans for distributed queries with Quality Contracts, in the presence of multiple replicas for each data source. Our scheme follows the classic two-step query optimization [21,11,13]: we start from a statically-optimized logical execution plan and then apply a greedy algorithm to select an execution site for each operator and also which replica to use. The overall optimization goal is expressed in terms of "profit" under the QC framework (i.e., the approach balances the trade-off between QoS and QoD).

4.2   RAQP Experimental Evaluation

We evaluated our proposed replication-aware query processing algorithm experimentally by performing an extensive simulation study using the following algorithms:

- **Exhaustive Search (ES):** Explore the whole search space exhaustively, thus guaranteeing to find the optimal allocation.
- **RAQP-G:** Greedy replication-aware initial allocation plus iterative improvement.
- **RAQP-L:** Bottleneck breakdown, local exhaustive search & iterative improvement.
- **Rand(k):** Random initial allocation plus k steps of iterative improvement (used as a "sample" of the search space).

Experimental results. One of the important features Quality Contracts hold is that users can easily specify the relative importance of each component of the overall quality by allocating the query budget accordingly. In order to observe the algorithm performance under different environments, we classify the users' quality requirements into 6 classes. We have three values for QoS and QoD: high (75), low (25), same (50) and two types of slope for the QC function: small and large, which produce 6 seperate classes. We report our results in Figure 5. Since our allocation initialization algorithm was aimed at response time improvement, QoS got more improvement than QoD in all the cases. Especially when QoS was assigned a higher budget, the effect on both QoS and total profit were obvious. When QoD was assigned a higher budget, the relative improvement of QoD also increased compared to the lower budget case. Our results clearly confirmed the functionality of Quality Contracts and our RAQP algorithm. Assigning higher "budget" to a quality dimension ends in that dimension achieving better performance by our optimization algorithm. The larger the budget difference the larger the difference in the resulting quality. This behavior is unique to our algorithm and allows the system to tailor its behavior according to the preferences of its users.

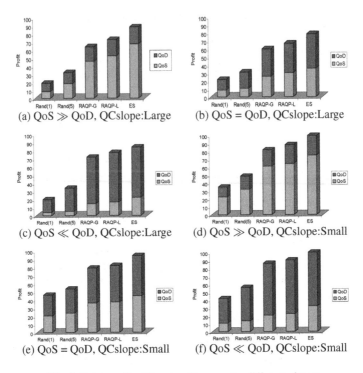

Fig. 5. Total profit of the algorithms under different classes

5   Conclusions and Future Work

In this work, we presented the Quality Contracts (QCs) framework that can be used to express user preferences for the QoS and QoD of submitted queries. QCs are based on the micro-economic paradigm and allow users to choose from a wide spectrum of QoS/QoD metrics, while, at the same time, indicating their relative importance. The QC framework is very intuitive, from a user perspective, and also provides a "clean" way for the system to quantify user preferences and allocate resources accordingly. It also integrates handling of both ad hoc and continuous queries that are crucial for real-time enterprises. Finally, we applied the QC framework in two different application domains: transaction scheduling in web databases and distributed query processing. For both cases, we introduced new algorithms that utilize the QC framework and also presented experimental results that illustrate the applicability of QCs and the high performance of our proposed algorithms.

Acknowledgments

This work was funded in part by NSF ITR Award ANI-0325353 and by NSF Award IIS-0534531. The authors also thank the anonymous referees for their helpful comments.

References

1. Abadi, D.J., Ahmad, Y., Balazinska, M., Cetintemel, U., Cherniack, M., Hwang, J.-H., Lindner, W., Maskey, A.S., Rasin, A., Ryvkina, E., Tatbul, N., Xing, Y., Zdonik, S.: The Design of the Borealis Stream Processing Engine. In: Proceedings of the 2nd Biennial Conference on Innovative Data Systems Research (CIDR 2005), Asilomar, CA (January 2005)
2. Abbott, R.K., Garcia-Molina, H.: Scheduling real-time transactions: a performance evaluation. ACM Transactions on Database Systems 17(3), 513–560 (1992)
3. Adelberg, B., Garcia-Molina, H., Kao, B.: Applying update streams in a soft real-time database system. In: Proc. of the 1995 SIGMOD conference, pp. 245–256, San Jose, California, United States (1995)
4. Balakrishnan, H., Balazinska, M., Carney, D., Cetintemel, U., Cherniack, M., Convey, C., Galvez, E., Salz, J., Stonebraker, M., Tatbul, N., Tibbetts, R., Zdonik, S.: Retrospective on aurora. The. VLDB Journal 13(4), 370–383 (2004)
5. Carney, D., Getintemel, U., Cherniack, M., Convey, C., Lee, S., Seidman, G., Stonebraker, M., Tatbul, N., Zdonik, S.: Monitoring streams: A new class of data management applications. In: Proc. of the 28th VLDB conference, pp. 215–226 (2002)
6. Chandrasekaran, S., Cooper, O., Deshpande, A., Franklin, M.J., Hellerstein, J.M., Hong, W., Krishnamurthy, S., Madden, V.R.S., Reiss, F., Shah, M.A.: TelegraphCQ: Continuous Dataflow Processing for an Uncertain World. In: Proceedings of the 1st Biennial Conference on Innovative Data Systems Research (CIDR 2003), Asilomar, CA (January 2003)
7. Chen, J., DeWitt, D.J., Tian, F., Wang, Y.: Niagaracq: a scalable continuous query system for internet databases. In: Proc. of the 2000 ACM SIGMOD Conference, pp. 379–390, Dallas, Texas, United States (2000)
8. Ferguson, D.F., Nikolaou, C., Sairamesh, J., Yemini, Y.: Economic models for allocating resources in computer systems. In: Market-based control: a paradigm for distributed resource allocation, pp. 156–183. World Scientific Publishing Co. Inc., River Edge, NJ, USA (1996)
9. Haritsa, J.R., Carey, M.J., Livny, M.: Value-based scheduling in real-time database systems. The. VLDB Journal 2(2), 117–152 (1993)
10. Hellerstein, J.M., Haas, P.J., Wang, H.J.: Online aggregation. In: Proc. of the 1977 ACM SIGMOD Conference, pp. 171–182, Tuscon, Arizona, United States (1997)
11. Hong, W., Stonebraker, M.: Optimization of parallel query execution plans in xprs. In: Proc. of PDIS, pp. 218–225. IEEE Computer Society Press, Los Alamitos (1991)
12. Kang, K.-D., Son, S.H., Stankovic, J.A.: Managing deadline miss ratio and sensor data freshness in real-time databases. IEEE Transactions on Knowledge and Data. Engineering (TKDE) 16(10), 1200–1216 (2004)
13. Kossmann, D.: The state of the art in distributed query processing. ACM Computing Surveys (CSUR) 32(4), 422–469 (2000)
14. Labrinidis, A., Roussopoulos, N.: Webview materialization. In: Proc. of the 2000 ACM SIGMOD Conference, pp. 367–378, Dallas, Texas, United States (2000)
15. Labrinidis, A., Roussopoulos, N.: Balancing performance and data freshness in web database servers. In: Proc. of the 29th VLDB Conference, pp. 393–404 (September 2003)
16. Labrinidis, A., Roussopoulos, N.: Exploring the tradeoff between performance and data freshness in database-driven web servers. The. VLDB Journal 13(3), 240–255 (2004)
17. Motwani, R., Widom, J., Arasu, A., Babcock, B., Babu, S., Datar, M., Manku, G., Olston, C., Rosenstein, J., Varma, R.: Query processing, resource management, and approximation in a data stream management system. In: Proceedings of the 1st Biennial Conference on Innovative Data Systems Research (CIDR 2003), Asilomar, CA (January 2003)
18. Qu, H., Labrinidis, A.: Preference-aware query and update scheduling in web-databases. In: Proceedings of the, International Conference on Data Engineering (2007)

19. Ramamritham, K., Stankovic, J.: Scheduling algorithms and operating systems support for real-time systems. In: Proceedings of the IEEE, vol. 82(1), pp. 55–67 (1994)
20. Sharaf, M., Chrysanthis, P.K., Labrinidis, A., Pruhs, K.: Efficient scheduling of heterogeneous continuous queries. In: Proc. of 32nd VLDB Conference, Seoul, Korea (2006)
21. Stonebraker, M., Aoki, P.M., Litwin, W., Pfeffer, A., Sah, A., Sidell, J., Staelin, C., Yu, A.: Mariposa: a wide-area distributed database system. The. VLDB Journal 5(1), 48–63 (1996)
22. Sutherland, I.E.: A futures market in computer time. Communications of the ACM 11(6), 449–451 (1968)
23. Xu, J., Labrinidis, A.: Replication-aware query processing in large-scale distributed information systems. In: Proc. of the Nineth International ACM Workshop on the Web and Databases (WebDB'06), Chicago, IL, United States (2006)

Author Index

Akilov, Alex   50

Benczúr, András A.   63
Berk, David   50

Ellmann, Curt J.   34

Georgakopoulos, Dimitrios   118

Han, Seung-Kyun   133

Im, Duksoon   133

Jee, Cheolkyu   133

Kawamoto, Eugene   92
Kim, Kwanho   133
Kim, Noyoon   133

Labrinidis, Alexandros   143
Lau, Phay   92
Lee, Wan   133
Liao, Hui   92
Lukács, András   63
Luo, Gang   34

Morris, Huong   92

Naughton, Jeffrey F.   34
Ngu, Anne   118

Orlowska, Maria   106

Padmanabhan, Sriram   92
Park, Jonghun   133

Pedersen, Torben Bach   4
Pirahesh, Hamid   77
Podorozhny, Rodion   118

Qu, Huiming   143

Rácz, Balázs   63
Reinwald, Berthold   77

Sadiq, Shazia   106
Schneider, Donovan A.   1
Sela, Aviad   50
Shan, Jing   92
Shani, Uri   50
Sidló, Csaba István   63
Sismanis, Yannis   77
Skarbovski, Inna   50
Srinivasan, Sriram   92

Tan, Kian-Lee   20

Watzke, Michael W.   34
Wisnesky, Ryan   92

Xu, Jie   143

Yin, Xuepeng   4
Yu, Feng   20
Yuan, Bo   106

Zhou, Yongluan   20

Lecture Notes in Computer Science

For information about Vols. 1–4534

please contact your bookseller or Springer

Vol. 4660: S. Džeroski, J. Todoroski (Eds.), Computational Discovery of Scientific Knowledge. X, 327 pages. 2007. (Sublibrary LNAI).

Vol. 4651: F. Azevedo, P. Barahona, F. Fages, F. Rossi (Eds.), Recent Advances in Constraints. VIII, 185 pages. 2007. (Sublibrary LNAI).

Vol. 4647: R. Martin, M. Sabin, J. Winkler (Eds.), Mathematics of Surfaces XII. IX, 509 pages. 2007.

Vol. 4632: R. Alhajj, H. Gao, X. Li, J. Li, O.R. Zaïane (Eds.), Advanced Data Mining and Applications. XV, 634 pages. 2007. (Sublibrary LNAI).

Vol. 4617: V. Torra, Y. Narukawa, Y. Yoshida (Eds.), Modeling Decisions for Artificial Intelligence. XII, 502 pages. 2007. (Sublibrary LNAI).

Vol. 4616: A. Dress, Y. Xu, B. Zhu (Eds.), Combinatorial Optimization and Application. XI, 390 pages. 2007.

Vol. 4613: F.P. Preparata, Q. Fang (Eds.), Frontiers in Algorithmics. XI, 348 pages. 2007.

Vol. 4612: I. Miguel, W. Ruml (Eds.), Abstraction, Reformulation, and Approximation. XI, 418 pages. 2007. (Sublibrary LNAI).

Vol. 4611: J. Indulska, J. Ma, L.T. Yang, T. Ungerer, J. Cao (Eds.), Ubiquitous Intelligence and Computing. XXIII, 1257 pages. 2007.

Vol. 4610: B. Xiao, L.T. Yang, J. Ma, C. Muller-Schloer, Y. Hua (Eds.), Autonomic and Trusted Computing. XVIII, 571 pages. 2007.

Vol. 4609: E. Ernst (Ed.), ECOOP 2007 — Object-Oriented Programming. XIII, 625 pages. 2007.

Vol. 4608: H.W. Schmidt, I. Crnkovic, G.T. Heineman, J.A. Stafford (Eds.), Component-Based Software Engineering. XII, 283 pages. 2007.

Vol. 4607: L. Baresi, P. Fraternali, G.-J. Houben (Eds.), Web Engineering. XVI, 576 pages. 2007.

Vol. 4606: A. Pras, M. van Sinderen (Eds.), Dependable and Adaptable Networks and Services. XIV, 149 pages. 2007.

Vol. 4605: D. Papadias, D. Zhang, G. Kollios (Eds.), Advances in Spatial and Temporal Databases. X, 479 pages. 2007.

Vol. 4604: U. Priss, S. Polovina, R. Hill (Eds.), Conceptual Structures: Knowledge Architectures for Smart Applications. XII, 514 pages. 2007. (Sublibrary LNAI).

Vol. 4603: F. Pfenning (Ed.), Automated Deduction – CADE-21. XII, 522 pages. 2007. (Sublibrary LNAI).

Vol. 4602: S. Barker, G.-J. Ahn (Eds.), Data and Applications Security XXI. X, 291 pages. 2007.

Vol. 4600: H. Comon-Lundh, C. Kirchner, H. Kirchner (Eds.), Rewriting, Computation and Proof. XVI, 273 pages. 2007.

Vol. 4599: S. Vassiliadis, M. Berekovic, T.D. Hämäläinen (Eds.), Embedded Computer Systems: Architectures, Modeling, and Simulation. XVIII, 466 pages. 2007.

Vol. 4598: G. Lin (Ed.), Computing and Combinatorics. XII, 570 pages. 2007.

Vol. 4597: P. Perner (Ed.), Advances in Data Mining. XI, 353 pages. 2007. (Sublibrary LNAI).

Vol. 4596: L. Arge, C. Cachin, T. Jurdziński, A. Tarlecki (Eds.), Automata, Languages and Programming. XVII, 953 pages. 2007.

Vol. 4595: D. Bošnački, S. Edelkamp (Eds.), Model Checking Software. X, 285 pages. 2007.

Vol. 4594: R. Bellazzi, A. Abu-Hanna, J. Hunter (Eds.), Artificial Intelligence in Medicine. XVI, 509 pages. 2007. (Sublibrary LNAI).

Vol. 4592: Z. Kedad, N. Lammari, E. Métais, F. Meziane, Y. Rezgui (Eds.), Natural Language Processing and Information Systems. XIV, 442 pages. 2007.

Vol. 4591: J. Davies, J. Gibbons (Eds.), Integrated Formal Methods. IX, 660 pages. 2007.

Vol. 4590: W. Damm, H. Hermanns (Eds.), Computer Aided Verification. XV, 562 pages. 2007.

Vol. 4589: J. Münch, P. Abrahamsson (Eds.), Product-Focused Software Process Improvement. XII, 414 pages. 2007.

Vol. 4588: T. Harju, J. Karhumäki, A. Lepistö (Eds.), Developments in Language Theory. XI, 423 pages. 2007.

Vol. 4587: R. Cooper, J. Kennedy (Eds.), Data Management. XIII, 259 pages. 2007.

Vol. 4586: J. Pieprzyk, H. Ghodosi, E. Dawson (Eds.), Information Security and Privacy. XIV, 476 pages. 2007.

Vol. 4585: M. Kryszkiewicz, J.F. Peters, H. Rybinski, A. Skowron (Eds.), Rough Sets and Intelligent Systems Paradigms. XIX, 836 pages. 2007. (Sublibrary LNAI).

Vol. 4584: N. Karssemeijer, B. Lelieveldt (Eds.), Information Processing in Medical Imaging. XX, 777 pages. 2007.

Vol. 4583: S.R. Della Rocca (Ed.), Typed Lambda Calculi and Applications. X, 397 pages. 2007.

Vol. 4582: J. Lopez, P. Samarati, J.L. Ferrer (Eds.), Public Key Infrastructure. XI, 375 pages. 2007.

Vol. 4581: A. Petrenko, M. Veanes, J. Tretmans, W. Grieskamp (Eds.), Testing of Software and Communicating Systems. XII, 379 pages. 2007.

Vol. 4580: B. Ma, K. Zhang (Eds.), Combinatorial Pattern Matching. XII, 366 pages. 2007.

Vol. 4579: B. M. Hämmerli, R. Sommer (Eds.), Detection of Intrusions and Malware, and Vulnerability Assessment. X, 251 pages. 2007.

Vol. 4578: F. Masulli, S. Mitra, G. Pasi (Eds.), Applications of Fuzzy Sets Theory. XVIII, 693 pages. 2007. (Sublibrary LNAI).

Vol. 4577: N. Sebe, Y. Liu, Y.-t. Zhuang (Eds.), Multimedia Content Analysis and Mining. XIII, 513 pages. 2007.

Vol. 4576: D. Leivant, R. de Queiroz (Eds.), Logic, Language, Information and Computation. X, 363 pages. 2007.

Vol. 4575: T. Takagi, T. Okamoto, E. Okamoto, T. Okamoto (Eds.), Pairing-Based Cryptography – Pairing 2007. XI, 408 pages. 2007.

Vol. 4574: J. Derrick, J. Vain (Eds.), Formal Techniques for Networked and Distributed Systems – FORTE 2007. XI, 375 pages. 2007.

Vol. 4573: M. Kauers, M. Kerber, R. Miner, W. Windsteiger (Eds.), Towards Mechanized Mathematical Assistants. XIII, 407 pages. 2007. (Sublibrary LNAI).

Vol. 4572: F. Stajano, C. Meadows, S. Capkun, T. Moore (Eds.), Security and Privacy in Ad-hoc and Sensor Networks. X, 247 pages. 2007.

Vol. 4571: P. Perner (Ed.), Machine Learning and Data Mining in Pattern Recognition. XIV, 913 pages. 2007. (Sublibrary LNAI).

Vol. 4570: H.G. Okuno, M. Ali (Eds.), New Trends in Applied Artificial Intelligence. XXI, 1194 pages. 2007. (Sublibrary LNAI).

Vol. 4569: A. Butz, B. Fisher, A. Krüger, P. Olivier, S. Owada (Eds.), Smart Graphics. IX, 237 pages. 2007.

Vol. 4566: M.J. Dainoff (Ed.), Ergonomics and Health Aspects of Work with Computers. XVIII, 390 pages. 2007.

Vol. 4565: D.D. Schmorrow, L.M. Reeves (Eds.), Foundations of Augmented Cognition. XIX, 450 pages. 2007. (Sublibrary LNAI).

Vol. 4564: D. Schuler (Ed.), Online Communities and Social Computing. XVII, 520 pages. 2007.

Vol. 4563: R. Shumaker (Ed.), Virtual Reality. XXII, 762 pages. 2007.

Vol. 4562: D. Harris (Ed.), Engineering Psychology and Cognitive Ergonomics. XXIII, 879 pages. 2007. (Sublibrary LNAI).

Vol. 4561: V.G. Duffy (Ed.), Digital Human Modeling. XXIII, 1068 pages. 2007.

Vol. 4560: N. Aykin (Ed.), Usability and Internationalization, Part II. XVIII, 576 pages. 2007.

Vol. 4559: N. Aykin (Ed.), Usability and Internationalization, Part I. XVIII, 661 pages. 2007.

Vol. 4558: M.J. Smith, G. Salvendy (Eds.), Human Interface and the Management of Information, Part II. XXIII, 1162 pages. 2007.

Vol. 4557: M.J. Smith, G. Salvendy (Eds.), Human Interface and the Management of Information, Part I. XXII, 1030 pages. 2007.

Vol. 4556: C. Stephanidis (Ed.), Universal Access in Human-Computer Interaction, Part III. XXII, 1020 pages. 2007.

Vol. 4555: C. Stephanidis (Ed.), Universal Access in Human-Computer Interaction, Part II. XXII, 1066 pages. 2007.

Vol. 4554: C. Stephanidis (Ed.), Universal Acess in Human Computer Interaction, Part I. XXII, 1054 pages. 2007.

Vol. 4553: J.A. Jacko (Ed.), Human-Computer Interaction, Part IV. XXIV, 1225 pages. 2007.

Vol. 4552: J.A. Jacko (Ed.), Human-Computer Interaction, Part III. XXI, 1038 pages. 2007.

Vol. 4551: J.A. Jacko (Ed.), Human-Computer Interaction, Part II. XXIII, 1253 pages. 2007.

Vol. 4550: J.A. Jacko (Ed.), Human-Computer Interaction, Part I. XXIII, 1240 pages. 2007.

Vol. 4549: J. Aspnes, C. Scheideler, A. Arora, S. Madden (Eds.), Distributed Computing in Sensor Systems. XIII, 417 pages. 2007.

Vol. 4548: N. Olivetti (Ed.), Automated Reasoning with Analytic Tableaux and Related Methods. X, 245 pages. 2007. (Sublibrary LNAI).

Vol. 4547: C. Carlet, B. Sunar (Eds.), Arithmetic of Finite Fields. XI, 355 pages. 2007.

Vol. 4546: J. Kleijn, A. Yakovlev (Eds.), Petri Nets and Other Models of Concurrency – ICATPN 2007. XI, 515 pages. 2007.

Vol. 4545: H. Anai, K. Horimoto, T. Kutsia (Eds.), Algebraic Biology. XIII, 379 pages. 2007.

Vol. 4544: S. Cohen-Boulakia, V. Tannen (Eds.), Data Integration in the Life Sciences. XI, 282 pages. 2007. (Sublibrary LNBI).

Vol. 4543: A.K. Bandara, M. Burgess (Eds.), Inter-Domain Management. XII, 237 pages. 2007.

Vol. 4542: P. Sawyer, B. Paech, P. Heymans (Eds.), Requirements Engineering: Foundation for Software Quality. IX, 384 pages. 2007.

Vol. 4541: T. Okadome, T. Yamazaki, M. Makhtari (Eds.), Pervasive Computing for Quality of Life Enhancement. IX, 248 pages. 2007.

Vol. 4539: N.H. Bshouty, C. Gentile (Eds.), Learning Theory. XII, 634 pages. 2007. (Sublibrary LNAI).

Vol. 4538: F. Escolano, M. Vento (Eds.), Graph-Based Representations in Pattern Recognition. XII, 416 pages. 2007.

Vol. 4537: K.C.-C. Chang, W. Wang, L. Chen, C.A. Ellis, C.-H. Hsu, A.C. Tsoi, H. Wang (Eds.), Advances in Web and Network Technologies, and Information Management. XXIII, 707 pages. 2007.

Vol. 4536: G. Concas, E. Damiani, M. Scotto, G. Succi (Eds.), Agile Processes in Software Engineering and Extreme Programming. XV, 276 pages. 2007.